THE ELEPHANT
IN THE CLASSROOM

Race and Writing

Research and Teaching in Rhetoric and Composition
Michael M. Williamson, series editor

THE ELEPHANT
IN THE CLASSROOM

Race and Writing

Jane Bowman Smith

Winthrop University

HAMPTON PRESS, INC.
CRESSKILL, NEW JERSEY

Printed in the United States of America

Library of Congress Cataloging-in-Publication Data

Smith, Jane Bowman.
    The elephant in the classroom : race and writing / Jane Bowman Smith
        p. cm. -- (Research and teaching in rhetoric and composition)
    Includes bibliographic references and index.
    ISBN 978-1-57273-894-2 -- ISBN 978-1-57273-895-9 (pbk.)
    1. English language--Rhetoric--Study and teaching--United States. 2. Racism.
in language. 3. African Americans--Education--United States. 4. African
Americans--Language--United States. I. Title.

    PE3102.N4S623 2010
    808'.042089--dc22

                        2010015991

Hampton Press, Inc.
23 Broadway
Cresskill, NJ 07626

For Dorothy Perry Thompson
beloved wife and mother,
teacher, poet, scholar,
friend.
June 25, 1944–January 4, 2002

Osprey

One attacks the other, mid-air.
The stronger one pulls the other
downward in a dangerous
spiral.

Doesn't he see the ground
is there for him too?

—D. P. T. August 13, 2000

CONTENTS

ACKNOWLEDGMENTS

Many people contributed to this collection. I think first of Dorothy Perry Thompson, with whom I began this book, and the many conversations we had—some difficult as we strove to be honest with each other. I also thank her family for their certainty that I and the contributors would see this work completed. They also kindly gave me permission to use Dot's unpublished poem, "Osprey," and her CCCC presentation that led to Chapter 10, "Dabbling in the Abnormal: Blackening the Text in the Composition Classroom."

The contributors worked hard and all-too-often displayed amazing patience with a lengthy process. I am awed by the depth of their commitment both to their students and to their vision of what a fair and equal education could and should be. I am very grateful to Winthrop University for both academic leave and a research travel grant which enabled me to study at the Perry-Castañeda Library at the University of Texas, Austin. The librarians there and at Winthrop's Dacus Library have been very helpful, answering endless questions and tracking down references for me.

I also have many intellectual and emotional debts to friends who listened, then challenged, responded to, and supported me. Two of my colleagues at Winthrop University in particular, Gloria G. Jones and Debra C. Boyd, also Dot's friends, have steadily encouraged me. Particularly after Dot's death, they urged me to continue when the work seemed too painful and too difficult.

Michael M. Williamson of IUP, Series Editor, was very helpful in shepherding the collection through the earliest stages of publication, going well beyond his responsibilities; Mariann Hutlak of Hampton Press, Inc., our Production Editor, was unfailingly generous with her time—I fear I often strained her patience. And I am very happy to thank Barbara Bernstein, the President of Hampton Press, for her belief in this project.

I must also say how grateful I am to my students—many of whom were a vital source of inspiration and support, and who shared their own triumphs and tribulations with writing and with education.

Finally, and always, I wish to thank the two important men in my life. My husband, Frederik N. Smith, has always understood both my frustrations and my joys and never doubted that what I called "the project" would eventually become a book. I also wish to thank my father who has always been—but most especially in the last five years—a model of intellectual commitment but also of determination and endurance.

INTRODUCTION

Jane Bowman Smith
Winthrop University

This book began in a series of conversations I, a White woman, had with my African American colleague, Dorothy Perry Thompson, as we attempted to answer a significant question: "What is it like to be an African American student in a writing class designed *by* Whites and *for* Whites?" After two presentations together at the Conference on College Composition and Communication (CCCC) in the late 1990s, we realized that this question furthered and served to focus our research; it has ultimately led to this collection.

Dorothy, who had herself been a student in that situation, passed away January 4, 2002. She would have found it both significant and appropriate that in 2003, some lines from Langston Hughes' "Theme for English B," written in 1959, were reproduced on the cover of the 2003 CCCC Program; the conference's title was "Rewriting Theme for English B: Transforming Possibilities." It is encouraging to believe that we are trying, perhaps more effectively now than even in the recent past, to listen to *all* our students, to see more of the possibilities inherent in our classrooms. Can those of us who are White finally hear the student in this excerpt from Hughes' poem?

> So will my page be colored that I write?
> Being me, it will not be white.
> But it will be

a part of you, instructor.
You are white—
yet a part of me, as I am a part of you.
That's American.
Sometimes perhaps you don't want to be a part of me.
Nor do I want to be a part of you.
But we are, that's true!
As I learn from you,
I guess you learn from me—
although you're older—and white—
and somewhat more free.

This is my page for English B. (410)

Hughes' poem raises issues that we are still addressing almost fifty years later. Can "he," Hughes' student, write today in a way that will be acceptable to members of an institution largely shaped by the assumptions of whiteness and especially to those members who may not be aware of those assumptions? Will the student be able to do this and simultaneously maintain his own voice and his sense of his identity? The student in Hughes' poem is not raging, threatening, sullen, or withholding—he *hopes* that he and his teacher can break free of the prejudice that each feels for the other. Underneath that sensitive language, the tentative words, he is very aware of the mutual resistance to an engaged connection. Neither he nor his instructor really wants to be "a part" of the other. Yet the student sees this paradox as American; we want to remain separate at the same time that we need to engage fully with one another. He believes the ultimate goal of education is for the student and the teacher to learn from each other. He has hopes for such mutual learning, yet he is not sure the instructor will be open to this; he says "I guess" rather than "I know." This collection of essays explores the complex situation that the African American student confronts in the composition classroom, and we hope it serves as at least a partial response to the student's "page for English B."

***

In this collection, we have chosen to focus primarily on those students who use African American English (AAE)[1]—not that we ignore or deny that students whose primary language is another stigmatized dialect do not feel the weight of prejudice in the classroom—but because we know that there have been well over thirty years of study of AAE, and yet this knowledge is neither accepted nor respected by many Americans.

The contributors and I hope to create honest conversations among Black and White teachers, a collaborative inquiry that writing teachers will find useful. Although much has been written about African American students and composition, this work tends to examine the *student*: his or her language, attitudes toward education, and successes and difficulties with writing. We hope to examine the social construct of the classroom itself, and the effects not only of race, but of class and gender. Clearly, the academy's traditions and expectations for writing and the teaching of writing affect the classroom in at least these ways. They influence not only the student's attempts to learn but the instructor's attempts both to teach and to reflect critically upon his or her teaching in the classroom. The composition classroom, which may seem straightforward and objective on the surface, is, in essence, a "danger zone," demanding that African American students expose themselves in a variety of ways—in the content of their writing as well as in the act of writing itself. Then, the instructor often unconsciously punishes them for what they have exposed, making vulnerable students even more vulnerable. The academy expects that students will come to it and change. However, to educate students effectively and respectfully, both the academy and individual faculty members must be willing to listen to students, to meet them halfway, and to change *with* the students.

In the chapters that follow, all of us who contributed to this collection are writing out of our own experiences with students, out of our own struggles to hear them and to respond effectively. As a result, our sense of an appropriate "authorial stance" has, I think, been affected—possibly because many of these essays are rooted in critical self-reflection. All the contributors seem to share, for example, the need to shift our stance from one of blame— "Why does she keep *doing* these things when she writes?!"—to one of openness and negotiation. As teachers and as scholars, we seek to ask students straightforwardly for information that will help us teach them more effectively, even when such directness might be difficult. Perhaps the most important aspect of this authorial stance is our conviction that we, as teachers, must work for greater racial understanding within the educational system and that such work involves ongoing reflection about our racial assumptions.

In writing chapters for this collection, we all have attempted to write complexly about these issues, perhaps sometimes at the expense of a clear answer to the question, a neat solution to a clearly delineated part of the problem. This complexity certainly comes from the demands we have made on ourselves first—to address these deeply troubling and painful issues as honestly as we can. In these chapters, we model good teaching, not simply to explain the steps in a process, but to reveal our own sometimes failed attempts. We hope this approach will more fully engage the reader in active learning and will also serve to identify what we see as the important questions.

Finally, and again possibly as a result of this critical self-reflection, many of us have used narrative—our own stories—and our personal voices in writing the chapters. Perhaps the sharing of our own experiences and stories was a natural result of questioning the traditional, hierarchical structure of the academy and its privileging of Standard Written English (SWE). Many of us responded to the problems that African American students confront in our classrooms by revealing ourselves within our work. In writing personally, of course, we are also responding to a shift in the way academic discourse is being created. Jane E. Hindman, in her article entitled "Thoughts on the 'Personal': Toward an Ethics of Professional Critical Literacy," written to introduce a special issue of *College English*, "The Personal in Academic Writing," reveals her own reactions to reading the essays submitted for her review; she was intrigued by the use of

> unfamiliar, "personal," gestures [to] replace or supplement convention-
> al gestures to an always-already-constituted disciplinary authority,
> familiar moves such as citing rigidly surveilled and highly specialized
> [bodies] of disciplinary knowledge; revealing contradictions within or
> between disciplinary positions; determining the nature and/or tradition
> of a discipline and whom it should include; or applying or testing a dis-
> ciplinary theory. (10)

I found myself similarly intrigued as I read these contributions. Some of us certainly share Hindman's concerns and are, as she is, attempting to create "a powerful alternative to masculinist discourse" (10). Our subject matter naturally leads us toward what she calls an "embodied rhetoric" (10). We also recognize the whiteness of this discourse. Many of us write from the stance of the self, as a person within a classroom; we are *seen* by our students as White, Black, Hispanic, Asian; as male or female; and as members of a specific social class and age group. All of these things are noted and taken into account by our students, just as we note and take into account— whether consciously or unconsciously—these same aspects of their identities. Race, age, class, and gender also profoundly affect the ways in which we have come to understand the intellectual problems we are addressing. Perhaps our inclusion of the personal and/or the narrative in these essays is also a response to our shared sense of the urgency of our subject matter and our authentic self-reflection.

Clearly, too, in writing the essays for this collection, we have been influenced by the work of African American rhetoricians and scholars—perhaps most notably Geneva Smitherman—whose skillful use of AAE as well as the personal inform and enrich their scholarship and our responses to it. It is difficult to pinpoint a cause-and-effect relationship here: Some of us, of course, have seen our own innate cultural strategies affirmed in scholarship that explains the power of the narrative to create relationships between writer and reader. In explaining the value of testifying, Smitherman asserted that

> The retelling of these occurrences in lifelike fashion recreates the spiritual reality for others who at that moment vicariously experience what the testifier has gone through. The content of testifying, then, is not plain and simple commentary but a dramatic narration and a communal reenactment of one's feelings and experiences. Thus one's humanity is reaffirmed by the group and his or her sense of isolation diminished. (150)

Those of us who are White do not necessarily share her particular cultural understanding, yet we are very aware of the power of this kind of connection between writer and reader. In an e-mail communication, Allison Shaskan, one of the contributors to this volume, said

> I felt that this personal narrative was a key element to the work I engage in, and to the way I see theory—work which can keep out those who don't fit a very rigid model of cultural norms. Because of life circumstances, I've dropped into the class that has to utilize social welfare programs, and due to my perspective into both class systems (upper middle and working class), I've had a unique perspective. My experience suggests that few professors have spent time in the working class, and thus lack the perspective of inclusion. What one hears, then, is usually "them" or "the poor," in other words, the "other." My utilization of the narrative stemmed from this frustration. I wanted strongly to reclaim "the other," and also to validate my credentials so that other working class women/men wouldn't see me as an academic without any street-level credibility.

Most of us don't want to give up our identities, our pasts, in order to survive in academe; we hope to negotiate our roles in a way that allows us to function in both worlds.

Just as I, in my role of editor of this collection, had not anticipated the more personal authorial stance in some of the contributors' writing, I did not envision the ways in which the authors would explore their subject matter. When I began this work, I imagined a neat and orderly collection of chapters in which each contributor dealt with a defined subject area, an element in isolation. It quickly became apparent that this was not to be. Thus, each of the following chapters might best be read as contributing to an *overlapping pattern*, a return to the same critical issues. As each author follows the particular thread of his or her subject matter—perhaps the contribution AAE makes to voice or style, for example—she or he tugs on other threads within the whole cloth of the classroom. Evaluative practices, for example, could not be completely separated from perceptions of language and language use, nor could it be separated from a particular teacher's relationships with the student, his or her own classroom goals and assumptions, and how these reflected the society at large. Ultimately, the chapters in this volume are concerned with the following three critical issues and attempt to answer at least some of the challenging questions that arise from them.

AFRICAN AMERICAN ENGLISH AND STANDARD AMERICAN ENGLISH: LANGUAGE AND THE CLASSROOM

Language is, of course, the central issue in the composition classroom. Erika Lindemann reminds us in *A Rhetoric for Writing Teachers* that "perhaps the most controversial questions writing teachers confront focus on language use" (61). She explores the vexed questions that surround "usage," "correctness," and "errors," and asserts that "[many] notions about language use have no basis in linguistic fact. Instead, they derive their strength from tradition and from the enormous value we attach to our own personal variety of English" (61). The contributors to this volume examined *both* Standard American English (SAE) and AAE through the lenses of tradition and personal value—the attachment each of us has to the idiolects and the dialects that help to establish our identities. In analyzing the effects of SAE in the academy, we have become even more aware than before of the public's linguistic ignorance; privileging a dialect does not make it the "best" or most "correct," yet this is the common belief about SAE. (Peter Elbow, chap. 8, calls SAE "Sanctioned American English" in order to reinforce this distinction.) Several writers touch on legislation—such as No Child Left Behind—that tends to maintain the notion of "correct language" within the schools. Yet we also understand the benefits to the student of mastering SAE and SWE in order to be fully competitive within the global economy.

In considering AAE, the contributors are of course aware of years of research that explain and clarify the language use of AAE speakers. However, some White and even some Black faculty members still do not fully understand the rhetoric and the language of AAE speakers, and some traits are still stigmatized rather than seen as strengths. We agree with the editors of *Making the Connection* who argue that use of the substantial body of linguistic research to help AAE speakers achieve academic success is clearly possible, but that "this potential has barely been acknowledged, let alone mined, because of unwarranted beliefs about language and because of disciplinary traditions, indifference, and racism" (Adger, Christian, and Taylor vii). Because we take pride in the belief that America is a "meritocracy," those who have not or choose not to master SAE are blamed, and AAE is still sometimes seen as proof not only of linguistic but of cognitive deficiency.

In the face of this complexity, then, the contributors saw these critical questions: How do we encourage all our students to make the best use of what they know? How can we validate what students bring with them, rather than seeing their language and rhetorical strategies as burdens that should be dropped, without regret, somewhere along the academic road? How do we explain to our students the wide diversity of language use in America and especially the privileging of SWE—the entrée into the academic discourse community? Can instructors approach these issues in ways that encourage *all* students' understanding and seek to end linguistic prejudice?

BLACK AND WHITE IDENTITY AND THE ACADEMIC CLASSROOM

Many of us tend to ignore or downplay our racial identities within the classroom, often with the intention of being "fair"—but should we, in fact, do this? Jan Swearingen's chapter in *Crossing Borderlands*, entitled "The New Literacy/Orality Debates: Ebonics and the Redefinition of Literacy in Multicultural Settings," asserts that because racism is ever present in our culture, it is dangerous to ignore race:

> Why, then, the flood of diatribes scorning Ebonics as the teaching of slang, lambasting the divisiveness of the liberal politically correct agenda, and claiming that twenty years of bilingual education and ESL [English as a second language], the counterpoint to the Oakland curriculum, simply don't work? I fear the thinly veiled racism that weaves its way through these hysterical, willfully distorted innuendoes. (245)

Several of the writers in this volume return to the Oakland School Board's Resolution (1996–1997) and the resulting media backlash. In doing so, they critically analyze cultural expectations for the public school system; these expectations are intended primarily to preserve society *as it is*, thus protecting and maintaining the status quo and White privilege. But we must also examine composition classes at the college level. Among other goals, the freshman writing course helps students to define "academic discourse," introducing them to the thinking and writing done in the academic community, and explaining both the rationale for its use and why students should ultimately internalize its demands. Yet the often unexamined, often unconscious assumptions that underlie most composition classrooms tend to privilege upper middle-class White students and to encourage conformity. Thus, the classroom works—even if unconsciously—against a real education for African American students, particularly for those of the working class, but also against White students who are not of the upper middle class. Even as we strive in academe to create diverse and multicultural classrooms, we can find shocking evidence of the imbedded racism of our culture.

Mainstream Americans remain largely ignorant of the Black intellectual tradition; much of what is known is devalued. Sadly, too many of us tend to accept that what we see in the media is "true." Given the complexity of these issues, it is not surprising that negotiation between teachers and students may be difficult, especially when some Black students participate in the rejection of AAE and see no place for African American culture within academe. Because our beliefs, our ideology, are clearly revealed in our pedagogy, we must engage at least the following questions about racial identities and the composition classroom. What does it mean to be Black in America? To what extent has the media, in its construction of "blackness," interfered with a healthy Black identity? How have we and how should we define the African American community, its history and traditions, the power of its language and rhetoric? How can we improve the relationship between the African American community and the public schools, which we see, of course, as a precursor for success or potential failure in the academy? Are there ways to end the paradox that can damage a Black student's successful education—that on the one hand, education is seen as an essential "acquisition" in our meritocracy, yet on the other, the child may have been warned of the prejudice directed against him or herself in the school?

CRITICAL SELF-REFLECTION AND RACIAL LITERACY

It is a given that excellence in teaching results from critical analysis not only of one's classroom but of one's own performance—the ways in which pedagogical methods, choice of text, and assignments impact students and encourage their learning. Jerome Bruner defines such learning in this way:

> Learning . . . is [climbing] on your own shoulders to be able to look down on what you have just done and then to represent it to yourself. Manipulation and representation, then, in continuing cycles are necessary conditions for discovery. They are the antithesis of passive, listener-like learning. Yet representation is not frenzied activity. Though active, it is still ratiocination, a going back over experience, a listening to oneself. (101)

Yet thinking critically about one's own performance in the classroom—and being honest—can hurt, particularly when one must confront vestiges of prejudice. Those of us who are White must recognize and move away from our cultural programming and come to an awareness of our privilege; the practice of affirmative pedagogy and racial literacy urges us to ask, how can we best educate ourselves? Many of the teachers encountered by African American students in the classroom—like the student in Langston Hughes' poem—are White. Both learning and writing can be more difficult for the African American student in this situation. Although the instructor may have thought with some sensitivity about the problems an African American student might face, this thinking may essentially be outwardly directed; he or she may not have thought critically about either his or her own "whiteness" and its possible impact on students or about the university as a "white" institution. The whiteness and its resultant privileges that are so obvious to the Black student are "silent" because they are never made subject to critical examination. This is also a problem when the instructor attempts to open these discussions, but the Black student is surrounded by White students who have not thought critically about their whiteness, who believe discussing race in America merely "opens old wounds," and that silence on this issue is appropriate. In some cases, the instructor may not be aware of this, and may assume that discussion has, indeed, taken place. Negotiation among the academy, the instructor, and the students becomes more difficult—if not almost impossible—as a result.

Yet the situation is equally complex when the instructor is African American. The personal dynamic of the African American teacher and the attitudes, assumptions, and experiences he or she brings to the classroom also profoundly influence the context in which students learn. Students, both White and Black, have learned throughout their education that whiteness is "normal," and that the study of African American language, culture, and history is not the norm. The goal should ideally be, then, to rewrite the racial script that has been given as the way that things "should" be. The contributors again agree that the answers—whatever they will be—are to be found in open and self-critical dialogue; our research revealed that students are not as open as they claim to be and prefer silence—a means to keep what they call "old wounds" hidden. But as we worked on these chapters we realized that we, as educators, tend to locate the concept of dialogue within our classrooms rather than within ourselves—and we need to make a start at an open dialogue with our colleagues.

All this leads us to the following questions. How does race complicate the negotiation between teachers and students as they attempt to establish relationships that can lead to better writing instruction? How can we best create space for open conversations among faculty members and among students that further learning? Can all members of the classroom learn to listen effectively, and if so, how? Can we learn to be honest with each other? What are the best ways to engage in affirmative pedagogy and encourage our own understanding of racial literacy?

* * *

The chapters in this volume resisted an obvious arrangement from theory to pedagogy or from problem to solution and have been arranged or "grouped" more by subject matter. The first two chapters discuss recent history and African American culture from two different perspectives—White and Black—and also African American students' potential attitudes toward academe. In Chapter 1, "Negotiating Racial Relationships: Case Studies in Freshman Composition," I briefly review the Oakland School Board controversy, presenting it as an exemplum of the American mainstream's failure to understand AAE. Using the work of John Ogbu and A. Suresh Canagarajah, I explore some of the difficulties a well-intentioned White instructor confronts when trying to hear African American students. In "Room for the Unfamiliar: Thinking about the Tradition of Self-Reflection and the Construction of Consciousness in the Black Community" (chap. 2) William Jones provides a history of the means through which consciousness is constructed in the Black community. Using the work of bell hooks and Cornel West, Jones asserts that teachers who wish to challenge their Black students intellectually must construct narratives that counter our culture's negative discourse about the African American community. He urges writing teachers to plumb the African American literary canon in order to construct positive alternatives to these often internalized negatives.

The next three chapters deal more specifically with AAE as a language— first within the classroom itself, then in the university as a whole, and then in the wider American society. In Chapter 3, "African American Voice and Standard English," Arthur L. Palacas furthers the linguistic work of John Baugh, John Rickford, Russell Rickford, and Geneva Smitherman. Acknowledging that using SAE can threaten the voice and self of African American students, Palacas offers useful strategies to help teachers learn *how* to teach "translation" from AAE to SAE. Throughout his chapter, however, Palacas also demonstrates techniques that enable the student to "mesh" elements of AAE into SWE in order to preserve voice and style. In Chapter 4, Jennifer Liethen Kunka broadens the focus on language in "Negotiating 'Interference': The Politics of Addressing Students' Writing Patterns." Aware that privileging SAE may affect students' learning, she urges us to consider a different argument to use with students—that the mastery of SAE is "linguistic capital" in our new global economy, citing the work of Thomas L. Friedman as well as Walt Wolfram and John McWhorter. She redefines the delicate balance among valuing our students' home dialects, teaching them that SAE is only one of many dialects, and enabling them to learn SAE as a means of being competitive in an ever-more-challenging global economy. Then, Allison Shaskan's "How I Changed My Mind—Or, A Bi-Dialecticist Rethinks Her Position" (chap. 5) also examines the idea of linguistic capital, but argues convincingly that mastery of SAE and SWE are not always the answer. Shaskan presents two narratives that probe the intersections between the academy and "life on the street." She questions our academic complacency, asserting that academic arguments do not always recognize real-life situations. Her first narrative presents the case of women who cannot speak SAE, and thus must work harder to escape the female world of social welfare. In a second narrative, she presents the difficulties that still exist for African Americans and other people of color who have mastered SAE but who nevertheless confront racism in a White, masculinist business world.

The next section, also comprised of three chapters, explores classroom practices. In "Can You *Re-present?*" (chap. 6), Richard W. Santana expands the focus on AAE as he examines some of its stylistic and rhetorical features. Santana refutes the assumption that African American students must be *taught* to assert, defend, or analyze ideas; he explains the rhetorical strategies that students of color use in their writing. Santana suggests both theoretical and practical ways to incorporate those strategies into a multicultural classroom environment. In Chapter 7, "Teacher Response to AAE Features in the Writing of College Students: A Case Study of the Social Construction of Error," Maureen T. Matarese and Chris M. Anson present a study of two White instructors' responses to AAE in their students' academic writing. Noting the students' lack of response to the comments written on their papers by the instructors, they call for further research on teachers' commentary in reaction to those specific linguistic features of texts that are tied to different minority language groups. The chapter ends with implications for educational reform, teacher development, and, therefore, enhancement in the area of writing instruction and language in multicultural and multidialectal settings. In "Why Deny African American Language Speakers a Choice We Offer Other Students?" (chap. 8), Peter Elbow furthers his own recent work; he encourages instructors to suggest to students that composing in one's "home language" offers significant benefits in terms of developing one's ideas. Elbow refutes two major objections—that students need to practice both SWE and academic rhetorical strategies throughout the process of composing in order to achieve mastery. He concludes by explaining his methodology for making the classroom more useful to these students.

The subsequent two chapters examine some of the difficulties African American instructors may confront in mixed-race classrooms and deal straightforwardly with "silent whiteness." Earnest L. Cox (chap. 9) examines the effect that his identity as a Black male has on his teaching; in "Play That

Funky Music . . . Black Man: Rhetoric, Popular Music and Race in the Classroom," he suggests some ways that popular music can be used in the composition course to address racial issues but also to demonstrate to students how rhetoric works in academe as well as in the popular culture. Thus, Cox creates a bridge between the university and the home. He concludes his chapter by reflecting on his presence within the classroom and cultural definitions of "being Black." In her introduction to "Dabbling in the Abnormal: Blackening the Text in the Composition Classroom," Teresa H. Redd explains the very positive reaction of Howard University's freshmen to her composition textbook, *Revelations*, a compilation of essays by Black authors writing about "Black subjects." When Dorothy Perry Thompson used this same text in a largely White, southern university, however, her experience was different. She argues that both White and African American students have been so "trained" by their public school education that they see whiteness as the "norm." Studying and writing about African American concerns was seen by both White and Black students in her freshman composition class as "abnormal." Thompson uses the work of Ann Louise Keating and Keith Gilyard to probe the effects of "silent whiteness" on all her students.

Finally, in the concluding chapter, Litasha Dennis and Kelly L. Richardson argue in "'We Are All Bound Up Together': Racial Literacy and Pedagogical Dialogue" that we must all engage in cross-racial conversations in order to further our knowledge of "racial literacy." Dennis and Richardson report openly and honestly on their own dialogues in order to model one possible approach. Using the work of Frances Maher and Mary Kay Thompson Tetreault on whiteness and Jane Bolgatz on racial literacy, they assert that the kinds of critical thinking and learning necessary to becoming more self-aware and more racially literate can be furthered in collaborative, cross-racial explorations, even when these conversations can be difficult. They conclude by offering a model that readers can use to begin their own explorations.

* * *

In 1997, Dorothy Perry Thompson presented a paper at the CCCC entitled "Colliding with the Elephant: Invisibility and the African American Student in the Composition Classroom." She asserted that "there is a silent whiteness in the classroom which renders the African American student invisible on two fronts: s/he does not see him/herself in the reader chosen for the course, and s/he cannot figure him/herself in the images created by classroom discussion." She went on to conclude that "African American students are asked to write and to speak about that whiteness which sits like an elephant in their faces — no one pointing to it, no one claiming it exists. It, and they, are both 'invisible,' but looming large toward that inevitable collision, the freshman essay." This book began shortly after her presentation, and mine, with the two of us in intense and sometimes painful conversations; because we were already friends, we valued each other's often hurtful honesty. Dot believed that the elephant that sits in all our classrooms should be foregrounded in this volume's title. I sincerely hope that we have, at least, sketched its outline in attempting to answer the question—"What is it like to be an African American student in a writing class designed *by* Whites *for* Whites?"

In late 2001, we were still writing potential contributors, only imagining that someday we would have a finished product. She would find it fitting that the book ultimately concluded in the way it does—with the chapter collaboratively written by Litasha Dennis and Kelly Richardson. These two women had been our students. They left Winthrop University to pursue their PhDs, and then accepted positions and returned to teach at their alma mater, in their old department. And so the conversation continues into the future.

NOTE

1. One of the first questions each contributor addressed individually was "What will I call the language or dialect spoken by many of my African American students?" Each contributor has selected her or his preferred terms for this language as well as for the language privileged by the culture at large. We believe that these variations in terminology suggest the breadth in the content of our scholarship and also our diverse beliefs on this, as well as other, issues. We cannot claim to agree in every detail.

   For a more complete discussion of the history of the terms used to refer to "Black English," "African American English," "African American Language," and "Ebonics," for example, please see Peter Elbow's chapter in this volume.

WORKS CITED

Adger, Carolyn Temple, Donna Christian, and Orlando Taylor. *Making the Connection: Language and Academic Achievement among African American Students*. McHenry, IL: Center for Applied Linguistics, 1999.

Bruner, Jerome S. *On Knowing: Essays for the Left Hand*. Cambridge, MA: Harvard UP, 1964.

Hindman, Jane E. "Thoughts on Reading 'the Personal': Toward a Discussive Ethics of Professional Critical Literacy." *College English* 66 (2003): 9–20.

Hughes, Langston. "Theme for English B." *The Collected Poems of Langston Hughes*. Eds. Arnold Rampersad and David Roessel. New York: Knopf, 1994. 409-10.

Lindemann, Erika. *A Rhetoric for Writing Teachers*. 4th Ed. New York: Oxford UP, 2001.

Redd, Teresa M. and Karen Schuster Webb. *A Teacher's Introduction to African American English: What a Writing Teacher Should Know*. Urbana, IL: NCTE, 2003.

Smitherman, Geneva. *Talkin and Testifyin: The Language of Black America*. Boston: Houghton, 1977.

Swearingen, C. Jan. "The New Literacy/Orality Debates: Ebonics and the Redefinition of Literacy in Multicultural Settings." *Crossing Borderlands: Composition and Postcolonial Studies*. Eds. Andrea Lunsford and Lahoucine Ouzane. Pittsburgh, PA: U of Pittsburgh P, 2004. 238-54.

1

NEGOTIATING RACIAL RELATIONSHIPS

Case Studies in Freshman Composition

Jane Bowman Smith
Winthrop University

It has been nearly thirteen years since the Oakland, California Board of Education attempted to do a reasonable thing: propose that the language actually used by African American children in their home community be used as a bridge to improve their chances of success in the classroom. The January 12, 1997 revised statement argued that these students' standardized test and grade scores "will be remedied by application of a program featuring African Language Systems principles to move students from the language patterns they bring to school to English proficiency" (Oakland Resolution 146). This was, by intent, a proposal to use African American English (AAE) to teach students Standard Written English (SWE).[1] To ensure that teachers and administrators did not misread the proposal and think that eradication of a student's home speech was the goal, the resolution also included this statement: "The Superintendent . . . shall immediately devise and implement the best possible academic program for the combined purposes of facilitating and mastering of English language skills, *while respecting and embracing the legitimacy and the richness of the language patterns*" (qtd. in Perry and Delpit 147, italics added). This decision—broadly misrepresented in the media as a proposal to "teach" in the schools the language children used at home—created a virtual firestorm; those linguists, both African American and European American, who attempted to validate and to explain this decision were outshouted by many who saw it as negating the importance of SWE; ignoring the intent of the Resolution, they claimed that the Oakland Board had "given up" on educating African American children. All aspects of this event have been thoroughly dissected, studied, and analyzed. But the decision and what followed are crucial to our understanding of race and writing in the classroom. It is important to view the Oakland decision, and the media frenzy that followed, as an exemplum of the enormous gap between what linguists and many teachers of English *know* as opposed to what many Americans *believe* about the variants of American English. The ability to use "Standard American English" (SAE), or what Peter Elbow (chap. 8, this volume) calls "Sanctioned American English," is tightly bound to the power class in our culture, yet many Americans ignore this connection and simply see this privileged dialect as "correct" English.

The conflict that arises out of this juxtaposition of knowledge and belief is critical to an understanding of what occurs in American classrooms. It is widely accepted in linguistic circles that if a child's primary language is AAE, then using that language to teach that child to use SWE is an effective tool. Yet, despite ongoing research and calls for action to improve the ways in which language and writing are taught, these African American students continue to face at least some teachers who are not well prepared to help them become bidialectal or bilingual. It is essential to understand why this situation continues to occur. One possible answer involves the complexities inherent in teacher education. John Baugh admits that it is difficult to prepare teachers to help their students become bidialectal or bilingual, because specific, straightforward strategies that work in every classroom are not known. However, he asserts that training is a necessity because of the potentially destructive consequences of teacher ignorance: "While linguistic prejudice represents an unfortunate form of sociolinguistic pathology, it takes on a particularly destructive form among teachers, student teachers, and teacher educators who conclude that students who do not speak mainstream American English have cognitive deficiencies or that they lack the capacity for abstract thought" (83-84). Thus, one would hope that the potential difficulties involved in discovering workable strategies would be clearly outweighed by the benefits to the children involved.

The Oakland controversy, however, if seen as an exemplum, suggests another view of the matter. Elaine Richardson asserts in *African American Literacies* that similar controversies have occurred regularly, "every other decade or so over use of African American language in the classroom"; moreover, she goes on, these controversies "point to the fact that educational institutions have not internalized and accepted systematic approaches that center African American discourse community students in the literacy experience" (15). Simply stated, colleges and universities have not fully accepted the task of training future teachers adequately. Anna F. Vaughn-Cooke, in tracing the source of the problem of teacher education, examines the culture at large: Perhaps the most "formidable challenge facing the profession and the educational system is the *American people's assessment* of the language of Ebonics speakers" (138). She asserts that the debates that result from the ongoing attempts to improve instruction clearly demonstrate that "a linguistically naïve public considers that Ebonics is inferior and unfit for classroom use, and that the children who speak it have limited intelligence" (138). It would seem that we have a self-perpetuating cycle in effect: The prejudice within the culture at large affects not only the students who are training to be teachers but the very system that trains them.

We arrive, then, at the end result of the Oakland controversy, in which the prejudicial beliefs of many Americans (as opposed to linguistic knowledge) determine what happens in the schools. Richardson argues forcefully that typical literacy practices are intended to maintain the status quo:

> One of the major roots of African American literacy underachievement is the ideology of White supremacist and capitalistic-based literacy practices that undergird curriculum construction and reproduce stratified education and a stratified society, that reproduce the trend of African American literacy underachievement. White supremacist ideology is insidious because it is entangled with the discourse of American meritocracy, which says that individuals are responsible for their own success. (8-9)

This is strong language. But a complex system is at work here. Teachers have embraced the idea that one language, SAE, is better than others; students who do not learn this language, for whatever reason, are made to feel responsible for their "failure," especially when they seem to choose to fail. Richardson condemns those of us who look for answers only within our "unsuccessful" students because they are being victimized by the system. By focusing on these students and their "problems," we continue the trend and don't break the cycle.

Treating AAE as a stigmatized dialect may seem to be a more destructive problem in the public schools than at the university and college level, but in fact it is not; students entering college need educated teachers, especially when the freshman writing course is a "gatekeeping" class. Faculty members need to understand the grammar of AAE as well as its rhetoric. This complex rhetoric is unknown territory for the White, middle-class teacher (and perhaps even the African American teacher) who does not participate in the African American discourse community and has not studied it theoretically. Furthermore, these teachers need to be both sensitive and strong; they will meet with resistance and will struggle to do the right thing amidst prejudice, often when those who are prejudiced have the mainstream community's beliefs and agreement on their side. Some of us have tried, often with the best of intentions, to invite students from other discourse communities into ours—the academic community. We have attempted to engage these students; we have pondered their difficulties and suggested solutions. However, this often becomes a "one-way" journey: The students are expected to come to us and change. The academic community and the classroom, its microcosm, have the potential to be truly multicultural, but only if we, ourselves, engage in the kind of critical thinking and analysis that we expect from our students. However, this analysis cannot be focused exclusively on the students and their challenges; we must engage in inquiry, critiquing our *own* assumptions and beliefs and the effect of these in our classrooms.

A first step in this inquiry process involves careful consideration of our assumptions about literacy, and in particular, "academic literacy." In *ALT Dis: Alternative Discourses and the Academy*, Patricia Bizzell (and others) examine the "new discourse forms that accomplish intellectual work while combining traditional academic discourse traits with traits from other communities" (Bizzell viii). In the first chapter of this book, Bizzell clearly connects the language and other features of traditional academic discourse with power:

> because academic discourse is the language of a community, at any given time its most standard or widely accepted features reflect the cultural preferences of the most powerful people in the community. Until relatively recently, these people in the academic community have usually been male, European American, and middle or upper class. (1)

She also provides a carefully crafted description of the key features of traditional academic literacy: one must master a grapholect that is "ultra-correct," as well as the "traditional academic genres [which] shape whole pieces of writing, such as the lab report, the reflective journal, the critical essay, the research paper, and so on" (2). Perhaps most importantly, Bizzell explains the typical worldview of the true academic, whose characteristics include being "objective," "skeptical," and finally, "argumentative, favoring debate." True academics believe that

> if we are going to find out why something is true or good or beautiful, the only way we will do that is by arguing for opposing views of it, to see who wins. In this view, only debate can produce knowledge. Knowledge is not immediately available to experience, nor is it revealed from transcendent sources. Additionally, the persona is extremely precise, exacting, rigorous—if debate is going to generate knowledge, all participants must use language carefully, demonstrate their knowledge of earlier scholarly work, argue logically and fairly, use sound evidence, and so on. (2)

It is worth noticing here how elegantly Bizzell presents this definition—and in academic discourse. And let me interject here how hard I struggled to master the dictates of my field through graduate school and beyond. I attempted to subdue my own preferred style—unfortunately replete with my own "emotions and prejudices"—as I wrote in order to master the "precise, exacting, rigorous" persona, the logical style. At that time, in graduate school in the 1970s, I was just beginning to be aware of the western European focus of traditional academic literacy; and of course, since then the academy has changed and become more diverse.

After defining academic literacy, Bizzell moves from the past and its traditions to the present and future to argue that as scholars come from different communities, they bring with them different discourses: while "gaining acceptance for these discourses . . . is an ongoing struggle, . . . slowly but surely, previously nonacademic discourses are blending with traditional discourses to form the new 'mixed' forms" (2). The work of Geneva Smitherman—with its blending of academic discourse and AAE—comes immediately to mind. It is very possible that the academic literacy required of students today is more pluralistic; certainly the literary canon, for example, now includes more women and people of color than I read in the 1970s. Yet I do wonder how long it will take for the "trickle-down" theory of change to come fully into being. How long does it take for theory to become established, and then to be accepted and applied within all our academic communities? The grading rubric that I am expected to use at my university even today privileges classical rhetoric; objective argumentation is favored, while persuasion is eschewed, and the academic dialect is clearly intended to be SWE. Students are not discouraged from using AAE and other dialects in their prewriting or their journals, but final drafts are expected to be presented in SWE. Another problem for those of us in academe is our own "egocentrism," for want of a better word; after years of work to intuit the demands of our fields, the ego urges us to know that the discourse we have painstakingly mastered over our years of study is of course correct. We have internalized these argumentative forms, this particular use of evidence, this organizational structure, and particularly the objective stance of our personae. Thus, when students resist what we are attempting to teach, it's all too easy to blame them rather than to question the underlying causes of their resistance.

A second step in this process of inquiry for those of us who have mastered academic discourse is to consider the impact that our unconscious privileging of our own language has on those students whose home dialects are most at distance from ours. Why might some of these students resist rather than embrace the changes expected by academe? Several important studies of the African American student's reactive coping mechanisms within the classroom suggest the potential destructiveness of an "unexamined" approach to teaching. The students' resistance begins early—when they realize that they are not fully accepted into the school's discourse community. In the introductory chapter to *Making the Connection: Language and Academic Achievement Among African American Students*, John R. Rickford summarizes several studies of "teacher expectations and pupils' performance" (7). He cites studies by Robert T. Tauber (1997), Jacqueline Jordan Irvine (1990), and Frederick Williams (1976), which report that teachers expect less of African American students than White students, and when African American students use AAE as their primary language, these teachers tend to believe that the students are "less promising and effective" (7). Some students are particularly vulnerable to these stereotypes and in some cases internalize them, fearing that they will "inevitably succumb to the low expectations and prejudices of their teachers and fellow students. A common response to this on the part of African American students is 'disidentification' with the academic enterprise" (Rickford 8).

John U. Ogbu's *Black American Students in an Affluent Suburb*, a study of middle- and upper middle-class African American students in Shaker Heights High School (Ohio), substantiates the depressing fact of disidentification: These students had been taught by both their parents and their community to view education as a means for upward social mobility *but also to believe* that the school, and White people in general, were prejudiced against them. However, Ogbu reports on his observations of a complex cycle of behaviors and expectations by both teachers and students. Lowered teacher expectations were only part of the equation:

> The problem with this explanation is that the situation involving low teacher expectations is more complicated than the proponents portray it. What is often overlooked is the role of students themselves in creating teacher expectations, low or high . . . in some classrooms we observed, low teacher expectations coexisted with students' unwillingness or refusal to do classwork or schoolwork. It was difficult to determine which came first. (37)

Disidentification, however, is still a significant part of resistance: "On the whole, what we heard and observed was that some Black students did not want to or should not behave in certain ways that they considered to be White people's ways in and out of school" (Ogbu 38). Resistance begins, then, with the student's recognition of the school or the teacher's "hidden agenda," and a distancing from the school's goals in order to protect the self.[2]

Disidentification, a student's internal recognition of dissonance in the school system, tends to lead to an outwardly directed form of resistance—the students create a survival mechanism to protect themselves. As Ogbu said, resistance often takes the form of an "unwillingness or refusal to do classwork or schoolwork" (37). Such a refusal may seem self-defeating, but these students have *chosen* to put forth little or no effort rather than to try and fail; furthermore, they turn away from the school in order to seek validation and support of their identities outside. Ultimately, the students in Ogbu's study believed that their efforts would not be rewarded equally to the efforts of White students. A similar pattern of disidentification followed by lowering of effort on the part of students at the university level is to be found in A. Suresh Canagarajah's dissertation, *Negotiating Competing Discourses and Identities: A Sociolinguistic Analysis of Challenges in Academic Writing for Minority Students*, in which Canagarajah studied ten middle-class African American students in an introductory writing course. These students, he noted, recognized the differences between their community styles and academic styles and, largely successfully, code-switched; over the course of the semester, however, they gradually lost interest in the writing course. They stated that academic writing was alien to them in terms of its values and the identity it imposed, and "[perceived] this discourse as reproducing them according to the ideology of the academy and the dominant social groups" (vii). Rather than overtly refusing to do the work, which would obviously cause them to fail, their means of surviving this attack was to "front," to act a role in their writing—to appear to do what was required while avoiding what they believed to be assaults on the self. Canagarajah sums up his study by arguing that "Literacy for minority students, therefore, involves more than knowing the 'standard' codes, necessary literate skills or the ability to switch language patterns as explained by current sociolinguistic and composition studies; literacy is an ideological act of negotiating between competing discourses and identities" (vii).

The competing discourses in these studies are clear: On the one hand, the students see the ideology of the academic community and the language of academic discourse; on the other, their own language and rhetoric, the strengths of which are ignored, or worse, seen as "ineffective" or "wrong" by the university. To agree that one's own language and rhetoric must be rejected is, of course, to reject one's identity. Canagarajah reports that the students he studied did not feel like equal members of the community; they asserted that the school wanted to "reconstruct" them. The questions then become, how can we help students learn to negotiate between personal and academic discourses? How can we contextualize this competition between languages so that our students understand the implications of the use of a language in as nonthreatening a way as possible? Can we make it possible for them to use this new language for their own purposes and goals without giving up one identity in order to assume another?

Canagarajah offers a partial solution to this problem of making choices between languages and identities in his recent essay, "The Place of World Englishes in Composition: Pluralization Continued." Agreeing with the contributors of *ALT Dis: Alternative Discourses in the Academy*, who argue that we are shifting toward a blending of discourses within texts, he urges us to move beyond "code-switching" to what he calls "code-meshing":

> Though code meshing was used in classical rhetoric as a high-brow activity (i.e., inserting Greek or Latin without translation into English texts), I am presenting this notion as a popular communicative strategy in multilingual communities and developing it even for cases outside such elite bilingualism.
>
> Code meshing calls for multidialectalism not monodialectalism. . . . My proposal demands more, not less, from minority students. They have to not only master the dominant varieties of English, but also to know how to bring in their preferred varieties in rhetorically strategic ways. (598)

Such "meshing" could be the best of both worlds for the student, a means to negotiate between two identities and two languages. Helping students to achieve this places demands on instructors, however, who must create a different classroom—one in which they demonstrate both an awareness of and an openness to varieties of the English language. Perhaps this new way of looking at language will enable us to respond to at least some of the silent resistance in our classrooms.

In a comparable but perhaps less dramatic way, James L. Collins urges us to see what underlies resistance in the classroom. In his book *Strategies for Struggling Writers*, Collins argues that students will succeed when

> adults and children work together to create an environment in which performance is enhanced by believing in self and others. Students who improved in our studies did so because they stopped standing outside the perimeter of the playing field and stopped participating in school only by running in place, all the while falling behind other, seemingly more "natural learners." (209)

Admittedly, Collins is discussing younger children here. However, he argues that "people become as literate as they need to be to participate meaningfully in the cultures in which they hold membership" (209). The challenge he issues us is great. Our goal is to consider thoughtfully how we can offer membership in our academic community. Not an easy task, particularly when our students—the source of much of our information—are so vulnerable and, realizing their vulnerability, often shift like chameleons, intuiting what we "really" want. Perhaps more aware of our "hidden agendas" than are we, they tell us what they think we want to hear as a means of self-preservation. Sadly, creating the ideal academic community that Collins envisions is far from easy.

* * *

Let me go back in time once again to my own personal exempla. These students and their stories reflect, or "shadow," the theory of the first section of my chapter. Essentially, like the Oakland controversy, they served as my wake-up call. At about the same time as the backlash to the Oakland Resolution was occurring in 1996, I taught three sections of freshman writing in the fall semester. One of the classes had enrolled primarily African American students; out of twenty, there were only three White students in the class. The other sections were more typical—out of the twenty students, in one class there were four African American students; in the other, there were only two. The African American students in the primarily Black section acted very differently than had other African American students in composition classes I had taught in the past at my small, southern university. They seemed to me to be much more comfortable, and they talked more, both with me and amongst themselves in group and class discussion, seemingly enjoying the class and willing to take risks. Students clearly react differently to teaching methods, texts, approaches; what works brilliantly at 10 a.m. may bomb at 11. But I was accustomed to our norm, in which White students were a majority in most classes. What puzzled me, then, was the behavior of the three White students in that class. Each of these students regularly and deliberately became "invisible" through body language that clearly stated "please don't call on me." I had seen African American students, when in the minority in a class, do this, but I had never realized it was an expression of race-related discomfort. This discovery, combined with the three students' stories presented here, brought me to a better understanding of how difficult it is to create a classroom community in which all members feel ownership and reinforcement of their identities.

Before I begin these stories, I need to describe my classroom. Certainly naively, back then I saw myself as a democratic teacher, one who valued genuine relationships with all my students, and I hoped to motivate them, to encourage them to try, and to take risks in order to learn. I hoped the ways in which I taught and the strategies I used would change their probably negative attitude toward writing, to shift or at least soften their focus from the fear of making errors to what they had to say.

Then, over the course of that one semester, I began to learn that I did not fully understand what was happening beneath the surface of the classroom that was so familiar and comfortable to me. As Jacqueline Jones Royster says, I was in actuality "away from home," trying to understand these students. I needed to be made aware that

> what we think we see in places that we do not really know very well
> may not actually be what is there at all. So often, it really is a matter of
> time, place, resources, and our ability to perceive. Coming to judgment
> too quickly, drawing on information too narrowly, and saying hurtful,
> discrediting, dehumanizing things without undisputed proof are not
> appropriate. Such behavior is not good manners. (32)

I sincerely hope that none of these students would report that I said "dehumanizing" things to them. But the three stories I present here resonated deeply for me, forcing me to re-evaluate my own certainties about teaching and my own identity as a teacher of composition—my role in "my" classroom. Royster might add here that the following stories have an unreliable narrator; all I can do is report what I think I saw—not what really happened in its entirety.

Of the three students, Andréa was the easiest to identify as the stereotypical "good student," as the one who seemed to be comfortable with her adaptations to the demands of academic discourse. She was enrolled in a special "honors" section of our second-semester class, which focused on argumentation. (The students enrolled in this honors section had been given credit for the first semester's writing class due to high advanced placement scores.) Of the fifteen students, two were African American students. Andréa demonstrated from the first day that she was *engaged*, not only in the work of my class, but in her own education.

The most telling detail of her engagement in her education and her ability to demonstrate her mastery of academic literacy was her reliance on writing as an aid to thinking—she took notes, jotting down advice, ideas from class discussion, and the titles of books I mentioned, and this was so rare as to be noteworthy. She did not use AAE in my presence, even when we were outside the classroom; she consistently wrote in SWE, even in her prewriting and her class journal. She rarely referred specifically to herself as an African American, nor did she position herself when writing from a specifically African American point of view; she seemed to have had a solid but traditional education. Perhaps she simply preferred not to reference it, but she did not seem to have had any schooling in African American history, culture, literature, or its intellectual tradition beyond the bare minimum. Of the three papers written in class for which she had some "leeway" in the subject area, two dealt with her major in elementary education. Her final research paper, for example, argued for the importance of parental involvement in the schools and in their children's education. Throughout her writing, she created a reasonable voice and supported her opinions with thorough research; she had no difficulty creating a persuasive thesis and supporting it with evidence.

The fourth paper assigned in this class, an in-class essay on our university's policy against hate speech and its potential infringement on students' right to freedom of speech, abruptly changed the students' conversational comfort level. The students as a group resisted discussion of this issue, and our usual lively debates dwindled to silence. Andréa was no exception. Normally one of the most active participants in class discussion, she distanced herself and maintained a carefully objective stance as we attempted discussions of the university's policy and the essays in our textbook that presented arguments that dealt with both sides of the issue. All of the students agreed that the university's intent—to create a community in which all students felt accepted and fully able to engage in learning—was admirable. They were not sure, however, that a policy that forbade the use of "fighting words" could work. One of the readings for the class was Charles R. Lawrence's essay, "If He Hollers Let Him Go: Regulating Racist Speech on Campus," which is often reprinted in composition textbooks.[3]

Lawrence argues that being called a racist term "is like receiving a slap in the face. The injury is instantaneous. There is neither an opportunity for intermediary reflection on the idea conveyed nor an opportunity for responsive speech" (159). The White students who spoke disagreed with Lawrence's assertion that "the racial invective is experienced as a blow, not a proffered idea, and once the blow is struck, it is unlikely that dialogue will follow" (159). They said that words were not the same as actions. But what is important here is not so much what they said but the way in which the discussion moved forward. The students seemed much more interested in preserving a polite façade, and the painfulness of the issue was "swept under the rug." Andréa finally said that she believed that freedom of speech was more important than freedom from this kind of language, and "if someone were ignorant enough to call me by the 'N' word, then that has more to say about that person than about me, myself. My parents have told me to let it wash off my back because language can't hurt you unless you allow it." The White students in the class were careful *not* to say that they agreed that her response to being attacked with "the 'N' word" was right, but one or two of them claimed they too had been taught to ignore comments directed at them by "ignorant people." The other Black student did not comment, and the White students seemed very relieved not to be pushed into a discussion of racism on the campus. Only one of the White students was brave enough to describe the shame he felt when a White student directed a hate term at a Black student in his presence.

Andréa's assertion that she could defuse the power of this word bewildered me. I know that at that point in my life I did not understand the quiet strength and determination that underlay those words. What I remember thinking at the time was that perhaps Andréa had been somehow forced by silent pressure in the classroom into acceptance of what I perceived as a "white stance"—while I had unconsciously expected her to agree with Lawrence, who seemed to me to argue persuasively about the wounding power of language and a student's right to be free from these denigrating terms. I think I hoped she would bravely speak out in favor of Lawrence's views, despite the response of other students whose silence suggested, "well, but we're all friends here." Was she forced to accede because, as an honors student determined to succeed, she dared not question and rebel, but had to embrace the educational values presented in the classroom? My failure was in my expectation that she would reveal her vulnerability and pain—if indeed it existed—to these White students, the very ones who might use these words against her. I kept silent, waiting to see what would happen in the class—but nothing really did. The polite, halting discussion began again and simply flowed over and around the incident, revealing how shallow my community truly was. We could not confront the issue of racism openly.

Keshia, the second of these students, was very different in personality from Andréa. She was a member of the first-semester composition class section that was predominately African American—there were only three White students out of twenty. Like Andréa, she was comfortable with an assertive role in the classroom; I never questioned her engagement with the reading or the work. However, when she came prepared to talk, it meant to *argue*, and pretty forcefully, too. It was harder to see her as a "good student" in terms of mastering academic literacy because she rarely changed her mind; she listened to other students in the class discussion primarily for evidence of weak logic or lack of evidence, which she gleefully pointed out to them. At that time, I did not understand the significance of her argumentative style, and the "debates" that Keshia engendered disturbed me because they were not topic-centered, carefully objective and text-focused; rather, they seemed to be based on "scoring points." She primarily used SAE in the class, but she often switched to AAE as an "exclamation point" when scoring in her debates. And when she could silence the opposition, her friends often made appreciative, celebratory noises.

Keshia wrote fairly consistently in SWE, but unlike Andréa, she referenced herself as "a Black woman" in her writing, and three of her papers dealt with African American issues. However, because she rarely discussed her high school years, I am not sure that her experience had been any more diverse or pluralistic than was the norm among my students. Her writing was consistently strong in its mastery of the grammar of SWE; her main problem in terms of academic literacy seemed to be mastery of the genre (in this class, the expository essay). In her peer-writing group, which was composed of four other African Americans from similar backgrounds (they had all told me with pride that they were the first to attend a university in their immediate families), she was an ongoing frustration to these same friends. She would come to class on the first of two class periods set aside for review of their essays with a finished draft. She was perfectly willing to read, respond, give her opinions, make suggestions—as long as the group was not dealing with her paper. When the group did deal with her paper, she would listen politely to each person's opinion, but ignore the advice.

Keshia's group asked me to intervene when they were discussing her paper on the television show *Moesha*, a situational comedy about a young Black girl and her family. The assignment had been to select one character from a television show and analyze the character in terms of any gender stereotyping that was present. The four students had been arguing with Keshia for several minutes about her response to the assignment. I listened to their comments, many delivered in tones of frustration, and then read her opening paragraph as they requested. Their advice was sound; Keshia had described each of the Black women characters on the show, making the point that television needed to present more women like these. I seconded the group's opinion, suggesting to Keshia that the paper as written was going to be powerful but did not fulfill the assignment. Keshia refused to revise. "This is my paper," she said, "and this is exactly the way I want it. Even if my grade isn't as good as I hope for, I don't want to change it to suit what someone else says I should do." She then added, "My mama told me that to survive, a Black woman gotta be strong and stubborn as a mule."

At that time, I honestly did not see that for Keshia, fulfilling the assignment in order to deal with gender stereotyping was not as important as her commitment to her own idea: that strong Black women should appear on television. Of course I agreed with her—it was about time!—but I could not, then, grasp the depth of her assertion's significance to her. It gave her power to write this paper, but I was much more concerned with her demonstration of an awareness of the demands of the academy, which necessitated learning to read an assignment carefully and to fulfill its expectations. These were the means, I thought, to survive her education. Keshia's stubbornness seemed to be yet another "attack" on my classroom as a community. It was only much later that I realized her "stubbornness" was actually a refusal to give up her sense of her identity.

The third student, Tyrell, was in the other freshman writing section, the one that had primarily enrolled White students. Tyrell was twenty, a bit older than most of the other freshmen; he had a strong and combative personality. Almost every time a student made a comment in class, Tyrell would respond to it, often sarcastically, usually not waiting to be called on. I spoke to him about his sarcasm after class several times, and after each of these discussions, he seemed almost physically to restrain himself from responding to what he thought—and sometimes said—were ignorant opinions in class discussion. Unlike Keshia, who somehow managed to present an attitude of playfulness when debating, a sense that "it's not personal, even though I'm scoring on you," Tyrell's comments made the other students angry. I can see now, of course, that much of this was the difference in the racial populations of the two classes, but at that point, it was simply difficult to have Tyrell in class. I sometimes dreaded entering the classroom, and this adversely affected my ability to help him with his writing.

Unlike Andréa and Keshia, Tyrell's speech seemed to be a meshing of SAE and AAE. Although he was articulate and powerful when speaking, Tyrell's writing was well below my (and departmental) expectations for the course. And, in fact, in his first paper of the semester, an analysis of his writing's strengths and weaknesses, Tyrell angrily wrote that he could see from his new "college perspective" that he had never been adequately challenged in public school, and that writing had consisted of sentences on tests—not the extended prose that he learned had been expected of most of the others in the class. Even Tyrell's handwriting appeared "unpracticed," as if he had not had much actual experience with the physical act of writing. When he used the computer, the text he created read as if he had typed as fast as he could to get his ideas down, as if his brain worked much faster than his ability to get the words onto paper. Unfortunately, in both modes, it appeared that he did not bother to reread his work; words were often left out, and ideas would be juxtaposed, often in a single sentence.

Unlike most of my students—then and now—Tyrell had prepared himself for college by reading widely on his own to counter what he often called a weak high school preparation. However, Tyrell's class notebook, a sort of writing journal, and his essays were frustrating to read. On the one hand, they revealed that he was remarkably well informed about world and national affairs; he wrote about both the Black experience and Black history, usually taking a theoretical stance. These challenging ideas revealed his energetic thinking as well as an occasional use of his sardonic sense of humor. On the other hand, he almost never developed or explored these ideas and sometimes appeared to be going through the motions. My comments on his work were amazingly redundant: "Great point—can you tell me more about this?" I also regularly read between the lines in an attempt to intuit his thought process.

Tyrell consistently wrote from an African American perspective in all six of his papers, often harshly criticizing the media, social institutions, and public education. Tyrell's most serious writing difficulties, given our rubric, were his struggles with the essay as a written form. Despite work in class on the thesis statement and organizing structures, Tyrell wrote passionate "statements" rather than academic discourse. His first four essays appeared to be single drafts, finished in one sitting, with no evidence of prewriting or planning. These papers had only implied theses, paragraphs that were not unified around a central idea, and very little evidence for his points. All four were repetitive, choked with what were apparently careless mistakes such as missing words, for example. There were also patterns of errors, particularly with punctuation, that suggested a lack of knowledge. However, like Andréa and Keshia, Tyrell did not use AAE when writing his essays and only rarely used it in his notebook.

Each time I returned his papers, we had essentially the same conversation: I attempted to validate his ideas and to show him I was listening—but this quickly degenerated into arguments about the way I graded. Tyrell could not understand how I could tell the students in the class that they needed to care about their subject matter but then to mark him down for losing objectivity. However, in his fifth paper, a research paper which he chose to write on affirmative action, Tyrell finally demonstrated real progress. He conducted an extensive survey of other freshmen and wrote out his responses to what they had said as well as to the reading. This final paper showed the benefits to him of this practice; he earned a "C-" and was triumphant. His final exam was not as strong, but he did have a thesis and unified paragraphs, which was impressive given the quality of his earliest work for the class. Despite this improvement, however, he earned a "D" in the class because of his earlier failing grades. He was required to repeat the course.

Tyrell needed and deserved to be rewarded for his ideas and honesty—and given my job and the grading rubric we used, I had to punish him, as he saw it, for his lack of organization and the errors that resulted from his hurried writing. Yet Tyrell did understand this problem, at least intellectually; in a self-evaluation late in the semester, he wrote:

> Another flaw that I have to rid myself of is getting on the soapbox in essays—this takes away from the quality of my papers, and turns them into a bunch of babbling by me. I think it's time to focus in on the subject without changing in the middle to some other topic. However, this has become a part of my writing ever since I wrote about important subjects that I have strong feelings about and I cannot help but voice them.

At least for that semester, the strong feelings continually overwhelmed Tyrell's ability to stay focused and write organized, linear, analytical prose.

So, ultimately, what is Tyrell's story—the fact that I did not know how to help him succeed—or what happened to him afterwards? The next semester, when he was repeating the class, I was approached by his professor, another White woman. She, too, was frustrated and unnerved by Tyrell's combative stance in the classroom and concerned about how to handle it. We discussed this, and I tried to suggest what I believed had helped him the most—allowing him leeway in his subject matter so that he could write about what interested him. She told me she was not willing to do that. She had selected a composition text (a reader/rhetoric) that did not include authors of color and planned to avoid any racial topics out of fear of "potential anger in her classroom." At the end of the semester, I learned from her that Tyrell had failed the course and would be placed in a class for "basic writers." No wonder he was angry.

* * *

In "Danger Zones: Risk and Resistance in the Writing Histories of Returning Adult Women," Anne Aronson defines a danger zone as a site in which an individual's identity places the individual

> at considerable psychological risk. These danger zones pervade the lives of many socially disadvantaged peoples; they are aspects of gender, class, race, and other hierarchies that shape the material and emotional well-being of those at both the top and the bottom. For many, the act of writing is itself a danger zone. (56)

As a White *woman*, I saw gender first, and in my thinking about Andréa and Keshia, at least, I emphasized our similarities. The fact that all three of these students were immediately vulnerable because of our racial differences was somehow below my level of consciousness. I simplified each of their situations, seeing class discussions and the resultant writing *only* as a means for them to become empowered, as it had empowered me over the years of my education. And I held to this belief despite my own experiences which had taught me that people can be damaged by the dominant discourse. Yet African American students' honest writing, particularly when they chose to write about racial subjects, only made them more vulnerable. I was implicitly asking the students to trust me enough in one semester to learn that writing could empower, when it takes years to learn this, and the more I expected or hoped that they would expose who they really were in their writing, the more vulnerable I was asking them to be. Their responses to these expectations should not have surprised me to this degree.

Stephen Brookfield, in *Becoming a Critically Reflective Teacher*, asks us to consider if we are teaching "innocently": "Teaching innocently means thinking that we're always understanding exactly what it is we're doing and what effect we're having. Teaching innocently means assuming that the meanings and significance we place on our actions are the ones that students take from them. At best, teaching this way is naïve" (1). He urges us instead to be "critically reflective," and argues that the first step in this process is to consider the assumptions that frame how we think and act. This is

> one of the most challenging intellectual puzzles we face in our lives. It is also something we instinctively resist, for fear of what we might discover. Who wants to clarify and question assumptions she or he has lived by for a substantial period of time, only to find that they don't make sense? (2)

This was certainly true in my case. Was I asking the right question when I said, "Why *won't* they learn from me?" Was I simply asking it in the wrong way? Perhaps a better way to learn from these students and what they experienced in my classroom would have been to ask, "What do they see and hear when I ask them to learn from me?" Brookfield goes on to argue that

> reflection becomes critical when it has two distinct purposes. The first is to understand how considerations of power undergird, frame, and distort educational processes and interactions. The second is to question assumptions and practices that seem to make our teaching lives easier but actually work against our own best long-term interests. (8)

Arnetha Ball and Ted Lardner argue that teachers must "raise [their] awareness of their own processes of pedagogical discoveries and change, to help teachers recognize what their own habits of reflection make accessible to them, and what their habits of mind may leave out" (477).

Perhaps Ball and Lardner would find it promising that these students and the incidents I have described have remained stubbornly in my head for years, an ongoing reminder of something I have not fully dealt with. It is certainly easier to reflect safely in my journal, to ask myself the same questions even now, than to ask the students openly to tell me what's going on. I see myself, when I read back over my old journals for these classes, tending to focus my reflective gaze outward onto the students rather than inward, into myself. In the past, fearing to say the wrong thing, I remained silent, my brain bumbling between alternatives like a horsefly in a bottle. Confrontation is not easy for me. In a mixed race classroom, saying "look, things aren't going well, let's talk" becomes almost impossible. It's certainly easier to reflect in comfortable, predictable ways after the fact than to come out and tell a student that I don't understand what she just said.

Even now, I do not have answers to the questions I should have asked ten years ago. Was Andréa protecting herself by writing on topics that were essentially safe and by appearing to embrace academic literacy? Or were these her real interests and goals? Keshia seemed to maintain her own view and definitely used her own rhetoric in debates; was she doing this to negotiate a space for herself within a community and discourse that demanded that she change, yet was itself resistant to changing? But surely, was not the most violence done to Tyrell, perhaps because we perceived his anger as an assault on the academic system?

As I was struggling to conclude this chapter, I was compelled to search out a relevant scene from James Baldwin's *Another Country*. Vivaldo, in the midst of a painful conversation with a white woman, his friend Cass, remembers "Ida's tone and Ida's eyes when they quarreled":

> *All you white boys make me* sick. *You want to find out what's happening, baby, all you got to do is pay your* dues!
>
> Was there, in all that rage, a plea? (234)

Ultimately, we all must decide whether or not we are willing to pay our dues—students and instructors, White and Black. Are we willing to think deeply and critically about these issues? Willing to confront the racism inherent not only in our culture but also in academe? Willing to engage in the learning necessary to educate ourselves so that we may better educate our students? I know that those of us who have contributed to this volume believe we *should*. More importantly, we believe we *can*.

NOTES

1. I follow Teresa M. Redd and Karen Schuster Webb's use of the term *African American English*, which they argue is "currently the most widely accepted term among linguists" (3).
2. Other studies have also been conducted, notably Signithia Fordham's *Blacked Out: Dilemmas of Race, Identity, and Success at Capital High*. For other, related interpretations of disidentification see Herbert Kohl's *"I Won't Learn from You": And Other Thoughts on Creative Maladjustment* and Mike Rose's *Lives on the Boundary*.
3. This essay has been widely reprinted over the past 10 years. I cite the textbook that I am using now in my freshman composition class, not the text that I used in 1996. My past students might be interested to note the changes that have occurred over time; present textbooks for use in composition present a much more complex, diverse view of the issue of "hate speech" versus "freedom of speech" on college campuses than they did in the past.

WORKS CITED

Aronson, Anne. "Danger Zones: Risk and Resistance in the Writing Histories of Returning Adult Women." *Situated Stories: Valuing Diversity in Composition Research*. Eds. Emily Decker and Kathleen Geissler. Portsmouth, NH: Boynton/Cook, 1998. 56–71.

Baldwin, James. *Another Country*. New York: Dell, 1960.

Ball, Arnetha and Ted Lardner. "Dispositions Toward Language: Teacher Constructs of Knowledge and the Ann Arbor Black English Case." *College Composition and Communication* 48 (1997): 469–485.

Baugh, John. "Considerations in Preparing Teachers for Linguistic Diversity." *Making the Connection: Language and Academic Achievement Among African American Students*. Eds. Carolyn Temple Adger, Donna Christian, and Orlando Taylor. McHenry, IL: Center for Applied Linguistics, 1999. 81–95.

Bizzell, Patricia. "Preface." *ALT Dis: Alternative Discourses and the Academy*. Eds. Christopher Schroeder, Helen Fox, and Patricia Bizzell. Portsmouth, NH: Boynton/Cook, 2002. vii–x.

____. "The Intellectual Work of 'Mixed' Forms of Academic Discourses." *ALT Dis: Alternative Discourses and the Academy*. Eds. Christopher Schroeder, Helen Fox, and Patricia Bizzell. Portsmouth, NH: Boynton/Cook, 2002. 1–10.

Brookfield, Stephen D. *Becoming a Critically Reflective Teacher*. San Francisco: Jossey-Bass, 1995.

Canagarajah, A. Suresh. "Negotiating Competing Discourses and Identities: A Sociolinguistic Analysis of Challenges in Academic Writing for Minority Students." Diss. U of Texas–Austin, 1990.

____. "The Place of World Englishes in Composition: Pluralization Continued." *College Composition and Communication* 57 (2006): 586–619.

Collins, James L. *Strategies for Struggling Writers*. New York: Guilford, 1998.

Fordham, Signithia. *Blacked Out: Issues of Race, Identity, and Success at Capital High*. Chicago: U of Chicago P, 1996.

Kohl, Herbert. *"I Won't Learn from You": And Other Thoughts on Creative Maladjustment*. New York: New P, 1994.

Lawrence, Charles R., III. "If He Hollers, Let Him Go: Regulating Racist Speech on Campus." *Writing the World: Reading and Writing about Issues of the Day*. Eds. Charles R. Cooper and Susan Peck MacDonald. Boston: Bedford/St. Martin's, 2000. 155–161.

"The Oakland Resolution." *The Real Ebonics Debate: Power, Language, and the Education of African-American Children*. Eds. Theresa Perry and Lisa Delpit. Boston: Beacon, 1998. 143–186.

Ogbu, John U. *Black American Students in an Affluent Suburb: A Study of Academic Disengagement*. Mahwah, NJ: Lawrence Erlbaum Associates, 2003.

Redd, Teresa M. and Karen Schuster Webb. *A Teacher's Introduction to African American English*. Urbana, IL: NCTE, 2005.

Richardson, Elaine. *African American Literacies*. London and New York: Routledge, 2003.

Rickford, John R. "Language Diversity and Academic Achievement in the Education of African American Students—An Overview of the Issues." *Making the Connection: Language and Academic Achievement Among African American Students*. Eds. Carolyn Temple Adger, Donna Christian, and Orlando Taylor. McHenry, IL: Center for Applied Linguistics, 1999. 1–29.

Rose, Mike. *Lives on the Boundary*. New York: Penguin, 1989.

Royster, Jacqueline Jones. "When the First Voice You Hear is Not Your Own." *College Composition and Communication* 47 (1996): 29–40.

Vaughn-Cooke, Anna F. "Lessons Learned from the Ebonics Controversy— Implications for Language Assessment." *Making the Connection: Language and Academic Achievement Among African American Students*. Eds. Carolyn Temple Adger, Donna Christian, and Orlando Taylor. McHenry, IL: Center for Applied Linguistics, 1999. 137–168.

2

ROOM FOR THE UNFAMILIAR

Thinking About the Tradition of Self-Reflection and the Construction of Consciousness in the Black Community

William Jones
Rutgers University

REFLECTIONS ON THE CLASSROOM

To assert the existence of an intellectual tradition among ordinary African Americans, a Black vernacular tradition, is to create dissonance for some readers. Since the popular imagination does not routinely include intellectualism as a core characteristic of the Black community, the response is expected. Curiously, these readers would find in social science and journalism elaborations of this popular view, particularly in reports on the Black poor and working class, reports that many readers internalize as representations of Black communities generally. From these reports emerge images of communities sharply differentiated from the mainstream, descriptions of populations under siege, poorly housed, welfare-dependent, underemployed, the young adult males in these communities disproportionately involved in the criminal justice system, children there raised in dysfunctional, matricentric families, those children aspiring to little that is socially sanctioned. Such characterizations exclude communal inclinations that foster intellectualism. Even schools in these communities cannot lay claim to that utilitarian orientation. In such contexts, the bedrock conviction is that Black students are incapable of high academic achievement. Such thinking clearly has currency among educators.

Teachers of Black students, then, may have to disarm the discourse on denigration and social ruin that defines their students and the circumstances from which their students come. If they themselves are, in fact, to function as the enablers they are supposed to be, they have to construct counter narratives for themselves, those narratives to become reminders that, whatever truths the negative discourse locates, those truths are only partial reports. And because the "news" about the African American world is historically dire, the news, although it must be reckoned with, can often be dismissed because it is not conventionally usable. James Baldwin puts it this way:

> All that you are ever told about being black is that it is a terrible, terrible thing to be. Now, in order to survive this, you have to dig down into yourself and re-create yourself, really, according to no image which exists yet in America . . . . [You] have to decide who you are, and force the world to deal with you, not its idea of you. (qtd. by Claude Brown in Carroll xvii)

Baldwin, in this instance, is commenting on a psychological process necessary for Black survival, but his comments are usable in the project for teachers that I want to propose. What teachers have to do would be considerably reduced if Black students, in the main, were as assertive and insightful as Baldwin is here. Students, then, in their own capacities, could escape the diminution that classrooms often subject them to. But teachers, simply as adults, have a responsibility for their students' welfare, for making certain that the classroom is the site of meaningful enterprises. Their challenge is to determine to what degree their own internalized processes permit them to maintain classrooms as unacknowledged racialized sites that accommodate the educational neglect of Black students. Teachers, whatever their racial identity, may have to accept, however, that there are few guides for creating the psychological circumstances that make possible the self-examination that is necessary for functioning in this self-critical capacity. The end result, whatever process they engage, must be the conclusion that teachers cannot teach those they despise. If teachers cannot make genuine human connection with Black students, recognize their intelligence, and value them enough to guide them toward clear academic accomplishment, what their students achieve will always be far less than what, in fact, is possible.

The project, then, for teachers is twofold: to create counter-racist narratives for themselves that enable them to maintain classrooms as sites of intellectual challenge for Black students, places where academic achievement is expected and made possible and, in doing so, to acknowledge their own probable ties to racism and to work against the active, negative effects of that attachment. I want to incorporate into this project attitudes and activities akin to those assumed and carried out by students in training to become

English as a second language (ESL) teachers. One feature of ESL training is the overt acknowledgment that those conducting the training are dealing with matters that their students, those in training, may be unfamiliar with. They are all in a "foreign" language situation. In this context of unfamiliarity, students are confronted with the need to be knowledgeable about the culture of the native speakers of language they will teach, the culture of the speakers of the so-called target language. Properly considered, acquaintance with cultural information is never secondary. The ability to locate and articulate that knowledge and impart it to others has an importance equal to the competence that ESL teachers need to reckon with the fundamentals of English sentence structure and with the intricacies of English sounds and intonation. Linguistic knowledge, of course, is of practical value but so is knowledge of culture, certainly so if students are to become skilled at using language in socially appropriate ways or when the teaching of literature becomes a part of language instruction. In either instance, because reading is often a powerful vehicle for becoming familiar with anything, teachers in training to become ESL teachers learn to mine the literature of the target language, the literature produced by those inside the culture, for cultural information, information that their students will have to respond to if they are to use the target language with full competence and if their reading of literature is to approximate the reading experience of native speakers. Incidentally and deliberately, writers expose readers to endless stores of cultural information: information about male–female relationships and the nature of families; details about religious practices, social customs and taboos; insights into intracultural hierarchies, interracial etiquette, and folk beliefs; information about the ways people use leisure and how they entertain themselves; information, as well, about their attitudes toward work and education. In short, these student teachers learn to read literature as cultural anthropologists might, unafraid to recognize differences and mindful of any inclination on their part to disparage what they discover.

Imagine, now, this activity positioned as personal, individual projects for the benefit of writing teachers who work with Black students. Imagine that these teachers undertake the activity with some awareness of its antiracist potential. They plumb the African American literary canon to begin to construct alternatives to the internal negatives that routinely influence their encounters with African American students. They accept that their interactions may include negative dimensions, not to immerse themselves in guilt but to open the way to self-examination and reflection. They acknowledge that it is not possible to be an American, aware of the negative associations attached to Black life, and not have at least some of the associations as part of their thinking. None of us, they accept, can live outside the influence of the negative discourse concerning Black life unless we prepare ourselves for lifelong struggle not to be. It is delusional to think otherwise.

To this end, teachers benefit from developing an orientation that maintains a critical frame of mind, one that positions them to engage information in ways that are the equivalent of Mitchell Duneier's critique of the work of sociologists and journalists, individuals whom he calls the "gatekeepers of the standard images of black life" (134). In *Slim's Table,* Duneier writes about the lives of working-class men, deliberately subverting the practice of framing them as ne'er-do-wells. He refuses to characterize their habits of living in negative contrast to Black middle-class respectability. He claims working-class rectitude instead, noting with directness "that the working poor are moral beings that can provide their own role models" (130), that they reproduce general civility in their relationship with others. There is no fabricating in this assessment. He does not overlook weaknesses. He can label families in Black communities, for instance, "more disorganized than [those] in mainstream society" (11), but he is observant enough to know that in such circumstances "people often develop substitute kinship ties, in which many of the functions served by families are taken up by other caring individuals" (10). Duneier is intent on constructing a fully nuanced picture of the Black people and manages to do so because he is insistent on working outside frames that reproduce stereotypical assessments of them. His intentions construct frames of mind that teachers can replicate.

What Duneier accomplishes in *Slim's Table* increases in value when played against bell hooks' comments on the habits of educated Black readers. Black readers, she informs us, work outside of conventional frames too. She notes that, in the all Black schools that she attended in Kentucky in the 1960s, it was common, as it was in schools across the nation, to read "white Western canonical literature" (16). She found it "stunning," however, when she learned that there were those who believed that, if Black people read the works of Black writers, they would not need an acquaintance with the Western canon. "It's really been the White reader," she observes, "who has focused on texts by White people and feels . . . [that] it's an either–or thing, that we have to choose one or the other. Black readers believe we should read everything" (17). What is missing here is the further observation that Black readers often come to Black writers on their own, frequently, but not always, outside the influence of what schools require. Certainly, this is often true in integrated schools. And whether we quarrel with hooks' description of the habits of White readers or not, the value of reading across racial boundaries can hardly be contested. It is a behavior to be encouraged in this project. It, too, like Duneier's revisionist work, has the potential of deepening teachers' conceptions of Black communities and, by extension, broadening their regard for Black students and increasing their resolve to develop greater competence in what they do in service of Black students.

I want to contribute "The Tradition of Self-Reflection and the Construction of Consciousness in the Black Community" as a text relevant to these ends. It adds a measure of complexity to how Black communities can be conceptualized. In its recognition of a credible intellectualism among ordinary Black people, it makes sensible the interrogation of the notion that intelligence is fixed, unequally distributed among individuals and, by extension, hierarchically distributed among races, and that in this arrangement Black people are positioned lowest. Some version of these ideas is often at play in classrooms, often unintentionally but not the less insidious in its effects for being so.

The research that founded basic writing as a writing specialty, for instance, constructed a deficit model to characterize the students who had served as research subjects. Researchers described them as those who wrote without intentions, who were satisfied with their first drafts and revised superficially, focusing principally on sentence-level matters, seldom on ideas that needed modification or expansion to improve the clarity and general communicativeness of what they wrote. The description became a taxonomy. Behavior that should have been seen as resulting from inexperience and instructional neglect became a fixed description of low intellectual functioning. Teachers accepted the research uncritically: Basic writers, in the main, particularly in metropolitan centers, were Black, Latino, and working-class White students, but interracial etiquette hid the overt marking of race behind the euphemism "basic writer." That phrase, functioning as code, allowed race to remain unacknowledged. However, only the acceptance of the notion of racial intellectual inferiority, inadvertent although it might have been, permitted the representation of behavior as fixed that should have lasted only as long as it took to eliminate it through instruction.

That such a situation developed is understandable: The research that helped to establish basic writing as a specialty brought a measure of respectability to what had been called remedial composition, a marginalized instructional area in English departments and special programs. The scholarly attention that researchers themselves garnered was extended somehow even to classroom teachers. That attention energized those in classrooms, brought them a modicum of prestige. Criticism, if they were inclined to voice it, was muted. Worshipful silence was the order of the day. However, the critical standpoint that this project requires encourages the opposite, necessitates the questioning of assessments that are reductive since such assessments inevitably point teacher expectations downward and perpetuate the negative regard of Black students and ensures their educational neglect. Quite directly, all evaluations of Black students must be challenged if the assessments accept inadequate performance as a norm, as a fixed display, as all-that-can-be-expected, as I suggest that the founding research of basic writing does. If educators insist on a critical stance, they will have established the basis for the creation of a circumstance in which Black academic achievement can be realized.

The New York Times (September 24, 2003) carried the headline, "A Private School That Thrives on Rules. Minority Students Excel at Brooklyn Site. Is It a Model or an Anomaly?" The story that followed detailed the work of administrators, teachers, and parents in the Trey Whitfield School, a twenty-year-old school for students up to Grade 8 in a working-class neighborhood in Brooklyn: "[B]leak" is the adjective that is used to characterize the neighborhood, but the phrase "consistently excel" indicates what students manage to do there (B1). Two things stand out here: The first is that the chief administrator, A. B. Whitfield, has created and maintained the circumstances—the administrative and instructional systems—that support achievement. The school is orderly; there are standards for behavior and dress that almost no one attempts to flout, students having accepted "that structure, calm and safety are prerequisites for learning." The atmosphere of the school alone, for me, is testimony that Whitfield, as an adult and educator, values his students. The second is that success at the Trey Whitfield School, for some outsiders, is suspect, hard to acknowledge as the result of efforts that can be replicated elsewhere and difficult to see as anything other than the product of dogged student selecting and weeding out, procedures that public schools, for instance, cannot follow. What is significant here is not the fact that students at the school routinely perform "two to three years above grade level on national achievement tests" (B6), but an observation that has, over time, become almost a dictum for me: Tales of Black academic success have to be told and retold. Even then, they are difficult to accept. Stories of Black academic failure told once, suffer no such fate.

REFLECTIONS ON THE TRADITION

The transgenerational practice of self-reflection and social criticism that has its beginnings in eighteenth-century communities of enslaved Africans and freemen survives in present-day African American communities as an intellectual tradition sustained by ordinary people. Paul Gilroy in *The Black Atlantic*, a study of culture in the African diaspora, acknowledges C. L. R. James's identification of this tradition as anti-hierarchical. Ordinary Black people, James observes, "do not need an intellectual vanguard" to tell them what to say or think (79). The mental acumen, the skill at seeing the world in its complexity and understanding its effects, is available to them and is not the sole province of an intellectual elite. Similar characterizations surface in John Langston Gwaltney's *Drylongso: A Self-Portrait of Black America*, written in 1980, where Gwaltney asserts that the racial context in which Black people operate necessitates analytical flexibility on their part. "[The context] demands," he says, "virtuosity at option sorting and general improvisation which places an often mortal premium on profound thought. It is a kind of indigenous analysis. . . ." Survival itself "is a preeminently analytical process" in this racialized circumstance (xxx).

Slave narratives offer some insight into the inauguration of the tradition and the centrality of truth within it that flourishes in present-day African American communities. Although large numbers of the narratives are of questionable worth as literature, that they exist at all in the face of systematic efforts to make literacy a near impossibility is testament to the determination of slaves to tell their stories and for us to see these narratives as responses to the assaultive, dehumanizing effects of slavery and as declarations of Black humanity and condemnation of the master caste. Originating in widely separated geographic locations, they present consistent stories of slave life, so that the problems of slave existence that emerge become partial evidence for claiming their authenticity and for valuing them as windows into the psychology of the slaves (Osofsky 14). We know that the purposes of men and women like Harriet Tubman, Sojourner Truth, and Nat Turner were shaped by religion, but the ranks of these familiar figures are increased by hundreds of less familiar men and women of God: self-styled slave preachers and priests and trained clergymen who went to divinity school after freedom.

Christianity, when the purview of Black preachers and their congregants, differed sharply from the Christianity of the slaving caste. Slave narratives comment on the corruption at the center of White Christianity, on its disassociation from the tenets of human embrace and connection, its distortion of Christian teaching on justice and personal salvation. The White preacher was an agent of oppression, bringing to slaves lessons that identified them as "hewers of wood and bearers of water," bound by the Almighty's plan to obey their masters, to embrace their suffering, and to seek recompense in the hereafter (Osofsky 34). Although some slaves accepted these lessons of subordination, slave narrators described the Black church as spiritual and psychological sites of refuge, places where human and spiritual identity were asserted and maintained, where connection with the ancestral past was made real. But the Black church was more, if not by intention certainly in achievement, for it was the place where a multiethnic African population forged a common African American identity under the leadership of the Black preacher who functioned as a community leader with residual powers akin to those enjoyed by African chiefs and priests (Stuckey 32 and 82-83).

The dual task of ancestral embrace and resistance to subjugation had the effect of Africanizing Black Christian worship, distinguishing it from White Christian practices. In this Africanized space, both prayer and testifying became principal vehicles for the establishment of truth and righteousness as core black communal values. Both testifying and prayer are governed by conventions of style, attitude, and presentation that determine how prayer and testifying are regarded both by those who engage in these activities and those who witness them. Those who testify and pray are always self-reflective, witnesses to God's ways in the world and to their own struggles to be upright, to lead righteous lives. To testify or to pray is to reckon with one's life circumstances and one's relationship with God as public, communal acts, understanding that the risk of humiliation is almost nonexistent, for the abiding faith is that the congregation will embrace those who, in all their wretchedness, stand or kneel in its presence because God is a forgiving God. The evidence of His mercy is all around them, on the lips of others who testify and pray, in the words of the songs they always sing, and in the sermons that are preached Sunday after Sunday. Salvation lies in laying all of their burdens at the altar or praying mightily to be able to do so. And since the flesh is weak and temptations ever present, a portion of every day must be given over to prayer. But it is the commitment to truth, the admonition against lying before God, that becomes a core value and enters the community from the Black church, the communal location that is the repository of traditional African-based values, values older than the first African on these shores.

The imperative to be truthful about one's life, to bear witness to God's mercy and His strengthening power, and to confront the vicissitudes that confound life as we recognize our own inadequacies mean that the impulse toward righteousness becomes an orientation. When multiplied among individuals generationally and recognized as historical extension and legacy, in a larger context of community, self-reflection, prayer, and testimony become spiritual forces that make truthfulness communal ethos and core values. Spirituality and its impulse to extend itself, in effect, embraces the secular so that goodness and rectitude have influence beyond the church and religiosity. While positing this spiritual dimension as core value in the African American community is clearly contestable, vulnerable to categorical dismissal in the face of sustained evidential documentation of dysfunction in African American communities, it is inappropriate to assign disproportionate importance to the ascendancy of so-called underclass values that coalesce in what Cornel West labels *nihilism* (12). To do so is fundamentally reductive, representing the current version of the stereotypical criminalizing and general denigration of the community that has been the hallmark of social scientific description of African American life.

Counterviews that still recognize negative qualities in the African American community offer a more accurate representation of the Black community. In 1982, Berry and Blassingame could assert that "since slavery most Black families have been headed by two parents . . . [and that even] in broken families . . . , the traditional kinship network has been maintained" (xviii). Anderson, examining the debilitating problems that characterized

Black Philadelphia in the 1980s, finds curious consistencies between W. E. B. DuBois' description of Black Philadelphia in 1890 and descriptions appropriate for current circumstances. DuBois' language, except for a certain quaintness in diction and phrasing, could describe contemporary conditions of Black Philadelphian drug dealers and users: "The size of the more desperate class of criminals and their shrewd abettors," DuBois writes more than one hundred years ago in *The Philadelphia Negro*, "is, of course, comparatively small, but it is large enough to characterize the slum district." He describes such people as:

> idlers, shiftless and lazy "ne'er-do-wells" who find themselves in court for "larceny or fighting" and often drift "into graver crime and shrewd-ness dissoluteness . . . in an environment that makes it easier . . . to live by crime or the results of crime than by work." (qtd. in Anderson 271)

Despite the persistence of conditions that make such historic comments appropriate for the present, Anderson concludes that most people in the so-called

> underclass communities are decent, law-abiding, ethical people who treat others with consideration, go to church and strive to have their own version of an intact family . . . . They have a sort of savoir-faire, are able to get along with people inside and outside the community and are . . . capable of working within the system. (271)

If such mollifying descriptions are difficult to accept, it is, in part, because they have to contend with the weight of negative descriptions that have become the almost uncontested conventional representation of the Black community in the popular mind. Nevertheless, the decency that Anderson identifies finds extended representation in John Langston Gwaltney's *Drylongso*, a compendium of autobiographical narratives that place before us the lives of Black people who in their range and variety are representative of Black communities generally and who reveal what Gwaltney calls "feeling[s] of personal and communal satisfaction . . . , rooted in the civil, principled survival in spite of the weight of empire that rests upon their backs" (xxi). The status of people in the Black community, accorded by the people who live there, is based on a person's fidelity to core Black standards. The effort to present Black people faithful to their conception of themselves, honestly in voices that display those standards, is facilitated here in considerable measure by Gwaltney himself. His familiarity with the barriers to faithful representation that Black people face at the hands of social scientists encouraged him to acknowledge his connection to the Black community and so validate the community's perspectives just by the grace with which he treated those he interviewed.

Because experience can become a context that makes communication an almost effortless activity, as it does in *Drylongso*, commentary and the exchange of ideas produce a continuous discourse that deepens analysis of the forces and currents that shape national life and affect the quality of life within Black communities. The honesty that is the hallmark of Black interchange is, in some ways, compensation for the absence of reciprocal honesty across racial boundaries. The critical insights that emanate from the Black community suggest the transformative power that honesty could generate if issues were addressed interracially. The Black community understands the costs that this lack of reciprocity has exacted on lives there and, without condescension, understands the ways of White folks, their worldview, and how it turns them away from the historical past, focuses on the present, denigrates Black life and makes it nearly impossible for them to reckon with the notion of White culpability and so perpetuates an inegalitarian social order that is, in fact, a racial hierarchy. Pronouncements about truth and lying, responses that are, at base, reaction to the reality of this hierarchy are common elements in Black vernacular discussions of ordinary people, as reported by Gwaltney:

> It will not kill [white] people to hear the truth, but they don't like it and they would much rather hear it from one of their own than a stranger. Now, to white people, your colored person is always a stranger, so you can't tell them anything. Now you know I'm right about that. They won't tell each other the truth, and the lies they tell each other sound better to them than the truth from our mouths. (29)

These words, spoken by an elderly Black woman, are routine utterances that are endlessly applicable in making distinctions between Black and White responses to institutionalized injustice, its presence submerged and revealed in the endless flux of behavior governed by civil interracial etiquette. Such utterances are an element in the continuous indictment of White innocence, ignorance, and indifference that is part of sane Black consciousness and its reckoning with the assaultive nature of racism.

It is in the context of such communal psychological positioning that an intellectual such as James Baldwin can best be understood. He is a pure product of the Black vernacular intellectual tradition, a mind that extends, refines, and elaborates thinking that is recognizably the intellectual property of ordinary Black folks. In describing his own response to Langston Hughes' poetry, Baldwin said that he could look up from Hughes' pages and see the folks that Hughes was writing about before him. Indeed, it was as though, when Baldwin himself sat down at his own typewriter, he set himself the task of establishing a similar eye–mind connection, particularly in his essays, with the Black folks he knew. The connection was achieved. Black people, for instance, who encountered Baldwin's photograph on the front cover of the Beacon Press paperback edition of *Notes of a Native Son* in the mid-1950s routinely and regularly testify to how taken they were by the audacious assertiveness of his face—pop-eyed, wide-lipped, his nappy hair descending in a point in the middle of his forehead—and even more by the assertive blackness of his words, the elegant reach of those long, rhythmic, carefully wrought sentences that embedded so many sentiments and ideas about this country, about who we, Black folks and White folks, were and who we had become. Those ideas and sentiments were recognizably part of the Black communal discourse, but they were presented with such clarity, with such crystalline incisiveness that Black readers responded to them with recognition, reporting that Baldwin had managed to put matters just the way they had been struggling to do: "Oh," they said, "that's exactly what I wanted to say." He had not said anything new, but his style and stance became standard, and writers as varied as Amiri Baraka and Henry Louis Gates, Jr. acknowledge to having been pulled into his language, attempting to appropriate his rhythm to embody ideas, for his language offered a frame to assert their humanity and a way to respond to the world. He suggested ways to be Black as well. Eulogizing Baldwin on December 8, 1987, Baraka said that Baldwin

> made us feel, for one thing, that we could defend ourselves and define ourselves, that we were in the world not merely as animate slaves, but as terrifyingly sensitive measurers of what is good or evil, beautiful or ugly. . . . That not only are we alive but shatteringly precise in our songs and our scorn. (129)

He went on to say that Baldwin had created "contemporary American speech . . . so we could speak to each other at unimaginable intensities of feeling, so we could make sense to each other at yet higher and higher tempos" (130).

Here, Baraka locates Baldwin's connection to the Black community as psychological and linguistic enabler, one who made it possible for us to communicate deeper and more authentically, trusting our experience, confident that our reading of the world was right. Baldwin's view of the world was a complex interplay of personal psychological stances, and as a writer and social activist, he enjoyed uncommon celebrity. Still, with his gifts, he had a nonhierarchical relationship with Black people. However complex his relationship with the Black community, that community, with its tradition of self-reflection and social criticism, produced him.

The church was the site where personal and sacred truth had been formed and the pulpit that he occupied as a preacher for a short time in his

teens was the place to tell it, and when he could no longer do that about himself and about his congregation and when he thought he could find no heal-
ing in spiritual power, he, alas, abandoned the church. The church, we know,
thank God, did not abandon him, and the fact that it did not resonates in
every sentence he wrote. It is a commonplace to say that Baldwin was a witness. It is not an overstatement to assert that he was a prophet. Clyde Taylor
says he was "[m]ore like an avatar, a seed person, distillation of a cultural and
human idea refined to the highest consciousness that could be attained and
still shared with one's fellow internees of this century" (35).

If we reach back past the current intellectualism that Baldwin represents, back to the nineteenth century to a representative Black intellectual
like Henry Highland Garnet, we may be able to see similarities in how they
both operated and so identify, tentatively, frames of mind and perspectives
that characterize the Black vernacular intellectual tradition.

Henry Highland Garnet died at age sixty-seven, having lived from 1815
to 1882. He is remembered for his radical position against slavery, an
unabashed stance that called for slaves to rise up against the master caste,
that position set forth in the *Address to Slaves of the United States* delivered
at the National Negro Convention in Buffalo, New York in 1842. Garnet's
radicalism, then, was opposed by Frederick Douglass, and it was not until
the mid-1850s that Douglass endorsed Garnet's call to revolt. Garnet himself was born into slavery in Maryland, but his father, who could trace the
family's beginnings to Mandingo royalty, effected the escape of the entire
family to New York City. There and in other northern locations, Garnet
acquired an unusual education. At the New York African Free School,
Garnet's classmates included Ira Aldridge, who was to become internation-
ally famous as a Shakespearean actor, and Alexander Crummel, who was to
enjoy a reputation larger than Garnet's as an intellectual in the mid-nine-
teenth century (Stuckey 145). There, teachers encouraged students to speak
out boldly against oppression so that Garnet was, on some level, prepared
for the hostility he met when he attempted to continue his education at
Noye Academy in New Canaan, New Hampshire—but where he and other
Black students were driven out (Stuckey 148). Clearly, teachers at the Free
School had attempted to prepare students there for the harsh life they were
certain to face. Such is illustrative of bell hooks' comments that Black educators, historically, have been natural Freirians when they are their most
authentic selves, properly focused on the existential realities of Black life, for
whatever lessons Black youngsters are taught, they must learn to stare reality down for life (hooks *Talking Back* 49; "A Conversation"). Seen from
another vantage, teachers at the Free School had simply accepted the conventional obligation of adults to function as guardians for youths.
Additionally, in Garnet's family, Black leadership was encouraged and seen
as natural for Black men (Stuckey 151). This particular aspect of encourage-

ment, in some measure, was bolstered by consciousness of and pride in the family's direct connection to African royalty although there is evidence that Garnet never fully appreciated the power of Africanisms in Black religious practice and in the general communal character, or the significance of Africanisms in shaping the character of Black intellectual discourse (Stuckey 145).

Despite that, I want make three generalizations about Garnet and about the Black vernacular intellectual tradition: First, the Black vernacular intellectual tradition finds first nurture in the Black community, most frequently in the Freirean support of Black adults, often teachers, sometimes Sunday school teachers, and ministers. This communal support supplements what the family in its most extended configuration offers daily over time. Overheard adult conversations, family stories, direct lessons for children, and correctives and admonitions aimed at adolescents become important elements in the familial–communal discourse continuum that initiates the Black vernacular intellectual tradition.

Garnet, as a thinker, is described as one who relied on himself intellectually and had a view of the world that was self-willed and insisted on with a confidence that took years for others to develop (Stuckey 150). I characterize this self-affirmation of his interior life as a frame of mind encouraged by the Black vernacular intellectual tradition: Audacious confidence is essential because Black intellectualism is not generally affirmed in the broader non-Black world and because denigration of it, subtle and brazen, is a constant. This audacious Black assertiveness, which is the second characteristic of the tradition, often results in the production of ideas and theories that are radical or revolutionary, or at least disturbingly uncommon, certainly not mundane. Sterling Stuckey, in *Slave Culture*, reports that Garnet's sustained reflection on the suffering of slaves produced a consciousness so attuned to the realities of their lives that his call for revolt among them could only be seen as coherent and logical (154). His thinking was contextualized in experiences that were peculiar to the Black community and thus almost guaranteed their separation from mainstream thought. Certainly, his call for revolt evoked an awareness of intellectual resourcefulness among slaves unrecognized in northern abolitionist circles (156).

Finally, the ideas of liberation and freedom that are central to Black intellectual discourse are not directly attached to the nation's founding documents—to the Constitution and the Bill of Rights. The abstract reality that these documents represent is not discarded or disparaged. Rather, it is undergirded by encounters with brutality that threaten and deny liberty, sometimes directly experienced, other times witnessed or made aware of and then internalized. Garnet lived in the deep shadow of oppression, and in his youth, while he worked as a seafaring cabin boy, his family's home in New York was invaded by slave catchers from Maryland in search of his fugitive-slave parents and sister. The family was assaulted and their furnishings destroyed so that, while they managed to extricate themselves from that circumstance, they had to start their lives anew with nothing (Stuckey 146). I contend that awareness of the vulnerability of Black life to racism's assaultive character, physically and psychologically, arbitrarily displayed and systematically maintained, is a constant, transgenerational feature of the Black vernacular intellectual tradition. That feature is the third characteristic to note, and it, perhaps more than any other, prompts reflection in African American communities and functions as a goad for ordinary people and the intellectual elite to reckon with the truth about themselves and about their circumstances.

WORKS CITED

Anderson, Elijah. "Drugs and Violence in the Inner City." *W. E. B. DuBois, Race and the City: The Philadelphia Negro and Its Legacy*. Eds. Michael Katz and Thomas J. Sugure. Philadelphia: U of Pennsylvania P, 1998. 258–77.

Baraka, Amiri. "Jimmy!" *James Baldwin: The Legacy*. Ed. Quincy Troupe. New York: Simon and Schuster, 1989. 127–34.

Berry, Mary Frances and John W. Blassingame. *Long Memory: The Black Experience in America*. New York: Oxford UP, 1982.

Carroll, Rebecca. *Swing Low: Black Men Writing*. New York: Crown, 1995.

Duneier, Mitchell. *Slim's Table: Race, Respectability, and Masculinity*. Chicago: U of Chicago P, 1992.

Gilroy, Paul. *The Black Atlantic: Modernity and Double Consciousness*. Cambridge, MA: Harvard UP, 1993.

Gwaltney, John Langston. *Drylongso: A Self-Portrait of Black America*. New York: Vantage-Random, 1981.

hooks, bell. *Talking Back: Thinking Feminist, Thinking Black*. Boston: South End, 1989.

_____. "A Conversation between bell hooks and Emma Amos." *UpSouth: Catalogue for the Exhibition "UpSouth."* Birmingham, AL: Space One Art Gallery, 1999.

Osofsky, Gilbert, ed. *Puttin' On Ole Massa*. New York: Harper, 1969.

Stuckey, Sterling. *Slave Culture: Nationalist Theory and the Foundations of Black America*. New York: Oxford UP, 1987.

Taylor, Clyde. "Celebrating Jimmy." *James Baldwin: The Legacy*. Ed. Quincy Troupe. New York: Simon and Schuster Touchstone, 1989. 29–37.

West, Cornel. *Race Matters*. Boston: Beacon, 1993.

3

AFRICAN AMERICAN VOICE AND STANDARD ENGLISH

Arthur L. Palacas
The University of Akron

My first memorable encounter with Ebonics[1] in the composition setting was an intense confrontation with an angry nontraditional (older) African American student who vehemently disagreed with a correction I had made on his paper. I was an unemployed linguist who had taken a temporary adjunct position at Cleveland State University to teach an innovative composition course with a linguistics slant. I had already taught linguistics for about five years, but I was not prepared for the intimacy of the composition classroom, where a teacher doesn't just deal with abstract concepts of language, including even enlightened abstractions about Ebonics, but tangles with another person's actual linguistic usage—with what comes out of their mouths and ends up on their papers. Although this encounter happened in 1975, I still remember explaining that "Being as" is not as usual or standard a way to begin a sentence as "Since" or "Because." The student's response let me know, in ways that I have grown to appreciate more and more over the years, that I had just experienced my first up-close and personal racial clash.

Looking back, I understand that "Being as" was the student's considered choice, based on his experience and background, to express himself in a formal and elevated way that he was certain was standard. My correction, the assertion of a White authority figure, came across as an assault on him and his race. I have since come to understand that my approach, with its incomplete grasp of linguistic-cultural identity, ripped into his self-respect and actually did constitute an assault at least on his person. It was far from my intent, emotionally or intellectually, to belittle the student. I thought I was doing a good, objective piece of teaching. But, as has been the case with many of us, I did not acknowledge the linguistic and intellectual validity of his choice, nor had I provided a background on language variation in which to embed my comments and give the student a way of understanding them—because I hadn't yet developed the mindset that would inform me of the importance of doing so. Thus, I had no way of undermining the stereo-typic antagonisms. Although the conflict between Ebonics and academic English does not always erupt into racial confrontation, the ingredients are always present with a White teacher in a classroom populated with any number of "Ebonics-strong" students, as I have termed them, students who are, by background, more comfortable or more confident with Ebonics than standard English; but there is always that underlying tension. The stronger the Ebonics background, the more likely that features of the language will cross over into their academic writing. Often, the treatment of this language conflict in class ends up demoralizing the student, with all the attendant harmful consequences.

Of concern to all of us, Ebonics-strong students in the college writing classroom pose an enormous pedagogical challenge for us as teachers, Black, White, and other. The retention and graduation rates for African Americans are among the worst (along with Latinos and Native Americans). The con-flict between standard English and Ebonics and the academic and personal consequences of the conflict are, of course, already severe in earlier grades, where Ebonics-strong African American students are among the lowest achievers and are already subject to demoralization.

The problem is not limited to Ebonics-strong African American stu-dents, however. Race is certainly an issue, because Ebonics-influenced speech and writing raise the worst stereotypes of inferior intellect and low expectations that often attach to African Americans. But race appears not to be the central issue since, intertwined with and beyond race, are the stereo-types and pedagogical challenges that come with all stigmatized varieties of English—those varieties of English that are judged by speaker and nonspeak-er alike as broken, impoverished, illogical, inferior forms of language. Across the nation, we experience many students bringing minority varieties of English to our classes, from Latino, Asian, Native American, Appalachian, and Hawaiian Creole varieties to Louisiana Creole, Gullah, and Ebonics—in general, the language varieties of students from linguistic-cultural minorities and lower socioeconomic backgrounds who are not fully acculturated to the norms of mainstream society. These varieties are not recognized as legitimate forms of language nor respected as such by most Americans, including teach-ers, and so the effort to successfully teach writing in an academically accept-able level of standard English is compromised. To be specific, this lack of acknowledgment and respect precludes any effort to train teachers how to handle language difference in the classroom. It precludes the very thought of training teachers and providing them with the necessary language skills. Instead, the students and their families are blamed for their academic failure. This is truly a national blindspot and a national problem.

LINGUISTIC BASICS

Thanks, however, to outstanding, familiar ambassadors of linguistic-cultural minorities, like Geneva Smitherman, John Baugh, Eleanor Kutz, William Labov, John Rickford, Walt Wolfram, and others, and the influx of ideas from linguistic science into composition studies over the past thirty years, we have come to accept certain axiomatic truths, which are reviewed here as a foundation for this chapter: that all languages and language varieties are rational and rule-governed and that the language of poor people is not poor language; that differences in language are simply products of different historical paths and social forces which, put simply, have brought some people together and kept other people apart. People who interact regularly and meaningfully speak alike; otherwise, they speak differently.

To elaborate briefly, the social isolation of large numbers of African Americans over time fully explains the existence and perpetuation of the linguistic differences that comprise Ebonics. And, in plain Chomskyan terms, the fact that African Americans are humans fully explains the linguistic and intellectual legitimacy of Ebonics. Human beings are linguistic by nature, making every child a linguistic genius. Language is instinctual in humans (the main theme of Stephen Pinker's best-selling *The Language Instinct*), which is why children come to language early, easily, and swiftly before they then use language to learn everything else. This means, of course, that those African American children who may not yet be fluent in the nuances of standard English come to school just as developed linguistically as children—of any race or social background—who are completely fluent in standard English. The problem that Ebonics-strong students face is not that they lack ability with language; their language abilities are as good as anyone else's. The problem is that their background language is not valued in the school curriculum, in fact, is not even acknowledged as a language or a valid variety of English. But Ebonics, like every other variety of English, is constructed with the same human genius for language that makes standard English what it is. Thus, it is no surprise that linguistic analysis of the speechways that are common in the African American community has proved over and over that Ebonics is rule-governed, that it has its own grammar and phonetic properties, and that it has grammatical characteristics that are often very different from those of standard English. Language scientists are not surprised that Ebonics is valid as a language; all languages and language varieties are equally valid in linguistic terms. After all, standard English is itself just a variety (or set of varieties) that has evolved over time, but a variety that has evolved with a highly prevalent mainstream prestige value that no one will deny.[2]

As a final note on linguistic basics, the terms *Ebonics* and *Ebonics-strong speaker* need clarification. Ebonics is intended as a descriptive term to mean the ethnic variety (or related set of varieties) of English that is commonly but not universally used among African Americans and includes those linguistic features that are the most distinct from standard (varieties of) English, especially standard written, academic, or professional English. However, to name and describe Ebonics is in no way meant to imply that any one person who knows Ebonics is ever limited to that language to the exclusion of standard English (any more than a speaker of Greek, like myself, is limited to Greek). In actual usage, a person who knows Ebonics is characteristically a code-switcher, whose speech may exhibit at times more Ebonics and at times less Ebonics, depending largely on the formality of the occasion and the relationship of the conversationalists. Typically, the languages are mixed, with code-switching occurring often within the sentence itself. Generally, the more formal the occasion, the more standard English will be evident, and, likewise, the less formal the occasion, the more Ebonics (along lines discussed in Baugh's *Black Street Speech*). The Ebonics-strong speaker is normally someone who is reared in a largely African American neighborhood where Ebonics is the preferred or dominant language of communication and who has little meaningful peer-pressured access to standard English. An Ebonics-strong person will evidence at least some and possibly a significant degree of Ebonics forms even in formal situations. Others who may know Ebonics but have experienced peer or parent pressure to acquire standard English, may evidence occasional features of Ebonics in their speech or writing, or may be completely competent, even elegant, in their use of academic or professional English. The degree of proficiency in Ebonics and standard English all depends on the individual and the individual's background.

THE PEDAGOGICAL SITUATION: THE NEED TO TEACH LANGUAGE

As cognitively intact and linguistically legitimate as minority Englishes are, the social reality is that every educated person needs to control standard English, whose written version is quite well prescribed. This means that all English teachers inherit the responsibility of helping students who are weak in the standard variety to learn its forms and nuances. It would be so much easier for us to teach writing and grade papers if our students did not pose any significant linguistic challenge. But many of them do, and so, as much as we might want to, and as much as we are tempted to blame the students for their lack of competence in standard English grammar and sentence rhythms, we cannot escape the need to teach language.

When it comes to Ebonics-speaking students whose speech and writing evidence features of Ebonics, we cannot escape the need to teach the differences between Ebonics and standard English. It is truly crucial to do so. Unfortunately, this is no simple matter; sometimes the differences are difficult to explain, and, more importantly, teaching the differences in a vacuum, as grammar lessons off to the side, or as a corrective, can be misunderstood and can meet with resistance. Students may not voice the problem in so many words, but when their language is shunted off to the side with remedial implications, they are left wondering if they will be valued and respected for who they are and where they hail from, if they will be valued for the potential of their intellect, or if they will be the object and victim of stereotypes that lower expectations. This is the current situation.

As I see it, large-scale success in teaching standard language to speakers of minority Englishes will requires major changes in teacher training and major changes in a curriculum that must be woven through with lessons on language awareness and culture. I have seen arguments that for the proper education of African Americans, including those who are not competent in standard English, all that is needed are highly qualified, dedicated teachers who hold their students to rigorous standards in a well-disciplined, stable school environment. In the past, it appears that there have been all-Black or largely Black high schools that could be described by this formula and that did well by their students (Sowell). Apart from the interesting implication of the merit of segregated schools where an African American student is naturally valued for his origins and person (Baugh *Beyond Ebonics* 108), the formula perpetuates an unfortunate message—that Ebonics is faulty English, slang, street talk, and a product of academic laziness with no intrinsic value. There is no evidence that such schools have become a force for truth about the linguistic heritage of African Americans or that they have done anything to alleviate the completely unnecessary linguistic shame and linguistic self-derision that speakers of Ebonics labor under (Baugh *Beyond Ebonics* 108-109). The only escape offered is the acquisition of very standard English and the culture of standard English. The acquisition of mainstream English and culture is not the question; school is supposed to teach these. In the usual English classroom in the usual school setting, however, this formula leaves the ingredients completely intact for resistance, self-deprecation, academic disillusionment and anger, and classroom tension, offering little hope for large-scale academic success of African Americans who are Ebonics-strong. It is not necessary to bequeath our nation with such a negative view of Black intelligence and potential, nor is it necessary to abandon Black students to the psychological burden of having to climb up out of that pit. It's enough to overcome the language and cultural differences posed by a standard English school setting without having to overcome, or continue to live with, the burden of linguistic-shame and self-deprecation, as well.

The formula also raises pedagogical issues: What in fact are the best qualifications for a teacher to teach standard English to speakers of Ebonics (or any other minority variety of English)? And what are the best ways to teach standard English to speakers of Ebonics? At the basis of any good pedagogy for Ebonics-speaking students (and students who speak other varieties) is the need to help them know that they are linguistically competent, that they have mental abilities equivalent to those of speakers of standard varieties of English. It is also clear that the best way to do this is to demonstrate to them that their home language is provably a legitimate language, different from standard, not deficient, with its own inner laws and beauties, its own history and heritage value. Thus, a central component of the preparation and qualification of teachers to best teach standard English to speakers of Ebonics is the knowledge of Ebonics grammatical properties and how Ebonics compares with standard English. This is not a shockingly new idea, but as simple as it is and as obvious as it should be, it remains controversial. If a teacher has a clear grasp of the linguistics of Ebonics, wouldn't it be unreasonable to forbid the teacher from using that knowledge if doing so could help Ebonics-speaking students more clearly understand the task before them of perfecting their knowledge of the standard? Wouldn't it be unethical in the training of teachers to hold back information about the similarities and differences between standard English and Ebonics when this information is available and could help teachers to help their students grasp the structures of standard English? And wouldn't it be foolish for an administrator of a school with an African American population to hire an English teacher who has no understanding of the relationship between Ebonics and standard English over an otherwise equally qualified teacher who had this knowledge? Clearly, a teacher who can credibly communicate to Ebonics-speaking students that they are intellectually okay because Ebonics is a legitimate language is more qualified than one who cannot communicate that critical piece of information. The mindset to communicate that piece of information was exactly the piece that was missing in my own approach to language difference in 1975 in my first confrontation with an Ebonics speaker in an English composition setting.

In today's world, where Ebonics is as deeply entrenched as ever, maybe more entrenched, and is a profound cultural marker and badge of identity, the most effective English curriculum with standard English as its goal is one that is linguistically friendly to the student. As I discuss further, and as emphasized in different ways repeatedly by Geneva Smitherman as well as

Eleanor Kutz, to be linguistically friendly also means to be culturally friendly;[3] this association is necessary because it is the surest way to let students who are at some distance from the mainstream know that they are intellectually and personally valued and that they are not being called to abandon their sense of self. That is, the English teacher/composition teacher can solve the motivational and practical issues posed by linguistic-cultural minorities by:

1. linguistic affirmation of the linguistic-minority student's intellect, person, and cultural background, and
2. explicit teaching on how the standard differs from the student's mother tongue.

THE WRITER'S VOICE AND STANDARDIZATION

The problem of the student can be formulated as a problem of voice. There are different kinds of voice—existential voices and a writing voice. Existential voices include social, cultural, political, personal, religious voices, and others having to do with a person's beliefs and role in society. In composition, voice usually refers to writing choices, both in content and style, by which writers make their minds known and by which they engage and capture the reader. In terms that are meaningful for composition, it seems clear that if students are not given the safety and freedom to express their existential voice(s)—which boils down to acceptance—they will be hard pressed to risk expressing themselves in a composition-style voice to make themselves known on paper.

In his "Inviting the Mother Tongue," Peter Elbow elaborates on the key assumption that the varieties of English are, in fact, mother tongues, that they have a linguistic reality and legitimacy in their own right and consequently deserve the respect that allowing them to be written would give. Elbow explores the value and the potential of writers expressing themselves in the language or language variety with which they are most comfortable. This is the language in which they can project their voice in familiar usage, phrasing, rhythms, and structures. Indeed, in the drafting stages of a writing project, it seems right that students be encouraged to write in whatever style they are most comfortable thinking in.

However, expression in the style that may be most comfortable and the most conducive to freedom of thought soon comes into conflict with the need to be standard in a language that may seem to the student to be distant, impersonal, unnatural, and voiceless. The movement to standard language is necessary, but the movement from comfortable language to the standard is a major linguistic-cultural leap for many students. Usually that movement is perceived by teacher and student alike as correction and improvement, rarely as a potential loss of voice, either existential or stylistic. In making the move to standard, students will do best if they sense the teacher's grasp of the dilemma and an acceptance of their language and thus of their person and voice. This move can take place on a street on which teacher and student walk together, not just in a professional relationship, but in a personal one with sometimes poignant moments, I can attest. For the Ebonics-strong student, it is a walk where disappointment threatens, but where student and teacher can work together to keep hope alive. This has been my experience in a composition course I teach that focuses on questions of African American language and culture, and where Ebonics-background students feel some freedom to express themselves. In my office one day, with the doors closed, when I had just made some suggestions about how to change a couple of sentences to make them sound more standard and to improve their clarity, the student grabbed hold of his hair, made moaning and groaning sounds, and rolled onto the floor, saying, "You're ruining my style." I was caught up short. He was right. I apologized and reviewed my suggestions in light of what he was trying to accomplish rhythmically to express the emotion of what he was saying. I saw that my standardization was dead in comparison and needed resurrection to recapture the student's purpose in terms that were academically acceptable.

THE INTERACTIVE NATURE OF EBONICS

What is so ironic and difficult about the intersection of language and writing is that Ebonics is by its very nature, in its very grammar, full of voice, that quality of engagement that we seek in compositions. So many mainstream students need to be taught or encouraged to write with a voice, but it is natural for Black students to do so. If Ebonics is anything, it is a language of engagement. In my view, Ebonics has inherent in it a certain literary quality where levels of intensity and linguistic empathy are paramount.

The famous Ebonics perfective pre-verbs *done* and stressed *BIN*, for example, are intensive and emphatic (Baugh *Black Street Speech* 74-77, 80-82). Thus, you can say "Tyrome forgot the money," but you can also say, "Tyrome *done* forgot the money." With the addition of *done*, the ante goes up, body language might come into play, and the communication becomes more dramatic; it begs for and elicits response. The same goes for the use of stressed *BIN*.[4] To use a well-worn example, if asked about a couple, one could say, "Yeah, they married," but one could also say, "They BIN married!", a way of talking that emphasizes the long-standing reality of their marriage and that gets the audience involved.

Ebonics also incorporates linguistic empathy. This is the subjective literary quality by which the writer shifts point of view to the person in focus or to the time in focus and makes it possible for the reader to feel the other's point of view or to feel that they are at the scene of an event.

LINGUISTIC EMPATHY AND INDIRECT QUESTIONS IN EBONICS

In Ebonics, linguistic empathy can be found in the fact that the line between indirect and direct quotation is very thin, and the fact that narration often has an immediate, present tense vividness to it. These properties can be seen in the following five student examples, three of which came from papers about a humorous "slang IQ test" that the students had administered to check out just who knew what current slang words. The highlighted portions of Sentences 1 to 4 are indirect questions, and as is characteristic of Ebonics, read or sound like questions. Examples 2 to 5 contain instances of present tense usage where standard requires the past. For comparison's sake, below the examples are standardized versions of the sentences at issue, and below Sentences 1 to 4 are direct quotation versions of the indirect questions.

1. I distributed the test to the Blacks first. None of them said a word, they just took the tests as if they were taking a final exam. When I had received the tests back, each of them had every single answer right. I asked them **what did they think of the test.**

   Standardized: *I asked them **what they thought of the test.***

   Direct quotation: *"What do you think of the test?"*

2. I asked ten people **what are their thoughts on Ebonics.**

   Standardized: *I asked ten people **what their thoughts on Ebonics were.***

   Direct quotation: *"What are your thoughts on Ebonics?"*

3. It really surprised me when I interviewed my boss. He got all the answers right, except three. I asked him **how *do* he knew most of the answers.**

   Standardized: *I asked him **how he knew most of the answers.***

   Direct quotation: *"How do you know the answers?"*

4. I told James that **I will be** back, I had to go tell my friends that I was chilling outside and **did they want to come chill with me outside** with everybody else that I **hanged around with** at school.

Standardized: *I told James that I would be back.*

Standardized: *I had to go tell my friends that I was chilling outside and ask them **if they wanted to come chill with me outside** with everybody else that I hung around with at school.*

Direct quotation: *"I will be back."*

Direct quotation: *"Do you want to come chill with me outside?"*

5. A girl came in to have her hair done. As she walked pass two clients getting there hair done, they immediately started **talking about how short the girl hair is and hope she will get a weave** (fake hair) put in her hair.

Standardized: *. . . they immediately started talking about how short the girl's hair was and hoped that she would get a weave (fake hair) put in her hair.*

Examining the highlighted portions in Examples 1 to 4 shows that the Ebonics indirect questions sound like questions and that the corresponding standardizations do not. Table 3.1 isolates the indirect questions and aids in the comparison of forms.

Notice that in Columns A and C of Table 3.1, a helping verb (*did, do, are*) occurs to the left of the subject. This is what gives the items there the sound of a question. This contrasts sharply with the standardized versions in Column B, where the standard indirect question has no helping verb to the left of the subject, so instead of sounding like a question, it sounds much more like a report. In other words, unlike standard indirect question style, Ebonics-style indirect questions have the life, voice, and engagement prop-

TABLE 3.1
Forms for Indirect and Direct Questions

COLUMN A: Ebonics-Style Indirect Question	COLUMN B: Standard Indirect Question	COLUMN C: Standard Direct Question
I asked:	I asked:	
1. what did they think of the test.	what they thought of the test.	"What do you think of the test?"
2. what are their thoughts on Ebonics.	what their thoughts on Ebonics were.	What are your thoughts on "Ebonics?"
3. how do he knew most of the answers.	how he knew most of the answers.	"How do you know the answers?"
4. did they want to come chill with me outside.	if they wanted to come chill with me.	"Do you want to come chill with me outside?"

erties of direct face-to-face conversation. This is a positive quality of Ebonics, one worth pointing out, and also one that English teachers would do well to be aware of for teaching purposes.

The final four sentences illustrate another difference of Ebonics-style writing. Where standard English has a sequence of tenses rules, Ebonics does not. Thus, as in these examples, often Ebonics-style writing will contain a present tense where a standardized past tense is called for. A side-by-side comparison (see Table 3.2) of the Ebonics-style forms and their standardization, focusing on the tenses of the verbs this time, makes this plain.

In Column B (Table 3.2), when the main verb is in the past, the subordinate verb in the representations of reported speech is also in the past. Quite the contrary in the Ebonics-style representations; the tense of the subordinate verb does not shift to match the past tense of the main verb; it is in the present tense. The effect is a more vivid, personal, right now feel that reconstructs the event, or gives the sense of being at the event rather than simply reporting it. This is another positive feature of Ebonics, and again one that teachers need to be aware of for the proper teaching of the standard sequence of tenses, while respecting the mother tongue of the student. It is not enough to tell a student that they have performed an illegal tense shift; the tense shift makes perfect sense in Ebonics. The student needs the understanding that a discussion of the linguistic realities would give.

Generally, one could say that Ebonics favors what are called main clause phenomena (Hooper, Green), structures or qualities that make speech live, as opposed to the subordinate noun clause type structures that can deaden sound and that have more the sense of a factual report than a relaying of someone's speech or a live event.

TABLE 3.2
Ebonics and Standard Tense Sequences

COLUMN A: Ebonics-Style Present Tenses	COLUMN B: Standardized Sequence of Tenses
I <u>asked</u> ten people what <u>are</u> their thoughts on Ebonics.	I <u>asked</u> ten people what their thoughts on Ebonics <u>were</u>.
I <u>asked</u> him how <u>do</u> he knew most of the answers.	I <u>asked</u> him how he <u>knew</u> most of the answers.
I <u>told</u> James that I <u>will</u> be back	I <u>told</u> James that I would be back.
they immediately <u>started</u> talking about how short the girl hair <u>is</u> and <u>hope</u> she will get a weave (fake hair) put in her hair.	they immediately <u>started</u> talking about how short the girl's hair <u>was</u> and <u>hoped</u> that she would get a weave (fake hair) put in her hair.

Another area of grammar where Ebonics evidences a main clause phenomenon and differs from standard is the apparent absence or avoidance of subordinate noun clauses in favor of paratactic—that is, side by side—structures. (This topic raises theoretical questions in linguistics that do not need to be addressed here.)

PARATAXIS AND LIVE SPEECH IN EBONICS

We regularly find students writing complementizer-free sentences (sentences without the subordinator *that*, known in linguistics as a complementizer) to introduce noun clauses. This is especially true of Ebonics-style writers. In an essay reporting on the highly controversial *The Bell Curve*, a student wrote the following sentences taken from different locations in the paper:

1. The authors opinion about Blacks as a race is we cannot help that we do poorly in socioeconomic fields and standardized testing.
2. I feel no kind of test can measure potential or a person IQ.
3. The information presented is East Asian typically earn higher scores versus White Americans.
4. To help support his notion, stated is the average Black person's IQ is 85, average White person 100.
5. Also implied is how could these test be wrong.

In each of the first four cases, standard English wants to insert or feels the naturalness of the complementizer "that" to head up the subordinate noun clause, as in these revised versions:

01. The authors opinion about Blacks as a race is *that* we cannot help that we do poorly in socioeconomic fields and standardized testing.
02. I feel *that* no kind of test can measure potential or a person IQ.
03. The information presented is *that* East Asian typically earn higher scores versus White Americans.
04. To help support his notion, stated is *that* the average Black person's IQ is 85, average White person 100.

The fifth example, of course, does not tolerate any added complementizer and is not standardized the same way; that is, you can't say:

05. Also implied is **that** how could these test be wrong.

The student who wrote these sentences was not satisfied with my suggestion of adding the complementizer *that* where it would have made good standard sense. Doing so changed the feeling of the sentences for him. From the academic point of view, I was offering correction, simple editing, fine tuning, to produce a little more appropriate formality. But I listened to him, and after some discussion, offered a rather different standardization solution, namely to use a colon. The student lit up and indicated that he preferred this solution, whose effect was to cordon off the noun clauses and keep them from being treated as subordinate clauses. I refer to this usage as "colon structure," where the addition of the colon standardizes the sentence just fine and suggests that the structures introduced by the colon are, in some sense, paratactic rather than regular subordinate structures:

001. The authors opinion about Blacks as a race is: we cannot help that we do poorly in socioeconomic fields and standardized testing.
002. I feel: no kind of test can measure potential or a person IQ.
003. The information presented is: East Asian typically earn high er scores versus White Americans.
004. To help support his notion, stated is: the average Black person's IQ is 85, average White person 100.
005. Also implied is: how could these test be wrong.

The paratactic idea fits perfectly with the live speech, main clause preferences of Ebonics.

The preference for paratactic structures over subordinate structures in Ebonics, it should be noted, in no way suggests that Ebonics speakers lack any ability to deal with complex ideas. Any such correlation of cognitive ability with particular grammatical preferences is completely uncalled for, as shown by the very examples discussed. The logical relationships are identical whether the ideas are presented in subordinate style, as in Examples 01 to 05, or whether they are presented in paratactic style, as in Examples 001-005. In other words, the two styles are cognitively equivalent even though they are grammatically or syntactically quite different. You can say and mean the same thing in either style.

To conclude this grammatical excursus, the very grammar of Ebonics is bent toward voice, and an understanding of the grammatical properties of Ebonics in comparison with the corresponding properties of standard English would help teachers and students to communicate with each other in a setting that is respectful of the students' linguistic abilities and maximizes their motivation and practical ability to acquire the standard version and express themselves accordingly.

In the larger picture, and in keeping with these comments about voice, Geneva Smitherman has emphasized that Ebonics encompasses much more than matters of form—it is the expression of a way of being (Smitherman "It Be's Dat Way"). As such, challenges to the language are perceived as challenges to the person. In one area of being, African American students emphasize that Ebonics is a language for "keepin it real." Along these lines, I love what one student said about her Ebonics in a paper she titled "Ebonics is the Best." Her words help me emphasize how important it is to show respect for Ebonics.

EBONICS IS THE BEST

In "Ebonics is the Best," a student named Brenda wrote plainly as a first-year student about the uniqueness of Ebonics, something she feels deeply. The portions given here do not hide the fact that Brenda is not yet completely comfortable with standard forms, but there is something very good about what she says and how she says it. Before I conclude this chapter, I want to quote from her paper. Brenda begins:[5]

> The one big question in college right now: Is Ebonics another language or is it just a dialect. Most educated people say that Ebonics is just "lazy talk" and the usage of slang words. My definition of language is a form of communication among people. The way I speak and the usage of words is what make my language it's own. What they fail to realize is that Ebonics has bonding power, body language, and soul, something that other languages do not have.

About the power of Ebonics, she says:

> The power for me, a strong Ebonics speaker, is that when I speak, often people do not know what I am talking about or what I am trying to express. When I am in my community and I get together with my peers we can start "rapping" (speaking) to where other people will not have a clue to what we are talking about. I can get so deep into Ebonics to where sometime my mother will say "Brenda what are you talking about? I can't understand a word you're talking." That power I have to communicate with my peers makes me feel so good inside because when I have that power to speak Ebonics it feel so good to know that I am in my community and relating to people that understand me, and do not have to be something that I am really not. I am an Ebonics speaker but when I go into society I have to be "phony" and speak something that is not I. The power feels so good when I can bond with

my culture. The only power in my eyes that Standard English has, is succeeding.

After a lively discussion of the role of body language in relation to Ebonics, where she says: "We women will move our heads, snap our fingers, roll our eyes, hold our hand in someone's face, place a hand on the hip and even stand with our feet at an angle," and "As for the men, they bop their heads, put their hands in the air, use a lot of hand gestures and stand real hard," she transitions into a discussion of the idea of soul in language. She writes:

> Ebonics has soul more than all of the things I talked about. Soul meaning that sometimes it feels like I have music in my ears as I speak Ebonics. I put soul into my speaking and try to make the listener feel where I am coming from. When I have this music in my ears that is where all the body language takes place. With the body language and soul it makes me have this rhythm when I speak. When I put soul into my speaking it helps me keep it real about whatever I am speaking about. That means neither biting of the tongue nor holding back anything that is on my mind.

As Brenda concludes her paper, she says, in her own way, what I am trying to say:

> My point being is that every language has some uniqueness. Society do not put other languages down in the gutter appose to the way they put Ebonics, so to say that Ebonics do not have any uniqueness is a lie because I just pointed out a few qualities that Ebonics have. Maybe if society took some time and try to learn something maybe they would see we are not dumb we just need help in learning how to use the two. To me I think they might be jealous because half of them could not use Ebonics. Another point, how could society judge something without taking the time to see what is going on.

CONCLUSION

The nearly universally disparaging and harshly judgmental view of Ebonics and other minority Englishes, whether in the university, the high school or lower grades, or the public mind, makes the task of improving the quality of education for speakers of Ebonics or any other linguistic-cultural minorities seem quite daunting. On top of that, the tough attitudes could combine with the usual resistance to new approaches and to the training that is needed. However, there is room for great optimism because the changes that are needed are not difficult to fathom nor strange, once the facts about Ebonics are understood. The clear presentation of the facts about Ebonics brings great energy where there is so often a simple, even regretful, resignation to the debilitating myths about African American intelligence and language ability. The vast number of teachers in our society, I believe, would dearly love for lower performing African American students to succeed academically and, so, would be thrilled if practical measures became available to them to achieve the goal, such as adequate language and culture teaching materials, suitable training in the materials, and the curricular space to implement them.

The first step is to face the negative views of Ebonics head-on, not with ephemeral politically correct values, but with solid, lasting, linguistic truth. This truth in a nutshell is that on scientific grounds Ebonics deserves respect as a language and as a variety of English. This truth has clear, obvious, and practical repercussions. These repercussions include the need to:

1. Give explicit teaching about differences between standard English and Ebonics (or other varieties of English).
2. Use linguistically and culturally affirming readings.[6]
3. Allow the student to use comfortable language in the composing stages of writing and in discussion periods when the flow of ideas and thoughts is paramount.

To carry out the first step, teachers may need to seek out specific training in language. Here, it becomes the duty of schools of education to offer such training, and it is the duty of people like myself to make practical materials available for the classroom. A good place to start is sources such as the books cited earlier and mentioned in the bibliography: *Spoken Soul* by John and Russell Rickford, *Black Street Speech* by John Baugh, and the classic *Talkin and Testifyin* by Geneva Smitherman, as well as my own article "Liberating American Ebonics from Euro-English."

Explicit teaching about language is the most needed and the most avoided dimension. The key for both teacher and student is the idea that Ebonics and English are plainly distinct varieties of English (see my "Liberating American Ebonics" for a fuller explication of this point). Making the distinction publicly, explicitly, and believably invites open discussion of language, of the beauties, power, and differing contexts of the language varieties (as encouraged in Eleanor Kutz's work), and, most importantly, dissolves the threat of self-diminishment and self-defeat for the Ebonics-strong student. In such a positive atmosphere, the teacher has the joy of bringing self-respect to students.

NOTES

1. The term *Ebonics* refers throughout to the same variety of English also termed African American Vernacular English, African American English, Black English Vernacular, Black English, and Soul Talk, among others.
2. This point is made very well by Roger Fowler in *Linguistic Criticism* and is worth quoting here: "Standard English derives from the dialects of the south-east of [England], developing since the fourteenth century as a result of the domination by London and its environs in the spheres of government, commerce, education, and communications. . . . The standard is inevitably associated with and used by people who have enjoyed higher levels of income, education, and power, and its resultant prestige may lead people to regard it as 'not a dialect'" (187).
3. Unfortunately, there are many who react negatively to the idea of Black culture because, for example, they over-associate certain controversial outlets, such as gangsta rap, rather than take into account the fact that church activity is still at the heart of Black culture, as evidenced by the power and national impact of gospel music as well as the strong family and community values that endure despite opposite pressures.
4. Linguists often use the spelling "BIN" to distinguish it from standard "been," especially because Ebonics overlaps with standard English in its use of regular "been."
5. I thank Brenda, an Ebonics speaker who agrees with the sentiments of this chapter, for permission to include her paper here.
6. The purpose of culturally affirming readings is not to promote minority cultures to the exclusion of mainstream culture. This is not what is being espoused here. What is being espoused is the simple idea that students need to know that they, who they are, and where they come from count, too. My focus is on the language-based changes needed to help minority-English speakers make greater strides toward the mainstream.

WORKS CITED

Baugh, John. *Beyond Ebonics: Linguistic Pride and Racial Prejudice*. New York: Oxford UP, 2000.

Baugh, John. *Black Street Speech: Its History, Structure, and Survival*. Austin: U Texas P, 1983.

Elbow, Peter. "Inviting the Mother Tongue: Beyond 'Mistakes,' 'Bad English,' and 'Wrong Language.'" *Everyone Can Write" Essays Toward a Hopeful Theory of Writing*. New York: Oxford UP, 2000. 323-50.

Fowler, Roger. *Linguistic Criticism*. 2nd ed. New York: Oxford UP, 1996.

Green, Georgia M. "Main Clause Phenomena in Subordinate Clauses." *Language* 52 (1976): 382–97.

Hooper, Joan and Sandra A. Thompson. "On the Applicability of Root Transformations." *Linguistic Inquiry* 4 (1973): 465–91.

Kutz, Eleanor. *Language and Literacy: Studying Discourse in Communities and Classrooms.* Portsmouth, NH: Boynton/Cook, 1997.

Palacas, Arthur. "Liberating American Ebonics from Euro-English." *College English* 63 (2001): 326–52.

Pinker, Stephen. *The Language Instinct.* New York: Morrow, 1994.

Rickford, John and Russell Rickford. *Spoken Soul: The Story of Black English.* New York: Wiley, 2000.

Smitherman, Geneva. *Talkin and Testifyin: The Language of Black America.* Boston: Houghton Mifflin, 1977. Detroit: Wayne State UP, 1986.

____. "It Be's Dat Way Sometime." *English Journal* 63 (1974): 16–17.

Sowell, Thomas. "Patterns of Black Excellence." *Education: Assumptions versus History.* Stanford: Hoover Institution P, 1986. 7–38.

4

NEGOTIATING "INTERFERENCE"

The Politics of Addressing Students' Writing Patterns

Jennifer Liethen Kunka
Francis Marion University

Scenario 1: During a faculty meeting, a White science professor introduces himself to a new English professor, also White. After a few minutes of conversation, the science professor launches into a long conversation about the quality of students' writing at their southern university. After complaining at length about students' poor grammar skills and ineptness with language, the science professor leans in and quietly proclaims, "They shouldn't let them talk that way at home."

Scenario 2: A White writing center director is greeted outside the writing center one day by a White composition professor. The composition professor has with her Danielle, a female African American student, who is visibly uncomfortable about the exchange that is about to ensue. After some small pleasantries, the composition professor introduces Danielle to the writing center director and states the student is having "some AAVE problems" and "issues with dialect interference." Watching Danielle cringe uncomfortably and shuffle her feet, the director knows that Danielle would rather be any place other than where she is at that moment.

Scenario 3: A White English professor from New England joins an English department in the South. During the first weeks of class, he is struck by the strong southern accent exhibited by his students. He notices one student, however, who seems to share his New England accent. The professor asks the student, named Michael, where he is from. Michael explains that he has lived in the South his whole life and grew up just a few miles away from the university. Surprised, the professor asks, "But how is it you don't have a southern accent?" Michael responds, in his best southern twang, "You mean, why don't I talk like this?" He continues in his New England voice, "I taught myself out of the southern accent a long time ago. I don't want people to think I'm stupid."

Scenario 4: *"Tammy," a White female student, meets with a White female writing center tutor for help developing a paper for her first-year composition class. Tammy has to write a narrative about a time in which language shaped the way she viewed another person. Tammy chooses to write about her parents and tells the tutor that they talk "real country." In high school, Tammy was reluctant to ask her parents for help with her homework, assuming that—because of their thick country accent—they were not very smart. One day, Tammy became so frustrated with her homework that she asked for their help. She was amazed how much her parents did know—especially about writing papers.*

The tutor finds this story interesting because Tammy also has a fairly thick, what-could-be-called "country" accent, rich with colloquialisms and dialectical distinctiveness. When the tutor asks Tammy with which areas of her paper she needs the most help, Tammy admits that she has been told her whole life that she does not "write proper." Tammy's paper was a bit unorganized, but she also exhibited sentence patterns consistent with what has been termed "regional dialect interference"—categorized by problems with subject–verb agreement, irregular verbs, verb tense and conjugation, plurals, articles, and prepositions. As they talk, it becomes clear that English classes are a constant source of frustration for Tammy because she never, as she said, "talked right" or knew how to write well.

After a few visits to the writing center, Tammy returns to see her tutor and pulls out her story—inked with lots of marginal comments about grammar. She has earned a "C" on the story and feels very depressed about it. Many of her grammatical problems stemmed from passages she revised on her own after her last meeting at the writing center. She feels bad about the "C," but particularly so because she is enrolled in school on a scholarship that requires her to maintain a 3.0 GPA in her classes. She begins to doubt if she will make it in college. If her language—far less "countrified" than that of her parents—is not enough to make it in this regional university, even after several revisions and trips to the writing center, what does that say about her? What does that say about where she comes from? What does that say about the language she speaks—and the academy's acceptance of it?

* * *

In 1974, *College Composition and Communication* published *Students' Rights to Their Own Language,* a background statement supporting the 1972 resolution on dialect passed by the CCCC Executive Committee. The resolution states:

> We affirm the students' right to their own patterns and varieties of language—the dialects of their nurture or whatever dialects in which they find their own identity and style. Language scholars long ago denied that the myth of a standard American dialect has any validity. The claim that any one dialect is unacceptable amounts to an attempt of one social group to exert its dominance over another. Such a claim leads to false advice for speakers and writers, and immoral advice for humans. A nation proud of its diverse heritage and its cultural and racial variety will preserve its heritage of dialects. We affirm strongly that teachers must have the experiences and training that will enable them to respect diversity and uphold the right of students to their own language. (Committee 2-3)

Thirty years after CCCC adopted this resolution, writing instructors continue to struggle with these same issues of language and dialect in the classroom, and the stakes are higher for both students and educators. In the wake of the No Child Left Behind Act, federal and state standardized testing of student mastery of Standard Written English (SWE) is directly connected to funding for schools, closures of failing schools, and dismissals of school administrators. The College Board's recent changes to the verbal section of the SAT and the addition of a writing component and editing test further testify to the institutionalization of SWE instruction in educational settings.

In 2003, the National Council of Teachers of English (NCTE) passed a resolution reaffirming the 1974 CCCC position statement, stating "that NCTE [encourages] its members, other educators, and all people interested in education to become familiar with the document and be guided by the principles of the statement in developing and adopting educational policies and practices." Today, writing instructors are generally more informed about the diverse linguistic backgrounds of their students; however, their ability and desire to defend and execute students' rights to their own language is compromised by the vociferous demands of the academy to teach students how to write "correctly" in SWE. Each of the scenarios at the beginning of this chapter highlight the types of struggles many composition instructors and writing center professionals face when addressing the challenges of dialect with their students. Tammy is not alone in her struggle with language. In my work as a writing center director in the southeastern United States, I have met many students who believe they do not "write proper"— in other words, conform to the protocols of standard written English that generally diverge from their own local dialectical patterns. Students like Tammy, who speak with strong home dialects, often find that their "right to their own language" must be subsumed by educational pressures to conform to SWE in order to be educated at all.

CCCC's 1972 position statement has succeeded in raising awareness about dialect issues with writing instructors. Writing assignments that encourage students to thoughtfully explore the role of language in their lives and identities can help students to understand SWE as a dialect. However, as Tammy's situation illustrates, students may have a right to their own language, but at the end of the writing process, they are still expected to produce SWE in the academy.

In other situations, well-meaning faculty members—even those who are knowledgeable about linguistics and issues of dialect—are sometimes too quick to make assumptions about race, patently diagnose students with African American Vernacular English (AAVE), and with good intentions send them off to writing centers for extra help. However, dialect issues are sometimes much more complicated than they appear and are not restricted by racial markers. For example, the regional dialect present in the eastern Carolinas is not simply a phenomenon of AAVE or Southern White Vernacular English (SWVE), but a compilation of the two categories, defined by differentiations with subject–verb agreement, verb tense and conjugation, plurals, articles, prepositions, double modals ("might could have"), and double negatives. Gaillynn Davis Clements has suggested some regional dialect patterns in central North Carolina can be traced back as far as the 1790s and may have evolved by a combination of immigration and migration patterns and speech contact between Black slaves and workers and White slave owners and employers (70-71). Today, many Black and White students in the Carolinas exhibit very similar dialectical traits, which colloquially have been termed by locals as "country" speech but linguistically can be attributed to a melding of AAVE and SWVE patterns.

Although educators may try to point out students' difficulties in adapting to the standards of SWE, the rhetoric of "dialect interference," as exemplified by the case of Danielle, can prove more damaging than productive to students. Dialects are simply systems "with distinct subsets of language patterns" (Wolfram and Schilling-Estes 4). Although *dialect interference* is the standard linguistic term used to describe variants between one dialect and another (such as SWE), as writing professionals, we need to acknowledge that the rhetoric of "interference" is not conducive to the classroom, that it depreciates students' self-esteem and devalues the discourse communities from which they emerge.

More importantly, with whom, and with what set of expectations, does this language *interfere*? In short, although the CCCC statement on dialect does succeed in acknowledging students' right to their own language, we still have an elephant in the classroom: How do we bridge the gap between respecting home dialects while engaging in the practical work of the academy? If we want our students to succeed in college and in the workplace, we must help them in more realistic ways to bridge the conflict between their home dialects and SWE. As educators, we must be open in acknowledging in our classrooms that SWE is just one of many dialects of English, but it is the one that is socially preferred in business, education, and law. We have a responsibility to teach SWE grammar instruction within the context of writing. Even more importantly, we also have a responsibility to teach students *how* to make linguistic choices, to understand the rhetorical situations in which they find themselves, and to use the appropriate language patterns to communicate in their respective linguistic markets and achieve their communication goals.

STANDARD WRITTEN ENGLISH AND THE LINGUISTIC MARKET

According to linguist Walt Wolfram, formal standard English is based on the "written language of established writers and is typically codified in English grammar texts" (7). Wolfram notes that there are "virtually no speakers who consistently speak Formal Standard English as prescribed in textbooks" (7). However, many people do more regularly conform to what he terms "informal standard English," which may carry slight variations due to local and regional speaking patterns. An accent is not a negating feature to achieving the sentence patterns found in informal standard English. Informal standard English also generally does not carry sentence constructions that are considered "nonstandard."

SWE developed through the privileging and standardization of speech patterns by early New England settlers. As described by the CCCC Executive Committee, "Americans sought to achieve linguistic marks of success as exemplified in what they regarded as proper, cultivated usage. Thus the dialect used by prestigious New England speakers early became the 'standard' the schools attempted to teach" (Committee 5). Although the CCCC Executive Committee notes that "there is no single, homogeneous American 'standard,'" it does acknowledge that the "need for a dialect to serve the larger, public community has resulted in a general commitment" to edited American English (EAE) (5). Northeastern cities like New York and Boston became the major hubs for publishing and the consequent production of English grammar textbooks. Therefore, the adoption of northeastern dialect and language patterns tacitly became the standard by which "good taste" in language was measured.

Whereas standard dialects "are largely defined by their *absence* of socially stigmatized structures of English," Wolfram notes that vernacular dialects are "characterized by the *presence* of socially obtrusive structures" (11). Such dialects develop in a number of ways, such as by migration, immigration, isolation, language contact, or invention (Wolfram and Schilling-Estes 29-34). Wolfram writes, "Since both formal and informal standard varieties of English are associated with middle-class, mainstream groups, they are socially respected, but since vernacular varieties are associated with the social underclass, *they are not considered socially respectable*" (Wolfram 12-13, italics added).

Wolfram is using the rhetoric of taste—social respectability—to describe why such regional dialects are considered "nonstandard." The exhibition of good taste in language can be approximated to the appropriate exercise of linguistic capital. In *Language and Symbolic Power*, Pierre Bourdieu defines linguistic capital as the value with which spoken or written utterances are endowed in specific cultural markets (Thompson 18). In the United States, expressions in SWE carry a high linguistic capital in systems of business, education, and law; the confident and competent expression of this dialect corresponds with socioeconomic power and respect in these communities. The well-educated upper classes have very little difficulty in "respond[ing] with relative ease to the demands of most formal or official occasions" (Thompson 21) because their dialect is very close to that which is expected for such situations. However,

> individuals from petits-bourgeois backgrounds must generally make an effort to adapt their linguistic expressions to the demands of formal markets. The result is that their speech is often accompanied by tension and anxiety, and by a tendency to rectify or correct expressions so that they concur with dominant norms. This hyper-correction of petit-bourgeois speech is the sign of a class divided against itself, whose members are seeking, at the cost of constant anxiety, to produce linguistic expressions which bear the mark of a habitus other than their own. (Thompson 21)

Such anxiety and frustration can lower vernacular speakers' self-esteem and may drive them to leave educational systems entirely (22).

The expectations of SWE usage in business, education, and law, as well as the codification of those expectations through institutions like the Department of Education, the College Board, universities, and K–12 school districts, all work concurrently to shape the linguistic market and the class stratifications within it. Bourdieu writes, "The constitution of a linguistic market creates the conditions for an objective competition in and through which the legitimate competence can function as linguistic capital, producing a *profit of distinction* on the occasion of each social exchange" (55). When applied to SWE in the United States, however, the profit of distinction of using SWE is less apparent because, as Wolfram explains, American audiences negatively appraise the *appearance of nonstandard constructions* as opposed to recognizing the absence of nonstandard dialectical features (Wolfram 11).

Thus, the set of grammatical rules identified with SWE in the United States has become an accepted linguistic standard for the enactment of American middle-class subjectivity. "Broadcast English"—that spoken by Katie Couric and other news broadcasters—carried more of a "flat" mid-western tone (McWhorter 9) but most closely resembles the language patterns of SWE in its oral form (Committee 5). Through its promulgation via institutionalized and commercial venues, SWE continues to be the dialect identified with success in American corporate and government systems. This emphasis, however, comes at the cost of disenfranchisement of many groups of Americans who come from home dialects that differ in language and grammatical structures from SWE—students like Tammy and Danielle. Furthermore, this disenfranchisement continues if K–12 schools, colleges, and universities do not provide students with sufficient education in the language and grammatical structures of SWE to enable them to use it correctly and confidently in rhetorical situations for which it is more appropriate than the students' home dialects.

EXERCISING CAPITAL IN THE LINGUISTIC MARKET

Student writers will find themselves limited in making choices in the linguistic market if they do not carry the linguistic capital—confident and competent usage of SWE—that continues to be privileged in many spheres of power. I have discovered that people like Michael—students from a variety of racial and ethnic backgrounds who have taught themselves out of dialects that contain accents and nonstandard grammatical patterns—are not uncommon in the South. Desiring not to be stereotyped as "rednecks," many Southerners like Michael determine they need to increase their options for exchange in the linguistic market, and through self-teaching or engagement with accent-reduction courses and English courses, choose to provide themselves with new forms of linguistic capital. Students like Michael are "market-savvy" in that they have already faced the reality that their home dialects are either not valued or negatively valued in spheres of business, education, or law, and, consequently, have sought to change the conditions of their linguistic commodification. By engaging in code-switching, Michael has created for himself a "bilingual identity," in which "the dominant language [is] used more often to discuss things like school, politics, and other subjects most likely to have been first encountered in it, whereas the local language is used mostly to talk about casual, intimate, or cultural things" (McWhorter 41).

This is not to say that home dialects do not carry their own linguistic capital in other markets. During my teaching experience in the South, I have also met students who have actually been shunned by hometown friends and family members for using informal standard English in speech and sounding "too educated." The point missed by the science professor described in Scenario 1 is that these students find that the linguistic capital expected in professional circles carries with it a negative value when applied to home situations. In some cases, speaking informal standard English at home can cause a speaker's credibility to be questioned in the same ways that credibility is questioned by speakers of nonstandard dialects in professional contexts.

In 1974, the CCCC Executive Committee proposed that a generation of English teachers could shape contemporary attitudes about employability and dialect, arguing that "English teachers who feel they are bound to accommodate the linguistic prejudices of current employers perpetuate a system that is unfair to both students who have job skills and to the employers who need them" (Committee 14). The Committee further asserted that "changing attitudes towards dialect variations does not seem an unreasonable goal, for today's students will be tomorrow's employers" (14). Consequently, during the last thirty years, the instruction of writing has shifted away from the acquisition of SWE grammatical and language skills and towards issues of personal expression. As written by the CCCC Executive Committee in 1974: "We should begin our work in composition with them by making [students] feel confident that their writing, in whatever dialect, makes sense and is important to us, that we read it and are interested in the ideas and person that the writing reveals" (15).

This shift in instructional emphasis has resulted in additional pressure on students who have strong vernacular dialects that carry nonstandard grammatical constructions. Thirty years after the publication of the CCCC position statement on dialect, SWE still carries privileged capital in the linguistic market, as reinforced by a contemporary educational culture that promotes continual assessment of SWE skills. Today, rather than finding that they are embraced in professional markets that value their dialect variations, these students are finding themselves further disadvantaged because they lack the linguistic background needed to perform SWE.

Instructional models that emphasize personal expression often presume that the written product will reach an audience that is interested in that personal expression, regardless of the form in which it is written. However, in the workplace, the form of writing—particularly if it reveals the presence of nonstandard constructions—may actually preclude an audience member from understanding the personal expression or considering it to be credible. In her study of white-collared professionals' response to grammatical error, Maxine Hairston identifies some SWE grammatical errors as "status marking" (796), meaning that these SWE errors will cause professionals to evaluate such writers as unintelligent or incompetent in the professional workplace. Many of the status-marking errors identified by Hairston—including subject–verb agreement problems, nonstandard verb usage, double negatives, and use of objective pronouns as subjects—are common features of nonstandard dialects. Today, students with nonstandard dialects who leave school without mastering SWE do not find the professional world as envisioned by CCCC in 1974—that employers are more accepting of dialect variations in the professional workplace. As Rei Noguchi notes, "we disproportionately put at risk students who speak a nonstandard variety of English since they are the ones most likely to reproduce in their writing the 'status-marking' and 'very serious' errors so roundly condemned by the professionals" (29). Rather, today's students find that they write in dialects that are not valued in the professional market *and* they are without the background necessary to perform SWE confidently and competently, should they so choose. Student writers cannot successfully code-switch to SWE if they are not provided with a sufficient educational background to execute that dialect successfully.

In the most cynical way, some may view a renewed emphasis on SWE instruction as a Foucauldian exercise of control by forcing nonstandard dialect writers to subscribe to the preferred forms of dominant discourse. We might question if retention of nonstandard dialects in academic institutions might be considered languages of revolt against the class-based institutionalism of SWE. We might also ask why English instructors should help students identified with "dialect interference" to co-opt the language of power rather than revolt against it.

Rather than working to destabilize the priorities of the linguistic market, writing instructors should concentrate on providing students with marketable linguistic choices—including the confident and competent ability to use SWE. The usage of SWE has very real socioeconomic consequences for our students. With an education in English, our students should be able to exercise the right to use the dialect which commands the highest linguistic capital in the American professional market. As John McWhorter writes:

> Always and forever, the standard variety will be indispensable to upward mobility, and always and forever, one of the main places children acquire comfort and fluency in the standard variety will be in school. When they come to school, children often have only limited ability in the standard variety. . . . What we must often recall . . . [is] that

> the job of school is to *add a new layer* to a child's speech repertoire, *not to undo* the one they already have. (15)

Efforts to increase SWE instruction need not impinge on students' rights to their own language, but offer students more choices for achieving linguistic diversity and value in professional marketplace.

In order to equip students with the skills they need to allow them to exercise linguistic capital in the professional marketplace, writing instructors—particularly in the K–12 level—need to refocus energy on SWE instruction. This instruction, however, must be reinforced with a concurrent instruction about the realities of the linguistic market. "English" is too often mistakenly defined as a singular, monolithic entity. Students need to know that SWE is just one of many dialects that form the American linguistic landscape, but they should know that SWE is currency in that its usage correlates to the highest wages in the American marketplace. By learning about the range of dialects available to them, our students will be in the best positions to define their own linguistic battlegrounds and choose their own battles.

The labor market has changed dramatically since 1974, and as Thomas L. Friedman describes in *The World Is Flat: A Brief History of the 21st Century*, workers around the world are exploiting the American linguistic market to their own socioeconomic advantage. American students today are not just competing for jobs with other American workers, but with a global workforce.

In *The World Is Flat*, Friedman shows the innovation with which corporations exploit the American linguistic market to earn a profit. He describes his visits to a call center in Bangalore, in which he watches Indian workers receive training in the language and speech patterns of various American dialectical groups. For example, workers who receive training in flat midwestern speech and dialect patterns will be employed to telemarket or answer phone queries for Midwesterners in the United States.

> On the surface, there is something unappealing about the idea of inducing other people to flatten their accents in order to compete in a flatter world. But before you disparage it, you have to taste just how hungry these kids are to escape the lower end of the middle class and move up. If a little accent modification is the price they have to pay to jump a rung of the ladder, then so be it—they say. (Friedman 27)

Speech-language acquisition classes help Indian workers to tap into American consumers' trusted home dialects. The success of these speech-language courses allow corporations to outsource call center operations to linguistically competent low-cost workers while improving their profit margins.

Corporate writing projects are also being outsourced to Indian workers versed in SWE. Friedman describes an Indian company called Brickwork (a division of B2K) that provides American executives with personal assistant services. Indian personal assistants prepare research, write brochures, and create PowerPoint presentations, sending the finished products through the Internet to their American clients (Friedman 31). Another such firm, Office Tiger, employs Indian "document specialists" who specialize in providing writing and document production services for Fortune 500 companies (Boo). At Office Tiger, located in Chennai, confident and competent fluency in SWE is needed because "a third of all work assignments must be sent back to the United States within an hour" (Boo). If American students are not prepared to write in SWE for the American workplace, other global workers are readily mastering this dialect and are more than willing to compete.

Indian workers see mastery of selected American dialects as linguistic capital with socioeconomic value in the marketplace. Mastery of American dialects does not devalue their home dialects; rather, American dialects are used as currency in a market that derives profit from their use. American writing instructors should feel a sense of urgency as a result of these developments. We must make students aware of the breadth of the linguistic market, as well as provide them with the linguistic currency that will make them most competitive in the American marketplace.

NEGOTIATING DIALECT ISSUES IN WRITING INSTRUCTION

In the 1974 background statement, the CCCC Executive Committee writes, "Students who want to write EAE [Edited American English] will have to learn the forms identified with that dialect as additional options to the forms they already control" (Committee 15). But in classrooms today—particularly in regions when the local dialect is at a strong variance with the language patterns and grammar of SWE—how do writing instructors communicate to students the reasons they should "want to write" in EAE or SWE? What kind of awareness do we provide to students about the linguistic market? And how careful are we in disassociating our instruction of SWE from implied value judgments about students' home dialects? A dissonance exists between actively respecting students' rights to their own language and providing SWE instruction. Similarly, there exists a dissonance between the idealism of the CCCC statement and the practicalities with which our students must face the professional marketplace.

Students cannot make the choice to use SWE if they do not have a strong enough education in the dialect to use it confidently. While compositionists and writing center professionals should approach SWE as a dialect and an "additional option" in their linguistic choices, they also have a responsibility to teach students how, when, and why to exercise those choices. Writing instructors need to make conscious decisions about their approach to dialect issues in order to equip students to compete in the linguistic marketplace while affirming their linguistic heritage. Taken together, the following steps suggest one such approach to providing a more equitable and practical pedagogy.

Make Students Aware That SWE Is a Dialect

In English courses throughout students' educational careers, writing instructors need to emphasize to students that English is not a monolithic, singular entity and SWE is just one of many dialects in English. Writing instructors should give students an awareness of the multiplicity of the linguistic market by showing students how their home dialects are valued *and* how SWE is valued in different rhetorical situations and marketplaces. By openly identifying SWE as a dialect, writing instructors can sidestep linguistic judgments that unintentionally emerge when evaluating writing. Telling students that their English instructor plans to "evaluate their mastery of English" is quite different than explaining to them their instructor will "evaluate their mastery of the SWE dialect." The rhetoric of dialect needs to be used more frequently in classrooms and should be accompanied by discussions about the linguistic market.

Respect Students' Right to Their Own Language While Giving Them Marketable Choices About Dialect Usage

Language usage is a pivotal feature of identify formation. The goal of English education, as advocated by the CCCC statement on dialect, should be to "respect the diversity" of our students, and to appreciate their dialectical distinctiveness as an inextricable part of their identities (Committee 3). Students need to know that their own dialects carry value in a variety of linguistic markets, especially at home. Writing instructors need to respect and validate those dialects while giving students access to SWE, the dialect that commands the highest monetary value in the professional marketplace. We have a responsibility to help our students become competitive in the global marketplace, and a strong command of SWE will help students to meet the needs of professional audiences. Writing teachers should view instruction of SWE as a step towards empowerment in the market, not a rescription of students' home languages.

Reinforce Dialectical Awareness in Teacher Training at All Levels

Since the publication of the 1972 CCCC statement, writing instructors have learned a great deal about theories of linguistic diversity. Yet many still struggle with the effective, practical application of such theories in their classrooms. Students like Danielle and Tammy have well-meaning writing instructors who are generally aware of the dialect issues in their classrooms; however, the manner in which these instructors discuss dialect needs refinement and sensitivity in order to maintain the egos of their students while providing quality SWE instruction.

Specific instruction about how to approach SWE as a dialect needs to be more overt in teacher training curricula at all levels. Although discussions of dialect interference may be helpful within teacher-training sessions to explain the linguistic disparities between vernacular dialects and SWE, the rhetoric of interference should not be used with students. The word *interference* carries obvious negative connotations. Students who enter the academy knowing only their vernacular dialects—the languages they have become acclimated to for their entire lives—should not be told that their words interfere. By extension, because language forms a vital part of our self-conceptions of subjectivity, the rhetoric of interference can make students feel as though they are "in the way"—that our society does not have room for speakers like they are.

Similarly, when young students enter grade school and have it regularly drilled into them that they—like Tammy—don't "write proper," they feel their home discourse communities are devalued. The consequential feelings of low self-esteem can negatively affect all areas of learning. Rather, teachers may find that discussing English as a broad linguistic market with a range of dialects that fit the rhetorical needs of different audiences will be a more productive route to SWE instruction.

Provide Tutors With Strategies for Managing Dialect Issues in Writing Centers

Writing center tutors are really in a delicate spot when addressing dialect issues. What are writing center professionals to do when a well-meaning teacher walks Danielle to the writing center for help with dialect interference issues? Often, writing centers become the default location in which dialect awareness must be addressed with students either because it is not sufficiently explained in classroom settings or instructors—particularly those in disciplines outside of English—do not have the capacity for addressing such writing issues themselves. Consequently, writing centers are uniquely tasked with helping students to negotiate the difficult and contested spaces between their home languages and the expected discourse of academic and professional environments.

Writing center tutors must be very careful in negotiating this sensitive rhetorical space in consultations. Rather than using the language of error, tutors may find that employing the language of audience awareness can be a more productive path towards demonstrating respect for dialectical distinctiveness while showing writers that learning to manage SWE can give them linguistic capital in the marketplace. Like English teachers, writing center professionals have an obligation to show student writers the means to acquiring the language of power, as well as making them aware that language is socially constructed and its use should be adjusted and negotiated for the social situation in which it is used. In tutor-training sessions, writing center professionals need to review strategies for discussing dialect issues in tutorials.

Revisit the Role of SWE Grammar Instruction in the Teaching of Writing

Writing instructors must appreciate the socioeconomic impact of language usage and work to help our students achieve the linguistic capital needed to compete in the professional marketplace. By overemphasizing personal expression in writing, we mislead our students to expect that the marketplace will value their written expressions in whichever dialect they choose to write. As Hairston's study shows, the professional marketplace negatively values nonstandard dialects. Are we teaching writing well if the written products our students create will not be valued by real-world professional audiences?

In 1974, the CCCC Executive Committee wrote, "No one can ever use all of the resources of a language, but one function of the English teacher is to activate the student's competence, that is, increase the range of his habitual performance" (Committee 6). I argue that a primary function of English instruction must be to provide students with competent and confident skills in SWE. A stronger emphasis on SWE grammar instruction within the context of students' own writing needs to be reintroduced to writing classrooms at all levels of education.

* * *

I must acknowledge the complexity of my own position as a White writing center director and English professor who is from the Midwest but working in the South. I was born and raised in a middle-class, suburban Wisconsin family and became acclimated to a dialect that is much closer to what is considered informal standard English than the dialect patterns of many of my students in South Carolina. Because of the privilege my linguistic heritage afforded to me, I did not travel as difficult a road to SWE acquisition as the one that many of my students face.

Because language usage in the South is a prime signifier for a "Yankee," which comes with its own set of social and status-marking expectations—often laced with suspicion and expectations of rudeness or directness—I wonder sometimes how students perceive me as the person on campus designated to help them get past their dialectical interferences to reach SWE. I too have found a need to negotiate my own linguistic position in the South. I know that although I may speak a dialect that is closer to informal standard English than many local speakers, I also know that my midwestern dialect prevents me from being fully included in some southern social circles. I am aware that I do not fully carry the linguistic capital that is valued in some southern social markets and know that there are still social and linguistic codes used by my students and people in my community of which I am ignorant and, by virtue of my outsider status, am excluded.

Some of my most meaningful teaching and learning moments over the last five years, however, have been moments of exchange in which students in my classes and in my writing center tutorials have taught me some of the words and phrases of their home languages. I deeply appreciate their decision to include me in the rhetoric of their discourse communities and respect who they are and from where they come. Likewise, I hope they see my approach to teaching them the dialect of SWE as a sign of respect and an action of empowerment.

WORKS CITED

Boo, Katherine. "The Best Job in Town." *The New Yorker* 5 July 2004: 56+. *Expanded Academic ASAP Plus*. Infotrac. Francis Marion U, Rogers Library, Florence, SC. 7 June 2005 <http://web7.infotrac.galegroup.com>.

Bourdieu, Pierre. *Language and Symbolic Power*. Cambridge: Harvard UP, 1994.

Clements, Gaillynn D. "Socio-historical Evidence for Copula Variability in Rural Southern America." *Historical Linguistics 2003*. Eds. Michael Fortescue, Eva Skafte Jensen, Jens Erik Mogensen, and Lene Schosler. Amsterdam: Johns Benjamins Publishing Co., 2005. 61-73.

Committee on CCCC Language Statement. *Students' Right to Their Own Language*. Urbana, IL: National Council of Teachers of English, 1974.

Friedman, Thomas L. *The World Is Flat: A Brief History of the Twenty-First Century*. New York: Farrar, 2005.

Hairston, Maxine. "Not All Errors Are Created Equal: Nonacademic Readers in the Professions Respond to Lapses in Usage." *College English* 43 (1981): 794-806.

McWhorter, John. *Spreading the Word: Language and Dialect in America.* Portsmouth, NH: Heinemann, 2000.

NCTE. "On Affirming CCCC 'Students' Rights to Their Own Language.'" *National Council of Teachers of English.* 2003. 1 April 2006 <http://www.ncte. org/about/over/positions/category/div/114918.htm>.

Noguchi, Rei. *Grammar and the Teaching of Writing.* Urbana, IL: NCTE, 1991.

Thompson, John B. "Editor's Introduction." *Language and Symbolic Power.* Written by Pierre Bourdieu. Cambridge: Harvard UP, 1994.

Wolfram, Walt. *Dialects and American English.* Englewood Cliffs, NJ: Prentice Hall, 1991.

Wolfram, Walt, and Natalie Schilling-Estes. *American English.* 2nd ed. Malden, MA: Blackwell, 1998.

5

HOW I CHANGED MY MIND—
OR A BIDIALECTICIST
RETHINKS HER POSITION

Allison Shaskan
El Centro College

THE NORTHERN FOOD STAMP
OFFICE EXPERIENCE

"Allison Shaskan? Your caseworker will see you now." I stood up to exit the bleak waiting room, smiling broadly at Ms. Caseworker as I shook her hand. She led me down a long corridor and finally to her room where I was instructed to sit in the chair opposite her desk. "Now this is just a routine re-examination of your case file. The government is looking for discrepancies between what people claim they earn and their actual bills. If the two don't match, we assume that there is unreported money, and then we begin a formal investigation." Ms. Caseworker became absorbed in my file, finally pausing to ask, "You teach composition at a community college. How do you like it?" This was no conversation between equals taking place, and I was filled with great trepidation. I managed to stutter something out about teaching being a great joy and that I enjoyed the students.

"I've always wanted to write; in fact I wish that I had the time. Once I took this job as a social worker, I haven't had much free time." She returned to my file and concluded her mandatory search with these chilling words: "You are a pleasure to work with, considering the usual people I have to *help*. I know that you aren't *the type* to cheat the government by hiding money, so there is no reason to be suspicious of you. Your food stamp benefits will continue."

I was confused. "Am I under investigation?" "Absolutely not, but we have to continually re-evaluate people to catch those cheating the government. We catch a lot of people that way. The government requires it in order to deter fraud. Frankly, talking to clients like you is the best part of my job."

Pleasantries were exchanged and I was escorted out of the office. I managed to look at the other people still left in the waiting room, and they were primarily people of color, with many small children by their sides. My four kids were at home with their father, because I knew that I would be evaluated more highly for this women and children's program if I didn't bring my children. My husband was also available as his PhD student status allowed him to be at home during the day.

After a two-month gap of not receiving any of the food stamps I was eligible to receive, these months were backdated. I would have to return to the office for the same procedure in another four months, in addition to filling out monthly report forms. Curiously, these monthly report forms are scarier to sign than one's taxes: One signs under the threat of prosecution and jail if there is any knowing *or unknowing* misrepresentation.

I spent considerable energy determining in what ways I differed from the other people with whom the caseworker normally dealt. Why did she absolve me of suspicion? What about me was different? I was educated, and spoke the most standard of English. I was also White, but more Whites are on the food stamp program than persons of other races.[1] Did my educational status and possession of standard English remove me from suspicion? Is it possible that the next woman who was evaluated did not get a free pass because she had an unfavorable accent, and was distracted by her small children's needs during the interview? I found myself able to successfully navigate a program intended to help the poor because I possessed a middle-class education and (presumably) middle-class manners. Of course, this leaves out the matter of race. At this point, however, I was thinking only of language and class issues. What did she mean that I wasn't the type to cheat the government? Why wasn't I *the type*? Finally, why was I under such examination in the first place, as my mother's Social Security application was accepted immediately? These programs operate with entrenched understandings of the poor.

I have argued, based on this experience and these questions as many in a long progressive tradition have done, that stereotypical beliefs that equate poverty with fraud must be changed. I thought that bidialectalism, the ability to speak both the middle-class dialect along with one's own nonstandard dialect, was integral to this attitude shift. Only bidialectalism would help these women achieve economic independence. However, this focus on changing one's language as a way to escape poverty was my old argument;

I'm not sure it is now enough. My above experiences with the welfare system led me down this bidialectalist path. Subsequent experience leads me down another.

Bidialectalism As a Way Out?

Because of my earlier experience in the welfare office, I came to suggest that code-switching—gaining Standard English proficiency—was a long-term way out of the trap of poverty, and out of the negative judgment the poor have come to expect, based on such experiences. Using the dominant language system, I thought, would allow one to remain distant from this threat. To recognize and understand this threat, to see that when one signs on the dotted line for one's $348 worth of food money is to see that this money comes with judgment. Based on this judgment, perhaps especially reflected by one's language, one either gets the money or not, is accused of fraud or not, and in the scariest cases, loses one's children or not. Therefore, being poor and trying to collect public assistance *is* inherently dangerous.

Michael B. Katz's *Improving Poor People* explores this phenomenon. He writes, "welfare reform has been as much about improving poor people by changing their behavior as about helping them with food, housing or cash" (21). This *changing of behavior* is what I believed my experience was showing—that if poor people, especially those of color, could change their language behaviors they, like me, could have an easier time of it. If women, the primary users of public aid, could learn to speak more powerfully, that is, to adopt more acceptable speech patterns, through a not necessarily unwholesome *bi*dialecticism, they should then be able to circumnavigate the trap set to ensnare them. For as Katz writes, "Distrust of poor parents' competence combined with fears of social disorder . . . override the sentimental exaltation of domesticity that shaped writing about home and family" (39). And it could be argued that one's language is very often used to judge one's competence.

Katz chronicles the historic distrust of poor parents, which leads in its most extreme state to the removal of children from poor homes. This point must be fully understood. The poor, whose lives are defined by their economic reality, are always subject to the removal of their children because of the developed perception concerning negligence. Katz describes the difference between relief and "social insurance" (Social Security) and explains that although both alleviate poverty, this artificial division and subsequent class demarcation continued the penalizing attitudes society has maintained towards the poor. He argues that

> The division between AFDC [Aid to Families with Dependent Children] and the social insurance programs . . . incorporated into the

> structure of the welfare state the gendered distinctions embedded in social thought about poverty, risk, and dependence . . . most recipients of outdoor relief and subsequent forms of public assistance have been women. By contrast, social insurance . . . reflected a patriarchal model of welfare that disproportionately directed benefits to male family heads, leaving problems distinctive to women either uncovered or relegated to public assistance, whose much lower benefits often have been administered in more intrusive ways. (24-25)

Hence, the language skills of, say, the well-to-do golfer in south Florida chasing his social security check are not nearly as important as they are for the poor woman chasing her welfare or food stamp allotment. The golfer has supposedly *earned* his social security rights, whereas the woman must *prove* her welfare rights. The level of danger to herself and especially to her children is of a different order entirely.

And yet, true as this analysis may be, to argue for the unfortunate if vital necessity of bidialecticism runs smack into the view that almost any devaluation of a "native" dialect is a racist act. James Sledd suggests precisely this point (see Freed). However, at the time I believed that although Sledd was an important pioneer in the preservation of dialects, he viewed this linguistic issue from the "Ivory Tower," neglecting the street-level realities I believed I was facing. Obtaining a usable bachelors' degree, I assumed, meant escaping the tyranny of the food stamp program. The price of this degree was *only* the suppression of one's native dialect. A trade off for sure, but one well worth it. I simply believed bidialectalism could lead to a usable degree, and a fuller set of language skills that could then provide a ladder out of poverty. My experience had suggested to me that Sledd's early 1970s arguments to equalize the valuation of nonstandard dialects were overwhelmed by the food stamp offices of the early 2000s. Indeed, as this student of language discovered, somewhat to my horror, the caseworkers weren't nearly as magnanimous as James Sledd could be.

So, although creating a worthy campaign and one that educated persons in English departments may subscribe to, Sledd had presumably never attempted to procure food stamps with a nonstandard dialect nor had he presumably felt the fear of losing his children due to poverty or inability to communicate in standard ways. I recognize that he wished to alter the perception of the poor through the valuation of their native dialects, but without everybody believing as he does, the campaign seemed hopelessly stalled. That is why in the meantime I wished to provide those recipients of poverty aid with a means out of poverty through the addition of Standard English to their native language.

Although farther than Sledd or his devotees would care to go, codeswitching seemed a small price to pay as an escape out of these dismal programs. I realized that some would say codeswitching carried with it an obsessive bias toward Standard English, yet this was again a very small price to pay when measured against hunger or shame. The argument for bidialectalism was a hard-headed position. It would not be the position taken by someone who might argue for the cultivation of an "alternative sensibilities" route. And this was because of the enduring fact that local attitudes dictate norms concerning the poor, and America has a long and proud history of blaming the poor for their poverty. Antipoverty programs are administered locally, they hire local workers to evaluate and distribute this federal aid, and it is known that these local evaluators are often themselves just out of poverty and hold strongly to stereotypical beliefs as a means of distinguishing themselves from *the poor* whom they serve.

When I was told by my case worker that I was a delight to work with because I wasn't *like them*, I thought then that it was my language and possession of middle-class manners that provided this illusion. Perhaps the colder reality of this experience was that I was also White. Materially I was no different, but I was never under investigation because my race and language suggested that I held the values society wishes poor women to possess. I had to keep silent during the interview, because in reality I was just as dependent on the approval of the caseworker as others. I wanted to explain to other English teachers that the work of education and easily recognizable language skills is quite significant to those living at the bottom of this social world. Enough of story telling, it was time to enter the middle class.

Based on this experience, here, then, is where I assumed our responsibility as rhetoricians to lie: to counteract the false and damaging stereotypes of minorities and poor; to give them admission to the Standard English club; to allow them to speak of their world while also, and more importantly, gaining access to another world. Yet the uncomfortable question that arises from more experience, an experience described below, is this: Is the adoption of bidialecticism sufficient to overcome this predicament? Is language the core issue?

THE SOUTHERN CULINARY EXPERIENCE

I am now the executive director of a culinary school in a mid-sized southern city. My restaurant experiences during graduate school, along with an exciting semester spent in Chicago attending culinary school, led to this position. One of my favorite duties at work involves placing students in culinary arts jobs. I recruit employers through cold-calling, asking them if they need workers, and determining the sort of workers they may want.

Do they want a pantry worker who works during the day? A pastry chef with cake decorating abilities? Do they need a baker who can work the night shift? Do they regularly perform urine drug tests? Does this restaurant have a high-turnover rate? Are they an encouraging place or do they aggressively perform on "the hot line"? These questions help me send the best student to their facility so that we can match their desires with the needs of my students to have a restaurant job.

However, I never anticipated employers requesting students based on their gender or race. Recently, an employer of a major facility called to put in his "order" for a student worker. This order included the following specifics: no African Americans, no women, and preferably a Mexican.

"Why not a woman or African American?" I asked this chef.

"Women can't lift anything, always get pregnant, and Blacks never show up for work. You can always count on Mexicans showing up for their shift," I was told.

Ignoring the fact that not all Hispanic immigrants are "Mexican" as this certified executive chef seemed to think, I was stunned by his attitudes toward the African American population as a whole. My response was to send him two women although I would have preferred to send him two African American pregnant women!

This attitude is reinforced weekly when I send my students into the community for jobs, and consistently the African American students are not hired. I must always vouch for the African American student. At one point, I had a transplanted New Orleans culinary student whose technical skills far exceeded the skills of the local students, but I had a very hard time locating work for him. He and another student of White descent applied for the same position at a small restaurant, and the White student—*with no restaurant experience*—was hired. Within one week, this employer called me back asking if he could swap workers, as this White student was worthless, lacking initiative, technical skill, and any interest in the culinary arts field. I swapped.

Ironically, the very habits this White student had were the habits that this restaurant owner believed African Americans as a whole possessed. I did not hear a diatribe about White folks being lazy, crafty stoners, even though I have witnessed my share of stoned White folks working in the kitchen. It was the African American who worried him.

This African American is now the restaurant owner's sous chef (a top position in the kitchen with a good salary comparable to an assistant professor's pay), and his most valuable employee. Nevertheless, I had to personally vouch for him, convince the owner that he was "different," and then convince this student that he had to ignore the slights of being passed over initially. A tall order and one that provided me with an unfortunate window into the myriad difficulties members of the African American community must endure in attempting to gain access to positions in the dominant culture.

Although proud that this student had been placed in a top restaurant, I overheard his peers making fun of his attempts to be White, to suck up to the administration, to try to act like the teacher's pet. It was brutal, and I immediately told these students that it would behoove them to adopt this man's habits if they too wished to rise to a high position in the restaurant industry. Yet, the group ribbing him consisted of a White woman, a Hispanic, and three White men: A group of students who do not need to be concerned with self-presentation.

The final concern was that this young man did practice bidialectalism, and yet even with Anglo-American speech patterns, and dress, he still could not find work on his own. The assumptions I previously held suggested language was the way up—that if African Americans played by the rules and learned how to speak in a "White" way they would then be able to enter the dominant White world. I have discovered the brutal reality while placing students in the restaurant community, that restaurant owners are no more enlightened than are teachers, caseworkers, or child-welfare workers, and that even the language patterns I had naively advocated are not sufficient to overcome the racism that I see on a regular basis here in this southern city.

What is the solution? Is technical education the solution to marginalized African Americans whose dialect reflects their other-ness? Or did Booker T. Washington ruin the possibilities of African Americans entering the mainstream White world in these problematic southern cities when he advocated technical education as the middle solution—the intermediate solution facing persons needing a trade, a skill, a job. A middling way that Whites seized on: imagining rural students of color as tradesmen was easy for southerners to tolerate as it did not alter their perceptions or beliefs of the African American individual.

Yet there were southern universities functioning in opposition to Washington's compromise. At Fisk University, President Fayette A. McKenzie's motto was "Let us dare to be a university" (qtd. in Wolters 30), and goals for student achievement were "as high for the colored youth as they are set for the white youth" (qtd. in Wolters 30). McKenzie asserted that Fisk University's goal was to demonstrate that "a negro as such, in his native mentality, is capable of the highest scholarship" (qtd. in Wolters 30).

Charles W. Eliot, president of Harvard from 1869 to 1909, became a member of the southern General Education Board, and advocated a peaceful compromise to this early debate between technical education and the classical curriculum. "This effort to make education contribute immediately to industrial efficiency is thoroughly wholesome in all grades of education; and particularly it is wholesome for a race which has but lately emerged from the profound barbarism of slavery; for it unites in one uplifting process all three of the civilizing agencies I have already mentioned—productive labor, home-making, and mental and moral training" (qtd. in Wagoner 466). Eliot's wide influence helped cement the field of technical education as that education most appropriate for the African American. His later unease with technical education arose from his observation that "industrial activities too frequently encroached upon the academic" and that "the education of the pupil is largely sacrificed to the demands of productive labor" (qtd. in Wagoner 466).

Culinary arts are productive labor. The field of culinary arts has undergone a recent makeover, in an attempt to professionalize it. The national guild that oversees certification for chefs is called the American Culinary Federation. To rise to the highest levels in the culinary arts field a chef must have an associate's degree, ten years of restaurant experience, progressive managerial experience and communication abilities, and finally must pass a written and practical exam administered throughout the country at regional and national competitions.

Years ago, according to a local certified executive chef, becoming a chef meant turning into a "sweat monkey." No longer is this the case. A chef is a member of a profession filled with career changers, attracted to the very high salaries and the excitement of the food industry created in no small part by the Food Network TV station. A certified executive chef in this city has an average annual salary of $65,000, with end-of-the-year bonuses exceeding $40,000 based on a complicated formula related to the chef's ability to keep food costs low.

Thus, with just an Associates in Arts and Sciences (AAS) degree, a worker can make a six-figure salary in this field. Although African Americans have historically been a presence in the food service industry, they don't generally rise to the highest levels of the field. With education such as our AAS degree, the idea is that they can make those professional salaries. Does the AAS degree in culinary arts lead to African Americans becoming certified executive chefs at higher rates?

In an article by Milford Prewitt, called "Changing the Culinary Landscape—Career Opportunities for African American Gourmet Chefs," the author argues that

> Despite the lingering perception that restaurant jobs represent a dead-end occupation, the U.S. Census Bureau reports that blacks slowly have been making sizable inroads in the culinary arts. In the 1980 census, approximately 248,700 black Americans listed their occupations as cooks, the vast majority so-called short-order cooks. By 1990, the most recent year for which numbers are available, the Census Bureau counted 386,900 blacks who called themselves cooks, a 56 percent increase. (The glaring problem with the Census Bureau data is that after the 1980 census, the government stopped trying to distinguish the degree of professionalism in the kitchen, lumping all occupations—from a McDonald's grill man up to a pastry chef at Tavern on the Green—under "cook.")

Those in the field say that they don't need Census Bureau numbers to see that African Americans are increasingly joining the ranks of professional chefs. In fact, certain individuals are making sure the trend continues by starting scholarship funds for young black students who want to pursue the culinary arts. While most of these efforts are less than two years old, the founders of these movements constitute a motivated group.

The very job I now hold places me squarely in an uncomfortable tradition of advocating vocational programs for African American students. This is very thin ice given the historical compromises that occurred during the Reconstruction era here in the South. As Booker T. Washington writes, "The students were making progress in learning books and in developing their minds; but it became apparent at once that, if we were to make any permanent impression upon those who had come to us for training, we must do something besides teach them *mere* books" ("Early Tuskegee" 347, italics added).

Again, historically advocating standard dialects or standard entry into the mainstream economy has deep roots as seen in Booker T. Washington's Atlanta Compromise speech of 1895:

> Our greatest danger is that in the great leap from slavery to freedom we may overlook the fact that the masses of us are to live by the productions of our hands, and fail to keep in mind that we shall prosper in proportion as we learn to dignify and glorify *common labour*, and put brains and skill into the common occupations of life; shall prosper in proportion as we learn to draw the line between the superficial and the substantial, the ornamental gewgaws of life and the useful. No race can prosper till it learns that there is as much dignity in tilling a field as in writing a poem. *It is at the bottom of life we must begin, and not at the top. Nor should we permit our grievances to overshadow our opportunities.* (350, italics and boldface added)

Washington's idea is that "correct education begins at the bottom, and expands naturally as the necessities of the people expand" ("Counter-Argument" 355) yet what happens when the very technical education that the African American is exposed to is obsolete within fifty years? In *Tuskegee and Its People: Their Ideals and Achievements* Washington lists thirty-six industries for which African American students could be educated. Among these were "bee-keeping; carriage trimming; cooking; electrical and steam engineering; harness-making; housekeeping; plain sewing; laundering; mattress-making; nurse training; shoemaking; tinning; and wheelwrighting" (v-vii).

Although a selective list, one can identify the misguided approach advocates of technical training asserted. Booker T. Washington again celebrates the work ethic of these former slaves by describing that "I can not find a dozen former students in idleness. They are in shop, field, schoolroom, home, or the church. They are busy because they have placed themselves in demand by learning to do that which the world wants done, and because they have learned the disgrace of idleness and the sweetness of labor" ("Atlanta Compromise" 349). Washington's approach to technical education is hinged on the belief that if persons gain a trade, they will be able to ply that trade and enter the mainstream economy, providing a task that the world wants done.

Is the advocating of yet another technical degree program for African Americans as misguided as Washington's so-called compromise? Is this kind of education actually the site of change? Are African Americans able to become gourmet chefs through bidialecticism, a technical degree program, or rather *still* only through the earnest (paternalistic?) assistance of a non-southern culinary arts director?

In this vein, recent analysis of segregation has moved away from education and the workplace and toward people's ability to purchase homes; neighborhoods demonstrate class status and thus, inequality. (See, for example, Kevin F. Gotham's study of Kansas City real estate.) Hence, teaching bidialectalism to emphasize the educational pathways, and teaching technical education such as culinary arts to address the workforce pathways, may no longer make as much sense as was previously assumed.

Research such as this forces me to ask: "If advocating bidialecticism and technical training for African American students ignores the racialized space African Americans ostensibly inhabit, am I an inheritor and now propagator of Booker T. Washington's misguided ideals?" My initial naïve belief that if African Americans could function with a high degree of bidialecticism, they would then be able to access the broader culture ignores the very deep beliefs that the dominant culture holds concerning the habits of African Americans. This has been the sort of personal education I have obtained here in the South as best (or worst) expressed by a local man: "If you aren't racist now, just give it some time, because it won't take long before you are."

In other words, exposure to *these types*, and we're no longer simply talking about language, seemingly will cement certain attitudes that I encounter weekly when I attempt to place yet another African American student in a kitchen. My time in the South has indeed created certain attitudes, but they mostly are centered on middle-class White Southerners. My outside–inside eyes see regular slights, constant insults and overt misunderstandings by Whites. "Don't live in that neighborhood because it is too rental" has come to mean a neighborhood that is in flux, and may be turning Black. Expect that regular contact with Blacks will turn your Northern sensibilities to racism is the most common attitude I have heard.

So, then, is the technical culinary arts degree actually valuable for the African American student given that *without* the support offered by a White administrator, he or she is still denied access? Will the degree program itself allow marginalized students access to the dominant economy, or is it a reshuffling of old and broken ideas that presume the mind of the African American student isn't strong enough to allow for book learning or scholarship? Is the nonstandard usage of English more accurately a product of racism such as we see in the overt racialization of space (Gotham) and educational ideals (Washington)? And do these—not language—prevent any real access of African Americans into the White world? Although once I thought I had the solution, now perhaps I am in fact complicit.

NOTE

1. 2001 USDA profile shows that 42% of food stamp recipient users are White; 35% are African American; 18% are Hispanic; 3% are Asian; 2% are Native American; and 1% are of unknown race.

WORKS CITED

Freed, Richard D. *Eloquent Dissent: The Writings of James Sledd*. Portsmouth, NH: Boynton/Cook Publishers, 1966.

Gotham, Kevin Fox. *Race, Real Estate, and Uneven Development: The Kansas City Experience, 1900-2000*. Albany: State U of New York P, 2002.

Katz, Michael B. *Improving Poor People: The Welfare State, the "Underclass" and Urban Schools as History*. Princeton, NJ: Princeton UP, 1995.

Prewitt, Milford. "Changing the Culinary Landscape—Career Opportunities For American Gourmet Chefs." *American Visions* April-May 1994. 15 July 2002. <http://find articles.com>.

United States Department of Agriculture. *Characteristics of Food Stamp Households in FY 2001*. www.fns.usda.gov/fsp/rules/Memo/03/2001/characteristics.htm.

Wagoner, Jennings L., Jr. "The American Compromise: Charles W. Eliot, Black Education, and the New South." *The History of Higher Education*. Eds. Lester F. Goodchild and Harold S. Wechsler. Boston: Pearson Custom Publishing, 1989. 459–72.

Washington, Booker T. "The Atlanta Compromise." *The Educating of Americans: A Documentary History*. Ed. Daniel Calhoun. Boston: Houghton, 1969. 349-51.

___. "Booker T. Washington Describes the Early Tuskegee." *The Educating of Americans: A Documentary History*. Ed. Daniel Calhoun. Boston: Houghton, 1969. 347-48.

___. *Tuskegee and Its People: Their Ideals and Achievements*. New York: Appleton, 1905.

___. "Washington Develops a Counter-Argument." *The Educating of Americans: A Documentary History.* Ed. Daniel Calhoun. Boston: Houghton, 1969. 355-56.

Wolters, Raymond. *The New Negro on Campus: Black College Rebellions of the 1920s.* Princeton, NJ: Princeton UP, 1975.

6

CAN YOU *RE-PRESENT*?

Richard W. Santana
Rochester Institute of Technology

Much has been written about dialectal differences among African American and mainstream college students and how these differences affect their respective experiences in the academy. Sociolinguists such as Jerrie Cobb Scott, Fay B. Vaughn-Cooke, Arthur Spears, William Labov, and others have examined questions of diverging "Black English," or, as Geneva Smitherman (and others) have termed it, "African American Language" (271)[1] (AAL) from "standard English" or "European American Language" (EAL). In this context and in relation to Standard English, I still hear some colleagues say, "'our students' [meaning African Americans] have no grammar." Certainly, AAL speakers have a grammar—it would be impossible to survive in the world without one—and *that* grammar can be used as a powerful communicative tool. The problem is not that "our students" have no grammar, but that the grammar that many of them use in their day-to-day communicative acts is one that is derided and debased by the dominant culture, and that grammar is similar to, yet significantly different from, what is used by the mainstream culture and what is used in the academy. There is similarly a difference between the discourse of American mainstream culture and the academy. These varying discourses need not be considered within a hierarchical framework; they are just different and operate relatively well in their own particular milieus.

In recent years, however, African American communicative practices have been co-opted by the mainstream media and the mainstream culture. In the media, AAL has been pressed into service in selling goods from Coca-Cola to Cadillacs; and in the culture, it is used as a marker of a certain hip urbanity, a voice or code "put-on" to gain a level of "street cred." In adopting an AAL phrase or posture, non-AAL speakers pay either mock or genuine tribute to the complex, emotive and potent communicative practices of the African American oral tradition; "Yo, all the kool kids be doin' it." This newfound respectability (if it is such) of what was once disparaged as "broken," "pidgin," or just plain "bad" (and not in a good way) English has yet to reach academia, where AAL may, to varying degrees, limit the potential of its speakers. The same is true in other segments of society; it may be just fine to use AAL in an ad campaign for a product, but I very much doubt that the company would hire an executive who used *it* exclusively.

Although spoken AAL has achieved a certain cachet in some areas of the mainstream culture, it represents only a part of the overall communicative practices of the African American oral tradition. As with any other legitimate form of linguistic communication, AAL requires a complex matrix of conceptual, symbolic, figural, and rhetorical systems in order to perform the work of communicating ideas. It is difficult to make meaning in any language without access to and awareness of the vast network of contextual undergirding that allows for nuanced interpretations of a speaker's meaning. To say a phrase like "get out of here!" in idiomatic English with certain intonations radically alters the phrase's meaning, and without access to the multidimensional, multifaceted network of meaning making linguistic and rhetorical machinery it becomes impossible to accurately render its intended meaning.

Languages do not function as parallel equivalents of one another, giving each correspondent concept and context equal measure. Each language is evolved by people, in the words of James Baldwin, "in order to describe and thus control their circumstances, or in order not to be submerged by a reality that they cannot articulate. (And, if they cannot articulate it, they *are* submerged.)" (E19). Every language, thus, functions within its own set of contextual, conceptual, and rhetorical parameters and it articulates the unique reality of its speakers. It is clear that as language is transferred intergenerationally within an oral tradition, rhetorical styles and strategies are also passed on. Rhetorical style, unlike the linguistic features of AAL, is not as readily perceptible in a thirty-second television commercial, nor can it be as easily recognized and mimicked by non-AAL speakers. AAL speakers thus function within a rhetorical mode that is concomitant with the linguistic features of their dialect, but it is difficult for outsiders to either understand or even recognize that this is going on.

Issues of language variance of speakers of AAL in the college composition class have justly received much attention from sociolinguists and composition experts. The question of rhetorical style, however, is an aspect of the African American academic experience in the composition classroom that goes unacknowledged. The academy demands a specific rhetorical model, which is not necessarily the model employed by students of the African Diaspora in their everyday rhetorical situations. Just as "our students" have a grammar, they have their own rhetorical methods and traditions; few people reach adulthood without some manner in which to refute, analyze or defend ideas. Again, the problem is that the traditional rhetorical modes used by many students of color are out of harmony with those of the academy. The academic model, dating back to ancient Greece, has been the basis for European academic discourse and modes of inquiry for centuries. We must, however, always remember that the primary reason for the prevalence of Western rhetoric is not an intrinsic superiority, but tradition and convention, and that these conventions are culturally rather than logically determined and open to change over time.

Students (*all* students) are not rhetorically born in the composition classroom; they do not enter the academy as empty vessels waiting to be filled. They bring with them their own fully formed set of rhetorical conventions and traditions, which may or may not incorporate features of both academic and African American or other styles. In arguing for acknowledgment of different traditions, we must be careful to avoid essentialism; we must not argue either that all African American students use a given rhetorical style or that only African American students use the rhetorical conventions associated with this culture. Although it is important not to engage in the essentialist argument, we can safely say that there are cultural linkages and shared experiences among diasporic African students that allow them some shared rhetorical practices. Several studies have engaged the historical, structural, sociological, and even spiritual elements of these practices, but pragmatic applications in the classroom have not yet been addressed.

In adapting their day-to-day argument styles to an academic setting, AAL speakers use (often unbeknownst to themselves) a number of rhetorical figures associated with the African tradition, including: *nommo* (a commitment to the transformative power of the word), argument from proverb (related to the Western figure of *autoritas*), and "signifyin'." I examine these rhetorical strategies and offer some theoretical and practical ways to incorporate them into the teaching of composition in a multicultural environment, and offer not just methods for incorporating a wider range of rhetorical strategies in the composition classroom, but also approaches for interrogating the dominance of European rhetoric. The rhetorical strategies that students outside the Western tradition bring to the classroom are not inherently inferior to the dominant modes (just as one dialect is not inherently superior to another). These strategies have a long history and may predate those employed in the academy.[2] Once this is acknowledged by students and composition instructors, it can be profitably studied and employed not only for the benefit of students of color but for all students. Teaching academic rhetorical style then becomes a comparative process, where rhetorical systems are examined. In fact, this method of comparative engagement with rhetorical conventions can become a "contact zone" in Mary Louise Pratt's sense. Thus, learning to be academic rhetors from a comparative rather than a normative perspective allows all students to interrogate the political and historical conditions that have led to the development of the traditions of Western thought.

The conventional rhetorical style of the academy is neither universal, nor unequivocal, and by no means is it the only method of argumentation. Although Cheikh Anta Diop, G. M. James, and others have asserted the African roots of much Greek learning, many rhetoricians justifiably trace the birth of Western rhetorical tradition to ancient Greece. The Greek tradition is arguable only because the emphases of the Western rhetorical tradition have wandered so far from those of the traditional African perspective. Even in accepting this Greek origin, however, we must acknowledge the African influences on Western philosophy. As we see later, the models, importance and teaching of traditional Western rhetoric have undergone major changes over time, and rather than a stable univocal, hegemonic, or homogenous space, the area of rhetoric represents a highly contested and controversial subject.

The rhetorical method currently in effect in the academy evolved as a result of certain historical and political exigencies. Although the case for a Greek and particularly Aristotelian basis for modern Western rhetorical tradition may be strong, this Aristotelian method has not remained fixed even within the European tradition. In the late medieval through the early modern period of European history, the scholastic-humanist debate of the sixteenth and seventeenth centuries focused precisely on the importance and applicability of rhetorical method and, to some extent, on the relative importance of rhetoric as a discipline. What is now the established rhetorical method took shape in this debate between scholasticism and humanism and in the later scientific revolution of the "age of enlightenment." According to Erika Rummel,

> Modern scholars are divided on whether humanism acted as a retardant or a stimulant to the development of Renaissance philosophy. Some see it as an impediment in the linear path leading from scholasticism to the scientific revolution, others think it breathed life into a moribund system. (153)

The humanist position was counter to the scholastics' devotion to Aristotelian method, and furthermore claimed that the scholastics misinterpreted Aristotle. As Rummel continues,

> In the teaching of the three branches of the *scientia sermocinalis*—grammar, rhetoric, and dialectic—the medieval curriculum placed the emphasis on dialectic. The need for grammar was acknowledged, but it was considered rudimentary art. . . . The value of rhetoric, on the other hand, was questioned by some. Its purpose was suspect in their opinion because it produced belief rather than knowledge and addressed emotion rather than reason. (154)

This emphasis on "belief" and "emotion" in disparaging rhetoric has two important consequences. On the one hand, it signals the continuity of the Augustinian synthesis of thought, through which most Greek philosophy was read in the early Middle Ages. Augustine provides a fusion of Greek philosophy with Christian doctrine, which until the ninth century serves as the framework for doctrinal law and philosophical inquiry, with philosophy, including rhetoric, as the handmaid of theology. What develops in the end is a rhetorical method that eschews empathic and emotional appeal and privileges instead cold dispassionate rationality. This is the basis for the Western rhetorical model. On the other hand, it is interesting that in the modern Western model the appeal to logical "Truth" is emphasized in contradistinction to the appeal to emotion and belief, which was the defining feature of rhetoric and that which rendered it most suspect for its detractors. Rhetoric, it would seem, came to be defined by its detractors, and, in this maneuver, we can see a moving away from those elements most central to the African tradition (with its emphasis on community and belief), which may have been the remnant African influences on Western thought.

In the contemporary academy, students are expected to develop their arguments along strictly "logical" lines, without resorting to such emotional appeal as *argumentum ad hominem* or the pathetic fallacy. The academy restricts any passionate appeal or expression of "belief" to prove a point. This is in direct contrast to the African American rhetorical approach, where the focus on the life-altering power of the word (*Nommo*) leads to a critical consideration of the emotional appeal an orator makes to the audience. The principle of *Nommo* according to Maulana Karenga, provides a framework within which,

> one perceives that the communal character of communicative practice and rhetoric is engaged, above all, as a course, and action oriented toward that which is good for the community and world. And it is here also that rhetoric is most definitively understood as a communicative

practice in the fullest sense, as both an expression of community and a constitutive practice of building community and bringing good into the world. (10)

Within this framework of rhetoric, the rhetor brings into being a speech, whose primary goal is not so much to persuade as to give or transform life and increase the common good. Thus, emotional appeal is focused on eliciting from the audience the best possible feelings, so as to engage them in a process of communal creation of the public good. According to Adetokunbo F. Knowles-Borishade, "Classical African orature occurs within a particular ritualistic format," within which the "caller," responders and chorus participate in creating a purposeful speech that will be of service to the community (490). Karenga quotes Molefi Kete Asante to make this point:

> The African sees the discourse as the creative manifestation of what is called to be. That which is called to be, because of the mores and values of society, becomes the created thing, and the artist or speaker, satisfies the demands of society by calling into being that which is functional. And functional, in this case refers to the object (sculpture, music, poem, dance, speech) that possesses a meaning within the communicator's and audience's world view . . . (qtd. in Karenga 10)

An examination of this principle's emphasis, therefore, reveals the transformative power of the word. The purpose of speaker in discourse is to create a communal object that has real existence and function for the community. In order to work in this manner the created object must possess a level of creativity that resonates with the community. A speech without aesthetic appeal would not serve even if its logic was flawless.

The traditional African rhetorical modes traveled with the enslaved African to America where they have evolved while maintaining some of their core emphases. According to Adisa A. Alkebulan,

> African American rhetorical methods including, Sermonizing, signifyin', playin' the dozens, stylin' out, soundin', lyricism, improvisation, indirection, repetition, poetry, spirituals, history, style, culture, rhythm, and the very creation of the language of Africans in the United States (commonly called Ebonics) are all significant aspects of language and African American rhetoric that are firmly rooted in the African oral tradition. (23)

In these rhetorical contexts, strict "logical" process in the Aristotelian sense is de-emphasized in favor of a more emotional and/or empathic response.

The rhetor is not expected to follow a logical sequence and is in fact deterred from a linear and noncreative path. To some extent, the rhetorical strategies of African American tradition are more literary and more lyrical than the Western/academic model. The orator seeks to instruct, delight and thus persuade rather than "prove" through a series of prescribed steps. A great deal of weight is accorded to the notion of invention and innovation, an emphasis which closely connects these strategies to earlier forms of Western rhetorical models.

Because the African American model is dependent on oral culture, its transference from generation to generation necessitates a constant repetition and reworking. According to Thurmon Garner and Carolyn Calloway-Thomas,

> Oral discourse is the mechanism by which interactants work out their daily routines. At the same time, cultural preparation implies a recognition of the rhetorical tactics in daily use and the names of speech acts that signal a particular rhetorical strategy. In African American culture, learning to act rhetorically is a lifelong process. How such practice develops—that is, how a culture goes about instructing members in rhetorical assumptions and rhetorical acts that lead to rhetorical understanding—will require continued exploration. (54)

By the time students get to a college composition classroom they have spent most of their lives being trained in their own rhetorical mode. This is as true for students from the mainstream culture as it is for AAL speakers. The problem for students who are speakers of AAL is that their "rhetorical understanding" like their cultural language is more in conflict with the academy's than that of the mainstream culture. From a constructivist position, the value of African American rhetoric both as a discourse strategy and interpretive tool is evident. For Richard L. Wright, "Rhetoric is the dynamic constructive force that frames and structures social reality" (97) and thus,

> it is productive to conceive of discourse or rhetoric from the perspective of the varied contexts within which realities are constructed and lives lived. Within such an approach, we come face-to-face with the realization (1) that there are alternative truths, (2) that there are alternative ways of truth telling, (3) that the tellers of truth must be responsible for the ways in which they tell their truths, and (4) that all constructed truth presupposes a community of truth consumers whose individual and collective consciousness emerge from their rhetoric or discourse practices. (93)

In this way, the day-to-day truths lived by African Americans are constructed by a rather different rhetoric than those of the mainstream culture. These truths come from a position of alterity, on the margins of American culture, and are framed by an oral tradition that has endured through the centuries of dehumanizing treatment by that culture. When African American students enter the academy, they bring with them the lived experience and the rhetorical strategies that have helped them endure that experience. It would be a disservice to deny their access to this rich history and successful tradition in favor of a normative hegemonic rhetorical form that allows for no dissension.

The purpose of acknowledging the existence of these rhetorical strategies should not be so that they can be discarded in favor of a more academic mode or strategy that is somehow more effective; rather, this knowledge will enable students to see that they already possess a method for argumentation, just as they possess a grammatically bound language/dialect that is no less powerful in communicating than the dominant mode of discourse. Once students can see the value of their own rhetorical style (and that they do, in fact, possess a rhetorical style), the transfer of that style to more dominant modes becomes a matter of translation, where the extent to which they can manipulate and transform language is emphasized, rather than allowing language to disempower, negate, or silence them.

When faced with questions of injustice, particularly when cultural construction is involved, students of color often respond with a dictum that resolves the issue permanently and straightforwardly. At first glance, this appears as an oversimplified and underanalyzed response. However, within an African American rhetorical model it is both more complicated and more sophisticated than would at first appear. The following is an example from a student essay. The prompt asked students to examine the notion of the social construction of beauty as it affects those outside the socially determined norms in a multicultural environment such as the United States. The students read two essays that examined the question from different perspectives. After an introduction that set up the main points and a discussion of the essays in one paragraph each, this is one student's concluding paragraph:

> In my opinion, everyone should be happy with their own beauty. Don't have your society or the media dictate to you what makes a person beautiful. You portray your image just the way you feel.[3]

If we read this paragraph for how closely it conforms to the rhetorical conventions of academic prose, a number of issues arise. First of all, the tone is too familiar; the second and third sentences in particular (with all those "you's," and written in the imperative mood) cause some concern for the composition instructor endeavoring to develop academic rhetors. Also, as a conclusion it lacks development; there is no show of proof here, no signal to the reader that the argument has been made and proven. It is overgeneralized; rather than analyzing the issue it seems to ignore it in favor of giving "everyone" a bit of sound advice, advice that nonetheless rings false because it cannot possibly apply to "everyone." Additionally, this stance appears to be naïve because it does not take the complexity of social construction and individual personal interaction into account, and, ultimately, advice is not what the prompt requires.

When I started teaching composition and encountered responses like this, my first reaction was to mark up the students' texts with all manner of "error" symbols: (l/l) logic lacking, (n/s) non-sequitur, (l/d) lacks development, and analyze, don't tell me what to do!—not to mention the grammatical marks. And, when the same students made the same exact "errors" on their next essays (or even worse, on revisions of the same essay), I just about lost it. After so many of these, and expending much red ink without seeing results, I began to reassess my approach. I began to think about why students were making these kinds of arguments.

One of the problems is that some of us (composition instructors) forget what it was like to learn to write academic papers. Our training as rhetors and rhetoricians either came too naturally, too easily, or too long ago to remember what we were like as novices in academic rhetorical mode. As I began to think about my students' writing issues, the memories came back. I remembered that I too was prone to occasional overblown diction, to vast generalization, and crisp, simple solutions to complex and weighty issues. In particular, I remembered this sentence from one of my own early compositions on the effects of immigration: "More than two score years have elapsed since I alighted upon these shores." Once the embarrassment of these memories passed, I began to read my students' essays from a different place. Rather than trying to fit them into the rhetorical mold of the academy, I wanted to see what it was my students were trying to do in their compositions.

Let's take a look at my student's paragraph more closely in this context. She argues not to win an argument or show proof of the validity of her position, that is already established; "all people, regardless of race, should be happy with who they are." She is not trying to justify a belief, the authority of which has been established proverbially. She is trying to rectify an injustice, disprove a prejudice and thereby bring into balance a situation that has long been part of the African American experience. In her resolute and impassioned plea, she stands against those who would criticize, those who would diminish and ultimately dehumanize her community. The insistence on community can be seen in the intimate use of the second person. "*You*, you who are part of me and have experienced the same prejudices, just don't put up with it anymore! Don't let *them* tell you, 'you are not beautiful!'" This student may not be familiar with the ancient Egyptian concept of Maat, the "quality of order, justice, righteousness and balance" (Asante qtd. in

Alkebulan 25), but she has lived through a search for order and balance in a culture that marginalizes her experiences. The imperative mood is precisely what is needed in this exhortation and the familiar tone determines an intimacy with the implied conspiratorial reader.

In the second sentence she says, "Don't have your society or the media dictate to you what makes a person beautiful." Here, there is an implicit distinction between "society" and "community." African American students often write of society as a force that exists outside of themselves, a force "out there" that shapes the unfortunate circumstances of the world. They write themselves out of society and into community. This is a justifiable position given the marginalized condition of the African American community in American society. Society is responsible for a host of injustices; it is the force against which balance and order must be restored and yet it is *your* society. For students, navigating through these contrasting ideas is very much like Du Bois's concept of double-consciousness. On the one hand, they see their society from their almost external marginal positions and yet they are a part of it. As they are both inside and outside their society, they are both inside and outside the academy. They must engage with ideas from an academic perspective and yet they cannot betray their community or their experience. This student argues that one should stand firm against the onslaught of societal pressure to achieve an internal harmony for oneself and all of those "you's" who are part of one's community.

The foregoing analysis may seem or even be an overdetermined reading of the student's intended argument. However, some of its sentiments are generally acceptable and easily recognizable by anyone who shares the experience. The experience of being a marginalized minority in the face of a dominant culture so imprints on one's psyche that one can recognize its expression with only the slightest hints. It is difficult, however, to operationalize this sense, to make plain the process through which one can understand another's lived experience with such few linguistic cues. There is no way to create an effective translator, an algorithmic table with predetermined meanings for African American discursive maneuvers where one would plug in a strategy and get back the Western equivalent. I am not arguing that this student's conclusion—or the entire essay—should be deemed successful in a composition context. What I propose is more of an attitude, an understanding that there is often more at work, or in play, than what is on the page. We composition teachers should err on the side of overreading in order to help students render these experiences more clearly within academic discourse by recognizing the value of alternative models of rhetoric.

This process becomes difficult because alternative rhetorical models most come into conflict with the traditional Western/academic model when they resemble missteps in the conventional mode rather than separate strategies. To illustrate, one of the major rhetorical modes used by some African

American students is the use of a proverbial proof for a premise. A student may begin an essay with the use of an ancient proverb or common expression and use its long-standing history to indicate its intrinsic truth. Once the truth-value of the proverb/expression is established, the next step is to argue analogically for the thesis.

The difficulty of this kind of proof lies in multiple causes. First, the most commonly used expressions or phrases appear to be clichéd or hackneyed. Second, students tend to blur rhetorical strategies (modes). A student may begin arguing by using her own, traditional modes of argumentation and switch in the middle to the more widely accepted academic modes. The result appears not as an alternative method, but as a lack of conformity to the conventional mode. It is not that the two traditions are incompatible, but that there is a lack of awareness that they even exist as separate methods of achieving similar goals.

As an example, in the essay cited above, the introductory paragraph reads:

> Beauty is in the eye of the beholder. Social construction of beauty should not be the basis of our social, emotional, or professional lives. It should be that beauty is in the eyes of beholder. Everyone is beautiful in their own way.

The paragraph begins with the restatement of a cliché that was mentioned in one of the readings. However, its occurrence in the reading is meant to be ironic. This student has misunderstood the attitude of the writer toward this expression and accepted it as a viable truism; because "beauty is in the eye of the beholder," society has no business defining it. Once again we see a reading of society as an external force that runs counter to the natural order of things. Here she interprets "social construction" as a negative and volitional act which positions some people outside itself, rather than a matter of fact.

The student argues for something she has heard all of her life and has come to accept as a true fact. It is a proverbial truth about which there can be no doubt, and she addresses it by arriving at her own personal interpretation. Although its status as a cliché may be clear to most instructors of composition, the personal dictum she elaborates out of it takes on an appositive position. "Beauty is the eye of the beholder" becomes "everyone is beautiful in their own way"; a sentiment whose apparent naïveté renders the world in best possible light and should call forth from an audience an overwhelmingly positive response. This rhetorical strategy shares some elements with the notion of *autoritas* in traditional Western rhetoric.

Where the Western notion *autoritas* necessitates a reading of an authority through a heuristic lens in order to create new knowledge based on the old, the African tradition relies more heavily upon the personal experience of the community to recognize the palpable truth of the proverbial authority. What is required is not a logic table that reveals the truth of the proverb, but its acceptance as truth by the community and its ability to function as an agent of the Good. The student in this example expects not only that the absolute truth of her statement is readily accessible to anyone who reads it, but that it will ultimately be useful to those who accept its obvious truth.

Often students conflate their traditional rhetorical styles with the academic model, without really noticing the contours and boundaries of either. This example comes from a student response to an essay by Elliot Aronson on the four causes of racism. The question was: "Do the causes of racism identified by Aronson continue to play a part in the United States?"

> In this society today economic and political competition might not be as the cases of prejudice in the mid-[19]60s, however, prejudice through economic and political competition still exists. For example, I have a friend that [sic] works at United Parcel Service and he told me most of the drivers are white and pre-loaders (the people that work inside UPS building) are Black people. That is a form of economic and political competition.

In this case, the student is commingling two rhetorical styles, but the apparent effect is a misuse of the conventional model. The student here uses "personal knowledge" to prove a general condition through exemplification. In traditional Western/academic rhetoric, this represents a movement from the general to the particular. Thus, the general structure of this paragraph is allowable; the student presents a general statement about her main thesis and provides an example that shows how the statement obtains in the real world.

Two problems arise, however, in the application of the provided example. First, the authority of the example amounts to no more than hearsay and the level of detail reported in the example does not give a clear indication of how the example proves the point. There is no signal, for example, of how working as a driver is preferable to working inside the building or how this represents an example of economic or political competition. The applicability of the example rests on a number of assumptions. Composition students, including those from the mainstream culture, often make many assumptions about audience. Students assume that all readers fully share their experience, so that all that is necessary is a hint at the interconnection of the argument. This student assumes that any reader can easily understand the implications of this example without further details.

In the context of this subject and in the form of address we can detect in this student's paragraph what Garner and Calloway-Thomas call a "Black presence." The assumptions that are made about audience in my student's particular example are that "part of the collective consciousness of African

Americans is that color still matters in the real world" (45). It is a safe bet that if the audience shares the student's experience, they would understand that if the Black people are working inside and the White people are working outside, there must be some advantage to working outside. The specific angle of relevance is almost beside the point; it would be both superfluous and unwarranted to give a detailed account of why this is so to any Black person living in this culture. Again in this example, as in the first, there is an unspoken but palpable disavowal of the society. Again the student writes herself in and out of society, positioning herself as an observer who can see clearly the impediments to justice and harmony that exist within the culture.

The student also assumes that the audience for her composition is also familiar with the text being discussed. The discussion of new concepts is joined, as it were, in *medias res*; there is no explication of "political and economic competition" as causes of racism; the audience presumably knows that already. Evident as well is the use of the personal as proof of the general. This harkens back to the intimacy of community. The position seems to be that we (the audience and the writer) have all experienced this and therefore the writer's personal word should be enough to guarantee the truth of the argument.

In a personal narrative essay, another of my students wrote this sentence, "Only through hard work can you make the inevitable happen." As I smiled at the apparent paradox, red pen in hand, poised over the paper, I contemplated the meaning of this statement. Could there be a deeper meaning to this? Or was it simply ponderous prose gone terribly wrong? At first, I thought maybe it referred to a Calvinist notion of predeterminism, where the predestination of being part of the elect is not enough to bring one to salvation. So that although it is inevitable, it requires hard work. Was my student a Calvinist with a very clear yet glib understanding of this very difficult doctrine? The context for his statement was his dream of becoming a star in the National Football League and his attempt to get a football scholarship at a top-tier university. The way he saw it, this dream was inevitable and yet he was aware that it would require a great deal of effort. The student in this case engaged in a bit of signifyin'. Contextually, the inevitability of his dream is dependent on the fact that he is willing to do the hard work necessary to achieve it. Verbally, he is playing with the signification of the terms. Inevitable here does not mean that it cannot be avoided, but rather signifies the optimism necessary to achieve that dream. Part of the "hard work" needed to achieve this inevitable dream is holding fast to the idea that is "inevitable." It cannot help but become a certainty, with devotion and faith the student is ready to give to it. This hyperbolic style presupposes the outcome without need for connection to present circumstances.

Rather than respond to these and other examples with the usual red pen comments, I choose instead to interrogate some of the assumptions about rhetorical style and the academic model. I gather many significant examples from students and we discuss them, not in the context of how far they stray from the normative, but rather how they were successful in what they were trying to accomplish. We discuss the concepts of African and African American rhetorical styles and address the development of the Western/academic tradition directly. Once we have sorted out some of the differences and similarities in rhetorical styles and interrogated assumptions made about the presumptive superiority of the academic model, I give students an assignment that allows them to transfer some of the success in their local rhetorical style to the academic mode. I attempt to give them a variety of assignments (not necessarily essays) that give them an opportunity to experiment with both language and rhetorical style. I also try to give them different contexts within which different approaches may be appropriate, and in each case I try to emphasize the verbal and linguistic play so central to the African American models.

In all these exercises I see my function as a facilitator and attempt to draw out student interaction with the concepts of rhetoric. My ultimate goal is always to allow students to become proficient academic rhetors. Although I completely agree with the CCCC language resolution on "Students' Right to Their Own Language" and would seek to extend that to "students' right to their own rhetorical style," I also believe it would be irresponsible to give students the idea that their language and their rhetorical style are fully accepted at all levels of society. What I suggest is a "both–and" rather than an "either–or" proposition. The complex, emotive, lyrical, rich, dexterous, and powerful communicative practices that many students bring to the composition classroom should be examined, encouraged, and celebrated, but they should gain the tools to master the conventions of the academy so they can successfully navigate their way through the system while questioning its authority. John Baugh and other sociolinguists have noted the relative ease with which African Americans can "switch codes" depending on contextual clues. In the approach I suggest, this ability is exploited to permit students to engage in academic discourse at several levels. The process then becomes teaching another code, rather than *the only* code. Once this is achieved, successful students should become proficient code-switchers, not only linguistically, but rhetorically as well.

NOTES

1. I am using Geneva Smitherman's term for this language advisedly. We should understand, however, that what occurs in the African American context is similar to what occurs in other areas of the African diaspora. The creolized English (or other European language for that matter) spoken by Africans in Jamaica or

Trinidad varies significantly from its local "standard" and developed through oral tradition and the similar conditions of enslaved Africans. In speaking of AAL, therefore, it should be understood that similar claims could be made for Diasporic Africans outside of the U.S. context.

2. Both Cheikh Anta Diop, in *The African Origins of Civilization: Myth or Reality*, and George G. M. James, in *Stolen Legacy*, propose that principal ideas of Greek philosophy are derivative of Egyptian thought.

3. These student samples are taken from essays written by my students at Medgar Evers College, City University of New York (CUNY) during regular freshman composition courses and as part of the regular requirements. All of the students were African American between ages 18 and 20, born and educated in the United States. Medgar Evers College is a small, traditionally Black, mostly liberal arts college within the CUNY system. A large number of students at Medgar Evers are nontraditional, the mean age is about 27, 65% are female and many are West Indian or Caribbean. I purposely chose examples from recent American-born high school graduates.

WORKS CITED

Alkebulan, Adisa A. "The Spiritual Essence of African American Rhetoric." *Understanding African American Rhetoric*. Eds. Ronald L. Jackson and Elaine B. Richardson. New York: Routledge, 2003. 23–40.

Baldwin, James. "If Black English Isn't a Language, Then Tell Me What Is?" *New York Times*. July 29, 1979: E19.

Baugh, John. "Research Trends for Black American English" *Language Variation in North American English: Research and Teaching*. Eds. A. Wayne Glowka and Donald Lance. New York: The Modern Language Association, 1993. 153–63

Diop, Cheikh Anta. *The African Origin of Civilization: Myth or Reality*. Chicago: Lawrence Hill, 1989.

Garner, Thurmon and Carolyn Calloway-Thomas. "African American Orality: Expanding Rhetoric." *Understanding African American Rhetoric*. Eds. Ronald L. Jackson and Elaine B. Richardson. New York: Routledge, 2003. 43–56.

Jackson, Ronald L. II, and Elaine B. Richardson. *Understanding African American Rhetoric: Classical Origins and Contemporary Innovations*. New York: Routledge, 2003.

James, George G. M. *Stolen Legacy*. 1954. San Francisco, CA: Julian Richardson Associates, 1976.

Karenga, Maulana. "Nommo, Kawaida, and Communicative Practice: Bringing Good into the World." *Understanding African American Rhetoric*. Eds. Ronald L. Jackson and Elaine B. Richardson. New York: Routledge, 2003. 3–21.

Knowles-Borishade, Adetonjunbo F. "Paradigm for Classical African Orature: Instrument for a Scientific Revolution?" *Journal of Black Studies*. 21.4 (1991): 488-500.

Pratt, Mary Louise. "Arts of the Contact Zone." *Profession* 91 (1991): 33-40.

Rummel, Erika. *The Humanist-Scholastic Debate in the Renaissance and Reformation.* Cambridge, MA: Harvard UP, 1995.

Smitherman, Geneva. *Talkin that Talk: Language, Culture, and Education in African America.* New York: Routledge, 2000.

Wright, Richard L. "The Word at Work." *Understanding African American Rhetoric.* Eds. Ronald L. Jackson and Elaine B. Richardson. New York: Routledge, 2003. 85–97.

7

TEACHER RESPONSE TO AAE FEATURES IN THE WRITING OF COLLEGE STUDENTS

A Case Study in the Social Construction of Error

Maureen T. Matarese
Teachers College, Columbia University

Chris M. Anson
North Carolina State University

Since the early 1960s, plentiful scholarship has identified, codified, analyzed, and historicized features of African American English (AAE), often in the written discourse of students at various educational levels (Labov; Smitherman; Wolfram, "Sociolinguistic"; Wolfram and Schilling-Estes; Wolfram and Thomas). Often ideologically neutral, this scholarship has nonetheless sparked heated debates about appropriate educational methods for teaching African American students who bring into their classrooms varieties of English that are popularly thought to deviate from the norms of academic or Standard (American) English (SE).

Although a growing body of research exists on teacher response to student writing and more recently on the intercultural dimensions of response (Anson, "Reflective Reading") and the social construction of error in teacher response (Anson, "Response"), scholarship on teachers' responses to specific linguistic features of texts tied to different minority language groups is sparse. Attributable to broad trends and culturally inherited beliefs, educational ideology ultimately exists in the minds and practices of individual teachers. We are interested, therefore, in the manifestations of such ideologies in the instructors who teach and must respond to the writing of students from a range of backgrounds and communities.

In this chapter, we report on a preliminary study of teacher response to AAE features in college students' writing. Our study lies at the intersection of a sociolinguistic categorization of AAE features appearing in five students' papers from first-year composition classrooms at a land-grant, research-extensive institution, and a descriptive analysis of teacher comments with respect to those features. The analysis allows for some observations on the nature and underlying ideological origins of response and the ways in which dialect features are socially constructed in typical composition classrooms. The results yield some prospects for further programs of research on these and related questions, and as well as implications for educational reform, teacher development, and enhancement in the area of writing instruction and language in multicultural and multidialectal settings.

THE SOCIAL AND POLITICAL CONTEXT OF AAE IN THE CLASSROOM

Although the historical *Brown vs. Board of Education* decision brought schoolchildren of different ethnicities together in 1954, it was not until 1979 that the Equal Educational Opportunities Act was extended to students who speak nonstandard dialects of English, arguing for "appropriate action to overcome language barriers that impede equal participation by its students in its instructional program" (qtd. in Jimenez 247). Research by the U.S. Department of Education showed that African American students scored significantly lower on standardized tests that measure language abilities than did Anglo-American students. Linguists addressed these low scores by suggesting that educators consider using students' home dialects as a bridge to learning SE (Wolfram and Schilling-Estes; Labov et. al.). In the mid-1970s, readers, school texts, stories, and other materials rendered in students' home dialects were introduced to facilitate reading acquisition and comprehension of SE (Simpkins, Holt, and Simpkins; Labov, "Can Reading"; Rickford, *African American*; Rickford and Rickford). Yet public reaction to the appearance of dialect features in such materials was often vociferous; the publisher of the *Bridge* dialect readers, for example, received so many objections from parents and teachers that it stopped all promotion and development of the series (Labov, "Can Reading").

After dialect readers fell out of fashion, the educational potential of using vernacular dialects to bridge students from one language code to another was disregarded until resurgence of the topic was prompted by the Oakland County School Board's 1995 decision to implement a curriculum allowing teachers to use AAE to assist SE learning. The Ebonics controversy, as it was popularly called, also met with widespread public concern and a general misunderstanding of the strategies designed to help AAE speakers' transition to SE (Rickford; Smitherman; Wolfram and Schilling-Estes). Thus, despite sociolinguists' attempts throughout the 1960s and 1970s to dispel popular misconceptions concerning the linguistic deficiency of vernacular-speaking students (Wolfram and Whiteman; Farr and Daniels; Labov, "Can Reading"; Rickford and Rickford; Wolfram, Adger, and Christian; Heck; Viechnicki; Rickford), the public—and, we would suggest, a significant percentage of teachers across the curricula of American schools and universities—remains largely uninformed about the nature, history, and cultural functions of AAE. As Longaker has argued, resistance to considerations of dialect difference, particularly concerning the Ebonics debate, is driven by powerful "market rhetorics" that limit teachers' agency in the face of powerful vocational interests and standardized assessments. Clearly, there is continued need for scholars and educators to reexamine the role of AAE in American classrooms and the theories that inform pedagogical response to its presence.

The need for continued exploration of language in the classroom is also supported by broader pedagogical trends. Current innovations in education, such as the enactment of critical pedagogy (Freire) and learner-centered teaching, do not support the behaviorist "banking" approaches of the past, which emphasized rote and passive learning. In place of this "blank slate" model, educational reformists propose techniques that help students to learn inductively, drawing on their existing knowledge and experience.

Parallel to these pedagogical distinctions, linguists and compositionists have proposed three "lenses" for viewing language variation in the classroom: eradicationism, code-switching, and pluralism. Eradicationism asks students to forsake their nonstandard dialect for SE norms (Howard). According to Gilyard, some teachers attempt to eradicate dialect features because they think AAE "represents deficient speech and interferes with the acquisition of Standard English" (70). Others do not perceive AAE as deficient speech but look to its social unacceptability and its departure from forms associated with power and prestige. African American scholar Lisa Delpit, for example, argues that because vernacular dialects will continue to be stigmatized, any dialect-related empowerment that the students receive only obscures the fact that real power lies in the ability to use and understand the SE prestige norms. She applauds teachers who understand "the need to help students to establish their own voices [as well as] coach those voices to produce notes that will be heard clearly in the larger society" (296).

Most recent literature concerning vernacular dialects in the classroom supports bidialectalism, or "code-switching" (although this has also been critiqued for simply masking attempts to eradicate the original "undesirable" dialect; see O'Neill). The code-switching approach to language variation in the classroom teaches students about the grammatical, rule-governed nature of dialects, but it also identifies the "standard" as the form that provides the students with the most power and prestige in many situations (Balester; Howard; Gilyard). Advocates of the code-switching model suggest that SE should be used in academic settings and the "mother tongue" dialect at home and in culturally cohesive communities and speech situations.

Support for this model has also found its way into literature on the teaching of composition to students in all dialect communities. Elbow, for example, describes serious dilemmas in deciding how to address vernacular dialects in students' work, wanting both to empower the students by not forcing them to conform to the standard and at the same time to help them to write "academically appropriate" essays. One proposed classroom strategy is to "postpone editing," which offers students the opportunity, if they choose, to use their "informal," vernacular dialects in the first two stages of drafting. Instead of concentrating on language in the early stages of drafting, the students work on organization, examples, concepts, and support. Students are encouraged to postpone final editing until larger issues have been addressed; then they can focus specifically on changing their language from "informal" to "formal" academic discourse. This is intended to provide the students with opportunities to use their most "authentic" and personally validating language to express themselves initially while allowing them a broader audience through a later editorial process.

Finally, some scholars and educators take a pluralistic approach to dialects in the composition classroom, arguing that students should be provided with ample information about prestige forms and dialect use but be allowed to make their own rhetorical and stylistic choices. Howard recommends a full multicultural experience for students, which includes dialects and "remove[s] the veil that so blinds a society to itself, that so limits the ways in which we describe ourselves, that allows us to engage in the willful ignorance that makes us believe that teacher-directed *code-switching* can be part of a 'liberatory' pedagogy" (279).

Unlike code-switching and eradicationism, pluralism rejects potentially hegemonic pedagogical structures that insist on SE forms in formal writing by allowing students to make more varied rhetorical choices based on audience and intended effect. We take into account these three approaches in our analysis of teacher comments, examining written responses for signs of underlying orientations toward language in the classroom.

RESPONDING TO WRITING: THE ISSUE OF DIALECT

In the context of the values associated with the use, legitimacy, and status of AAE in the classroom, response to student writing constitutes an important and underexplored area where ideology and pedagogy meet. Perhaps nowhere in writing instruction are personal beliefs about language more clearly expressed than in teachers' reactions to, assessments of, and suggestions for students' written work.

In the field of composition studies, scholars have explored in some detail the nature of teachers' responses to students' writing. The delivery of such responses can vary from one-on-one oral conferences (Murray) to peer-group feedback (Ede and Lunsford; Weiner) to tape-recorded comments (Anson, "Talking"); yet most composition teachers continue to provide response, either on drafts or final texts or both, in conventional ways: through marginal and end comments written by hand on hard copies submitted by the student. It is in this form that teacher response has been most commonly investigated.

Research on teacher response has examined various aspects of response, describing the form, nature, and intent of different teacher comments (Straub; Connors and Lunsford) and revealing how teacher response manifests the knowledge, learning, and writing views of the teacher (Anson, "Response and Social"). Most of this scholarship has shown that commenting is a delicate art, directing a student's writing process and use of language. The commenting styles that teachers use can encourage or discourage a young writer, "appropriating" a text and taking the student away from her own focus (Knoblauch and Brannon; Sommers) or providing valuable feedback for revision. Response can simply call attention to errors, or it can explain what affect errors have on the teacher as representative reader; it can express a meaning-based reaction to something the writer is saying, or it can treat the text as an artifact for linguistic analysis (Anson, "Reflective"; Hunt). Through marginal commentary, a teacher can inspire or disappoint, give praise or overwhelm with criticism (Daiker). The response can take control or it can "facilitate" (Straub); it can demonstrate understanding of the student's struggle to communicate in a sophisticated secondary language code, or it can portray writing as a process in which, as Shaughnessy says, the text exposes all the writer does not know and then passes "into the hands of a stranger who reads it with a lawyer's eyes, searching for flaws" (7). As Knoblauch and Brannon point out, the key to response lies in the "attitudes, postures, and motives that teachers communicate both through and apart from their reactions to particular texts" (288).

An important development in the literature on response is the creation of schemes for classifying the kinds of responses teachers make on students' papers. Such taxonomies provide categorical lenses through which to look for patterns in response in different educational contexts. Lees, for example, offers seven modes of response in order to "examine what kind of comments an instructor uses and importantly on whom the burden is placed in each type of comment":

Correcting, emoting, and describing . . . put the burden of work on the
teacher; the next three—*suggesting, questioning,* and *reminding*—shift
some of that burden to the student. The last mode—*assigning* . . .
provides a way to discover how much of that burden that student has
taken. (266)

Lees' study shows that teachers paradoxically comment on students' writing
as if they have already created the authorial persona that it apparently takes
an entire semester (or more) to achieve (267).

The complicating of the simple dichotomy between facilitative and
directive response, as noted by Straub and Lunsford, paved the way for
more sophisticated taxonomies, among them that of Searle and Dillon,
whose categories involve elements of form and type, with subcategories of
each. Types of response, for example, range from *evaluation* and *assessment*
to *instruction* (which includes subcategories such as *didactic/correction,*
encouragement, comment on attitude) and *audience,* which includes subcategories such as *clarification, elaboration, reaction,* and *taking action.* In their
categorical study of response, teachers focused on issues of form more than
twice as often as they focused on issues of content, and *evaluation* and
instruction were the most frequent types of comments, with *assessment* placing third. Searle and Dillon suggest that teachers correct mechanics most
often because grammar and sentence structure "are more apparent and cor-
respond to some well-established standard" (239).

The most fully theorized system of response categories is that developed by Straub and Lunsford in their well-known study *Twelve Readers*
Reading: Responding to College Student Writing, which theorized response
by exploring the comments of twelve "well-known, well-informed teachers and scholars . . . mainly for the perspective their work would provide"
(1). The authors believe that much can be learned from examining the
response patterns (and the underlying pedagogical sources of those patterns) of successful, experienced teachers who are also themselves composition scholars.

Straub and Lunsford break down the traditional directive/facilitative
dichotomy into a series of categories (see Table 7.1). These categories fall
under either *focus,* which describes specific writing-related elements the
teachers' comments focus on (e.g., comments on student ideas), or *mode,*
which identifies the type of comments that the teacher uses (e.g., comments
correcting student work rather than asking questions about it). Unlike previous linguistic definitions of mode such as Halliday's, Straub and
Lunsford's concept is not characterized by specific language, dialect, or register use; instead, *mode* is defined through syntactic structure (e.g., *questions*
as opposed to *imperative* statements) and through tone (e.g., *praise* rather
than *correction*).

TABLE 7.1
Taxonomy for Assessing Teacher Comments

FOCUS	MODE
Ideas	Corrections
Development	Evaluations
Evaluation	Qualified negative global structure
	Imperatives
	Advice
	Praise
Local structure	Indirect requests
Wording	Problem-posing questions
Correctness	Heuristic questions
Extra-textual	Reflective questions

From Straub and Lunsford (159)

Finally, much of the scholarly work on response has admitted that the impact of teacher comments on students and their work can be significant, yet generally it has not addressed this impact from a social constructivist perspective—that is, viewing language as central to the construction of knowledge, self, and social identity—perhaps because some scholars believe that social constructivism tends not to apply easily in the classroom nor to satisfy the goals of student-centered pedagogy. Recently, however, scholars have been challenging more traditional response theory by asking how the "relationship between the changing status of socially constructed norms of language use" and response to error affect teacher response (Anson, "Response and the Social" 7). Lexical differences and style registers, for example, can lead teachers to create a persona of the student that shapes their instructional response in potentially unhelpful ways. A more lexically complex and stylistically elevated piece of writing may cause a teacher to overlook important syntactic, organizational, and focus-related issues. By contrast, a piece of writing that is not as elevated in word choice and style may portray the student as a poor writer, regardless of the essay's content or degree of insight. The recognition that error is socially constructed and that teachers create personas from texts (with their errors) out of complex ideologies of language and culture represents, we think, a significant advancement in theories of response. Furthermore, preexisting attitudes toward language difference may affect the more specific response and evaluation practices of teachers (see, e.g., Bowie and Bond; Hill and Milner). However, little work has applied this recognition to the analysis of teachers' comments on students' texts—both in draft and final form—that contain elements of written vernacular dialects.

Our study critically explores teacher comments and student revisions in order to hypothesize the ways in which language use is constructed in typical composition classrooms. We utilize a comparative case study methodology (Denzin and Lincoln; Yin) to compare and contrast the written comments of three teachers on their students' work over the course of a college semester. Drawing on previously established sociolinguistic variables of AAE (J. Rickford; Wolfram and Schilling-Estes) and adopting the Straub and Lunsford taxonomy as well as the three previously described approaches to AAE in education to shape our coding and interpretation of the data, we sought to (a) identify features of AAE in the writing of African American college freshmen, (b) examine how or whether their teachers responded to these features in their drafts, (c) discern any ways the students revised or edited their texts as a result of these responses, and (d) speculate about the teachers' underlying ideologies of language and dialect as a result of the analysis.

METHODOLOGY

To gather a corpus of writing that potentially included AAE features, we collected more than 400 graded rough and final drafts from three professors over the course of a college semester: roughly 37% from African American students, 54% from Anglo-American students, and 9% from students from Pacific-Islander, Native American, Latino, and unspecified backgrounds. Each of the three instructors taught at a large research-extensive university in the southeast. One instructor, Professor Johnson, taught three sections of English 111, the institution's standard composition course into which the majority of first-year students are placed. Because all of the students enrolled in this course were Anglo-American, they were used only as a control to ensure that a particular feature identified in the texts of African American students was common to AAE (i.e., not present in the Anglo-American students' papers). The second instructor, Professor Smith, taught two sections of English 110, the institution's basic writing course, and the third instructor, Professor Jones, taught one section of Upward Bound, an optional, college preparatory writing course. All sections of these courses required five essays; each final draft collected in the corpus included a series of marked rough drafts. Student, teacher, and administrative consent were obtained, and the teachers arranged to make copies of their students' papers and attach predetermined numbers for identification purposes. All names of teachers and students used in this text are pseudonyms.

Participants

Of forty-five total participants in the final corpus, twenty-nine were Anglo-American and sixteen were African American. Of the African American students, five appeared to demonstrate spoken-language influence in the form of AAE in their writing (as determined by the relevant literature); all were between eighteen and nineteen years of age and indicated that they were from middle-income families. Seven of the sixteen students had taken honors courses, and four students noted that classes such as creative writing, debate, and public speaking were offered at their school, although only two of those four took any of those courses. Only two students noted that they took advanced placement English courses for college credit. These aspects of the students' backgrounds and education, among other factors, may explain the relatively low incidence overall of AAE features in their writing (see Table 7.2).

Professor Smith (Essays 1-4) and Professor Jones (Essay 5) were both White males under the age of thirty who taught the Upward Bound and English 110 courses, respectively, from which the corpus was created.

TABLE 7.2
PARTICIPANT INFORMATION

Name (Altered)	Rough Drafts	Final Drafts	High School Courses Offered (Student Reported)	High School Courses Taken
Daunte	5/5	4/5	Required courses, honors, AP, creative, college prep	Required English
Kasha	3/5	4/5	Required courses, honors, AP, creative, college prep, public speaking	College prep
Michael	4/5	5/5	Required courses, honors, AP	Honors
Tamara	3/5	4/5	Required courses, honors, AP, creative, college prep, public speaking	College prep, honors, creative
Vanessa	4/5	1/5	Required courses, honors, AP, college prep	Honors, college prep

AP: Advanced Placement

LANGUAGE VARIATION IN FRESHMAN COMPOSITION

To examine the collected essays for AAE features, we needed appropriate operational definitions of such features. Although a review of the literature provided some degree of consensus about approaches to language variation in writing and teacher response, we also considered the differences between the essays themselves. Thus, we first determined what variables we might encounter and then read all the essays and drafts, highlighting anything that did not conform to the rules of SE. We then read the essays again, marking the types of problems that we saw, based on the scholarship of linguists who have established a set of credible features for AAE. In the interests of space, we have focused only on a few of the most clearly AAE features in the African American students' writing, leaving out many features that suggest a potential case of language contact and dialect interference.

Of sixteen African American students, the writing of only five students contained enough patterned repetitions (instances of one variable type) of AAE variables to be considered regularly occurring AAE features. In these texts there were six discernible, regularly occurring features: multiple negation, third-person singular–s absence, copula absence, plural, possessive, and consonant cluster reduction (CCR). We briefly discuss the evidence of such features in the sample compositions before moving to the analysis of teacher comments.

Of the AAE features that surfaced, one of the most frequent was CCR (Farr and Daniels; Labov, "Can Reading"). The reduction or simplification of consonants is discussed in Labov's ("Some Sources") seminal article on reading difficulties of African American English-speaking students as being one of the "most complex variables [that appear] in black speech" (148). Labov suggests in his chapter on the reading problems of AAE speakers that those clusters ending in /t/ and /d/ are often reduced. Simplifications of words ending in /-st, -ft, -nd, -ld, -zd, -md/ are common, and a word like *laughed*, which is realized phonetically by a word-final /ft/ consonant cluster, becomes *laugh*. Wolfram and Schilling-Estes note that clusters are also reduced in standard dialects in preconsonental environments (such as *use to* for *used to*). Importantly, CCR can occur in either monomorphemic (such as *graft*, *first*, and *send*) or bimorphemic (such as *used*, *graphed*, and *cursed*) constructions. Bimorphemic CCR can be mistaken for syntactic error to an unaware teacher, whereas monomorphemic CCR may be corrected in earlier stages of language development and in spelling class by teachers who care more about communicative language ability and less about grammatical accuracy. For this reason, bimorphemic forms may persist, whereas monomorphemic forms do not.

In our corpus, CCR that reduces clusters associated with bounded verb morphemes was one of the most frequently observed variables. Some instances of this variable included the following: (a) *The essay by Wolf, she talks about women looking pass, fighting for equal rights* (Tamara, Professor Smith); (b) *I think have because they are becoming more conservative then what they use to be*; and (c) *Darling-Hammond would not feel that Affirmative Action is insignificant, but it* **design** *to protect job opportunities* (Michael, Professor Smith). These CCR examples reveal the confusion that such a feature may cause for teachers who do not know about it. For example, cases of simple reduction of /nd/ (as in *design for designed*) and reduction of /ft/ (such as *laugh* for *laughed*) can be misinterpreted as erroneous tense switches from past to present. Labov ("Can Reading") notes that CCR is a good example of a phonological dialect process common to AAE that is often misinterpreted as a grammatical error.

Cases of AAE in the corpus of rough drafts are also manifested in a variety of verb phrase variations such as copula absence, various irregular verb manifestations, leveling, and third person–*s* absence. Scholarship on these linguistic variables, beginning in the late 1960s, is extensive. In some of the earliest studies of copula deletion, Labov ("Contraction") showed how the complexities surrounding copula deletion relate to the ever-changing dialects of English. In continuing research, Labov ("Can Reading") suggests that "copula and auxiliary verbs of the verb *to be* may be difficult to recognize on the printed page, because of the high rate of deletion in many contexts" (21). Labov was focusing on difficulty with *reading* copula be; however, in our study the copulas are deleted in writing, a feature associated with mapping oral language forms into written forms.

The following excerpts contain auxiliary deletion: (a) *She has strong points of view when she explaining the different events that happened*, and (b) *but when you go to the store to see how many African Americans working you don't see but a few* (Kasha, Professor Smith). Labov ("Can Reading") suggests that such problems in written language indicate a loss in confidence in the alphabet in younger children. Such confidence can decline further when teachers mark "errors" that seem perfectly natural to the student—an issue to which we return later.

Another verb-related AAE feature realized in our corpus is third-person singular–*s* absence. This feature, described by Wolfram and Schilling-Estes as an issue of vernacular subject/verb agreement, is noted as most common in AAE and more fully described in analyses of its frequency among older and younger African American speakers (J. Rickford) and also among New York, Detroit, and Washington, D.C. speakers (Labov, Cohen, Robins, and Lewis; Wolfram, "Sociolinguistic"; Fasold).

Our data also indicate instances of–*s* absence in the writing of the African American students. Furthermore, the feature is one of the most frequent of any AAE found in these essays (i.e., *All three authors had their own*

way of saying discrimination continue in schools [Daunte, Professor Smith]),
and its incidence indicates that diagnostic features of AAE persist in the
written language of some African American students. Such features were not
present in the essays extracted from Anglo-American students.

Multiple negation, more commonly referred to as double negatives, are
also relatively common in the essays, existing both in nonstandard forms,
(e.g., "I can't think of no time I have not been discrimination" [Kasha,
Professor Smith]) and standard forms ("I'm not trying to say nothing has
improved since the last century because things have improved" [Daunte,
Professor Smith]). However, despite the fact that many dialects share this
nonstandard feature, we did not find cases of multiple negation in the SE
essays.

Another vernacular feature common to AAE involves the attachment of
inflectional-marking affixes to nouns. The only inflectional affix that is
specifically diagnostic for AAE varieties is the "general absence of plural
suffix," as in "Lots of boy_ go to school" (Wolfram and Schilling-Estes).
This feature was widely used in written compositions by the AAE-speaking
students such as in the following excerpt: *White male supports were representing less than 8 percent of all household.* The absence of plural–*s* on nouns
is also confirmed by Labov ("Some Sources"), who suggests that the
Thunderbirds, which in his study were the youngest set of speakers who
represent "the groups which respond least to middle-class educational
norms," deleted plural–*s* moderately before consonants and only rarely
before vowels (32). This claim finds support in our data, as only one of the
examples of plural–*s* is deleted before a vowel. All other cases of–*s* absence
are before a consonant. Labov suggests that plural–*s* deletes the least when
compared with third-person singular absence and possessive absence; however, all of these forms are present at one time or another. An example of
possessive deletion in the essays is *While the women equal rights movement
was still in progress the middle-income earners were still against working and
middle other things* (Kasha, Professor Smith).

As some theorists have noted, certain vernacular features may not
"interfere" with the processes of communication. Labov ("Can Reading"),
for example, questions whether the structural vernacular differences
between AAE and SE matter in the development of written literacy. He suggests that the features do not interfere with writing and reading, and sees little indication of serious literacy failure associated with dialect in composition. Instead, he notes that dialect awareness programs for teachers have
resulted in a more accepting attitude in schooling. We have little doubt,
however, that the speech students bring into the classroom variously affects
teachers' conceptions of them. As one of us has noted, teachers' attitudes
toward error cause them to create personas of their students while reading
their writing (Anson, "Response and the Social"). Without sufficient understanding of the nature of dialect and the relationship between spoken and

written language, teachers' commentary may be misguided or unhelpful in cases where spoken dialect influences written text production. In the following section, we explore the awareness of and attention to AAE in composition among the teachers in the study.

TEACHER RESPONSE IN STUDENT DRAFTS

In our analysis of teacher comments, we used Straub and Lunsford's taxonomy (see Table 7.1), as it provided a way to focus on both the issues addressed by each teacher and the nature of his or her comments. In this section, we analyze the *mode* of commenting in thirteen AAE rough drafts before examining students' final drafts to determine if the errors persist. The *focus* in the essays is predominantly *local* because all comments relating to the AAE features centered almost entirely on problems at the word and sentence levels. Although it would be attractive to examine the use of global and extra-textual comments and praise, indirect, problem-posing, and heuristic questions in our corpus of nonstandard-speaking essays, these instances were extremely rare. Instead, we are compelled to focus on the tendency for teachers to address vernacularity in terms of local commenting, corrections, evaluations, imperatives, and the occasional problem-posing question.

Because of the frequency of AAE features, we conducted an analysis of these students' rough drafts, looking for how Professors Smith and Jones commented on AAE features at this stage of composing. The teachers who wrote comments did so with the full knowledge of their authors' identities and backgrounds as African Americans.

Smith's overall response style is consistent with a general pattern of teacher response in which local items such as grammar are given overt corrections, whereas global comments regarding contextual and organizational issues are addressed using interrogative, imperative, and declarative statements. This pattern is supported by literature that recommends closer attention to contextual, idea-related issues in writing rather than focusing on smaller mechanical issues.

When reading the papers of the African American students in the corpus, Smith often chooses the local correction response technique, not perhaps noticing the inherent content embedded within the grammatical feature's use. For example he marks both grammatical and ungrammatical instances of double negation as incorrect, as shown in Fig. 7.1.

Despite the grammatical well-formedness of Sentence 1 in Fig. 7.1, Professor Smith crosses out the first negative, completely changing the intended meaning of the sentence. This first comment is a correction in both mode and focus. Using a strikethrough, the teacher notes the appropriate usage.

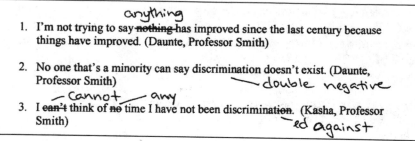

1. I'm not trying to say ~~nothing~~ *anything* has improved since the last century because things have improved. (Daunte, Professor Smith)

2. No one that's a minority can say discrimination doesn't exist. (Daunte, Professor Smith) *— double negative*

3. I ~~can't~~ *cannot* think of ~~no~~ *any* time I have not been discriminat~~ion~~ *ed against*. (Kasha, Professor Smith)

FIGURE. 7.1. Instances of comments on multiple negation in student drafts.

Similarly, the second comment, although it could be construed as focusing on a wording problem, also is a correction, and it loosely indicates that the sentence is double negative. Labov ("Some Sources") suggests that multiple negation poses a semantic contradiction to nonspeakers of AAE, as the multiple negation used by African Americans tends to mean the opposite of what Anglo-Americans would posit (131). As seen in Fig. 7.1, such a semantic difference seriously jeopardizes a teacher's ability to comment on multiple negation in terms of a student's intended meaning.

The use of correction here suggests that the teacher is in a proofreader's role according to Straub and Lunsford's taxonomy, although it is necessary to note that the teacher uses more interrogative and problem-posing statements when he is not commenting on sentential and word-level errors. These corrections do not explain why the student's construction is awkward or "wrong." Although *teacher* errors in commenting—misidentified mistakes, incorrectly labeled errors, misunderstandings of the student's intended meaning, and the like—must be accepted in the context of typically unreasonable workloads in composition instruction, the pattern of problematic comments on this student's multiple negation demonstrates the teacher's lack of knowledge about this feature of AAE. More importantly, it may reveal a tendency for this teacher to *hypercorrect* (a linguistic term usually referring to a speaker's tendency to correct him- or herself in error in formal situations, but here adapted to mean a teacher's tendency to "see" errors through a construction of the writer's language background and culture). These kinds of comments could be seen as one mistake made by the professor; however, the second instance of negation demonstrates the teacher's lack of knowledge regarding negation, and, more importantly, a specific example of the socially constructed persona that the teacher potentially has created for this student. Encouraging, however, is Smith's choice for Comment 2. Unlike Comment 1, Comment 2 does allow the student to determine what a double negative is for himself, which is seen as important for drawing the students' attention to the "error" and considering it on his own time.

In another set of drafts, Professor Smith neglects to write any comments with regard to other AAE features. In one essay, there are several AAE features that go unmarked. One example is the use of *does* for *do* in the following excerpt: "But Wolf and Faludi does not think there is a conspiracy." A second instance is the same student's use of multiple negation: "Something else she is trying to get through is women can not achieve nothing else so why try if they have everything." In yet another case, CCR goes unmarked in the sentence "Men, I think have because they are becoming more conservative than what they **use** to be" (boldface added). Although it is tempting to speculate that the teacher is withholding local, sentence-level comments in favor of a focus on content, this does not seem to be the case, as there are few other comments on the essay.

Similar trends in grading are seen in reviewing Professor Jones' comments; however, Jones generally uses questions and declarative statements more often overall, although he too may cross out sections or not comment on a section at all, as shown in Fig. 7.2.

In this section of Tamara's essay, corrections concerning how to address the term "essay," word choices, and imperative decisions about how to construct the paragraphs do not detract from the importance of how Jones constructs his comment about his student's CCR "looking **pass**," in which he asks the student to rethink or examine a certain word choice. He comments on several aspects of writing, focusing, as Smith did, on addressing local concerns, which include dialect use. In Jones' response to "looking pass," he relinquishes control of writing and revision to the student, whether he intends to or not, and asks the student to make a decision about his or her language. Although this mode of response is focused at the word level, it is evident that the interrogative nature of the statement returns more power to the student than would the comment "fix" or "looking pa<u>st</u>."

"The Beauty Myth" by Naomi Wolf

What does looking Pass mean?

The essay by Wolf, ~~she~~ talks about women looking pass, fighting for equal rights and looking for the beauty within themselves. She also discussed the political and economic influence ~~reasons~~ women are having on the society.

(Tamara, Professor Jones)

FIGURE. 7.2. Comments by Professor Jones.

In Fig. 7.3, Professor Jones circles and corrects many grammatical mistakes, in addition to commenting on larger wording and sentence-level problems. The paragraph's comments in Fig. 7.3 indicate several problems with tense, although some of the nonstandard dialect features in the sample are confused with what appear to be fairly standard problems with tense and subject/verb agreement. In the following sample, Jones makes judgments about what problems the student has, which focus on tense variation and subject/verb agreement.

In this example, Jones notes several problems with tense. In marking several past tense verbs, the teacher also corrects the *seen* in the phrase *she seen Rae Ann leave school today*. Although the occurrence of subject/verb agreement and consistent tense markings are common problems in many students' writings, this teacher makes no distinction between the common grammatical mistakes of students and a nonstandard dialect feature (*seen*). *Seen*, as used in this context, is an irregular verb in which the participle is used for past forms. Instead of paying more attention to this particular feature, the teacher corrects it along with everything else, reinforcing the teacher's image as a proofreader and diminishing his role as an educator.

Professor Jones does not address the student's hypercorrection of CCR ("that is their lost and someone's else gain" [Tamara, Professor Smith]). The rationale behind such a decision might be that the teacher marked overall content and idea formation instead of minor grammatical issues; minor issues might change with the scope of the piece anyway, so the changing of small details would become moot. The methodological decision of this teacher is speculative; however, the comments through the rest of the essay, although overwhelmingly imperative, indicate the teacher's desire to show the student where the content and focus of the essay fall apart.

In general, then, Professor Smith's and Professor Jones' methods of response are primarily directive (Straub), making corrections on wording,

---

The other problem Rae Ann (was) having (was) that she (did) not know how to tell ~~tense~~ *Good!*

M'Dear that she was bleeding. Rae Ann was afraid of M'Dear because she had used

up a lot of towels and things as remedies to her problem. Even though Rae Ann was

afraid of telling M'Dear, she ~~had already~~ (knew) that something (was) going on with Rae *Knows*

Ann, because a lady that lives on their street told her that she ~~seen~~ Rae Ann leave *Saw*

school early. (Vanessa, Professor Jones)

FIGURE. 7.3. Professor Jones' comments on a student paper.

local structure, and grammar, crossing out improper verb tenses, and using imperative statements to direct the student's revisions. In order to more accurately determine the utility of the comments, we now explore the final drafts to see whether the errors persist.

TEACHER RESPONSE IN FINAL DRAFTS

In this section, we return to the examples from students' essays, paying particular attention to those AAE features in final drafts that received a second round of written comments. Those features that were not commented on in rough drafts categorically persisted. For example, Kasha, who had relatively few comments on her essay, maintains all instances of AAE (including using *does* for *do*, multiple negation, and CCR).

Of those features commented on in the rough draft stage, the most striking is the example in which Daunte uses entirely grammatical modes of negation, as in "I'm not trying to say nothing has improved" and " No one that's a minority can say discrimination doesn't exist." Professor Smith, in his commenting, alters these sentences in the draft stage. In Daunte's final draft, he writes the following sentences in place of the former ones: "I'm not trying to say anything has improved since the last century because things have improved" and "Any minority can say discrimination doesn't exist." The meaning of the sentences is entirely changed. The first two sentences of the student's essay are now illogical, ill-placed, and potentially misinterpreted as even more "incorrect" than in the first draft. The sentences surrounding those with multiple negation are confused by the lack of cohesion among ideas. The first sentence is obviously introducing the idea of discrimination, whereas the last sentence is explaining where discrimination comes from. Both sentences, although not directly stated, in conjunction with the sentences previous to the sample, discuss affirmative action and minority status. For this reason, the sentence "Any minority can say discrimination doesn't exist" makes little sense in context. The teacher has inadvertently turned a perceived grammatical problem into a problem of meaning and coherence.

In a draft by Daunte, Professor Smith crosses out two words and corrects them as seen in Fig. 7.4.

"Three ~~authors has~~ *Writers have* an opinion on those issues."
(Daunte, Professor Smith)

FIGURE. 7.4. Subject/verb agreement.

In the final draft, Daunte does change the sentence to reflect the teacher's correction. However, he also appears not to apply this correction to a similar case later, continuing to use *has* with a plural noun (i.e., "Schools predominately minority has around a very high two though students and up to three thousand students"). Although this sentence contains several errors, we were struck by the lack of cognitive recognition of the change from an AAE feature to SE, a detail that perhaps demonstrates the futility of a model in which students are supposed to learn to recognize dialect interference in their writing by having errors marked in their papers.

Somewhat problematically, this same student uses multiple negation in the final draft of a paper, which this time is corrected by Smith (who neglected to point them out on the rough draft). Yet in the final draft, both marked and unmarked instances of multiple negation persist. As this case suggests, there is considerable misunderstanding of the use and nature of multiple negation in the student's writing; the almost arbitrary and even misleading way in which some of the cases are marked and the fact that others are left unmarked can only be seen to frustrate or confuse the student, whose AAE features persist until the end of the semester and earn her low grades.

Kasha's final essay also contained multiple negation in her rough draft. Smith responds to this instance as shown previously in Item 3 of Fig. 7.1: "I ~~can't~~ cannot think of ~~no~~ any time I have not been discriminat~~ioned~~ against." Kasha appears to mean that she has consistently experienced discrimination. This differs from the incident in which Professor Smith changed the meaning of the student's sentence (see Fig. 7.1, number 1). In both cases, Smith exerts corrective control over the writing. More importantly, however, these two cases demonstrate the semantic inconsistency and, at times, inaccuracy of Smith's rephrasings, providing an unreliable model of SE for students and perhaps suggesting a lack of knowledge about multiple negation in AAE.

Similar to Kasha's essays, Michael uses several AAE features that, although "corrected" or "marked," do not change in the final drafts. Of the four excerpts from the essay, Michael changed only Items 2 and 3 (see Fig. 7.5).

Adverbial –ly deletion is common among many students, regardless of dialect, but the fact that the features in Items 1 and 4 persist indicates that vernacular features related to irregular verbs and consonant clusters are not those that can be explained to a student simply by crossing them out. Instead, more interrogative, indirect, and heuristic comments that question the reasoning behind certain types of language might be more useful if the trend in the final drafts continues.

Professor Jones's students react in similar ways to Professor Smith's students. In Tamara's essays some instances in which we might examine her learning of distinctions between AAE and SE are complicated by her avoidance of the problem Jones identifies. For example, Jones comments on

1. After 1988 the gap begin *a* to widen

2. Darling-Hammond resourcefully told how the federal, state, and local governments discriminated against black students, by showing how the government **use** the tracking *ly* system to segregated students within the same schools." [emphasis added]

3. Due to the fact that many schools are already partial *ly* segregated because of the trend that blacks usually live in urban cities and whites live in suburban cities; discrimination of the schools are easily shown..." *areas* *within*

4. Darling-Hammond would not feel that Affirmative Action is insignificant, but is design *ed* to protect job opportunities...."

(Michael, Professor Smith)

FIGURE. 7.5. Professor Smith corrects Michael.

Tamara's use of *pass* in the phrase "she talks about women looking pass, fighting for equal rights. . . ." by asking, "What does looking pass mean?" In the final draft, Tamara omits the idea of women looking past discrimination and instead writes, "she discussed how women are realizing how unhappy they are with their appearance," which does not seem to match the focus on equal rights and discrimination in the earlier draft.

Other instances of vernacular dialect in Tamara's papers—both those identified by Smith and those not identified—remain unchanged. For example, in her final draft, Tamara edits the sentence, "that is their lost and someone's else gain" to "that is their lost and someone else's gain." She corrects the possessive marker, but she preserves the case of hypercorrection in the use of *lost* for *loss*.

In another essay, Vanessa is grappling with the use of past tense, in addition to using the participle form for past tense forms (see Fig. 7.3). Although Jones has crossed out her *seen* and written *saw* clearly above it, Vanessa does not correct this in her essay. Similarly, both Tamara and Vanessa have third-person–*s* absence. Each instance is marked with a circle and an "S" by Professor Jones. Despite their teachers' persistent identification of–*s* absence in every draft, these students, like most in this group, did not change this feature in their revisions. It appears that the students were unable to act on the admonitions in their teachers' comments and corrections, perhaps because, as Seymour shows in a dialogue between two Black schoolchildren trying to understand why the verb "is" appears in a sentence, their underlying linguistic knowledge and structures make such corrections seem incorrect or "sound wrong."

"Wha' da wor'?"

"Da' wor' *is*, you dope."

"*Is*? Ain't no wor' *is*. You jivin' me? Wha' da wor' mean?"

"Ah dunno. Jus' *is*."

Instead of seeing the lack of correction as a consequence of the students' negligence, we might see it as a consequence of pedagogical negligence—teachers uninformed about the use of vernacular dialects and unable to employ appropriate strategies to address some of the grammatical issues in the essays. Clearly, the response strategies used by Smith and Jones to help these African American students to gain an understanding of SE, including the ability to recognize AAE forms and to edit them to their SE counterparts, are a near-total waste of the teacher's energy and the students' learning potential.

CONCLUSION

From an examination of the teacher comments on the rough and revised drafts of five students who exhibit features of AAE in their writing, it is not possible to reach generalizable conclusions about either the source of the teacher comments or the precise comprehension of AAE and SE syntax by the students. However, we can make some inferences about why the teachers used the response techniques that they did. We propose that the teachers' comments can be interpreted in two possible ways: either they had full knowledge of the nature of AAE dialect features and were intentionally using eradicationist and directive commenting to assist the students in learning SE; or, in the absence of such knowledge of language differences and dialect patterns, they were unable to comment on AAE features with any regularity.

If the teachers were deliberately using eradicationist and directive commenting, some evidence of systematicity in their approach would appear in the focus and nature of their comments. There is, however, nothing systematic about their approach, for although the comments are overwhelmingly directive, there are many instances in which no comments are written at all, and instances in which the teacher appears not to understand the underlying meaning the student was conveying—as would be clear from an understanding of the nature of the dialect and its features. In the absence of the theoretical, linguistic, and pedagogical knowledge necessary to help novice writers to recognize the ways in which their home and community dialects are manifested in their writing, the teachers in this study appeared to be responding through an ideological lens we might call "nescient eradicationism," in which they identify errors in a scattershot way for all students, without knowledge of the norms and patterns of dialect use. In their self-constructed role, they feel obliged to edit and proofread students' papers, but we cannot blame them for not providing richer, more pedagogically useful response—even as eradicationists—because they lack the training and background necessary to do so. Although their directive response style on both rough and final drafts may provide a kind of behavioral model for students—reinforcing trial-and-error learning—it does not yield the desired results, either behaviorally or textually. The extent to which corrections and directive commentary solve issues of AAE usage remains, as Hillocks has shown, quite dubious.

Although disconcerting, the results of this study must be interpreted cautiously. The study was designed to serve as a preliminary investigation of the relationship between AAE features and the responses of teachers in a typical college setting. As Fife and O'Neill remind us, considerable research on response to student writing has focused too strongly on texts (student essays, teachers' marginal and end comments, etc.), and not on the broader contexts in which such texts function. Our study did not, for example, explore the underlying ideological and pedagogical sources of teachers' responses more directly through interviews with the teachers or retrospective accounts of why they wrote the comments they did. Nor did we study the students' interpretations of their teachers' comments, a direction that has been profitably taken in some research on response (see Auten; Fuller; Ziv). Further research could extend our exploration of the relationship between dialect features, response, and learning through more descriptive and ethnographic methodologies. Moreover, our analysis focused primarily on details within a narrow band of textual features. Recent research on broader rhetorical, pragmatic, and discursive characteristics of the writing of AAE-speaking students has revealed the presence of circumlocution, indirection, call/response, and persuasive features found in these students' oral culture (see, e.g., Redd and Schuster Webb; Syrquin), suggesting profitable new areas of research on teachers' response to these features in student writing.

Furthermore, our study was generally external to the classrooms from which our corpus emerged. As Fife and O'Neill remind us, even studying teachers, students, and texts may not reveal the full range of discourse and information that affects learning:

> Textual analysis of teacher comments can suggest important characteristics of response that encourage students to see themselves as writers, but we need to look at the broader structure of the exchanges about writing that go on in the classroom to see how these dynamics can encourage or inhibit a real conversation with students about their writing. (311)

Although our general knowledge of the classrooms and pedagogies surrounding our corpus would suggest that little attention was paid to issues of linguistic and cultural variation, further research should explore the many sources of information, attitudes, and dicta that emerge from specific classrooms in their fullest sense (e.g., Campbell).

Our study does, however, suggest an urgent need for more attention to issues of dialect variation in the teaching of writing. Many excellent teacher-development programs now prepare instructors to meet the challenges of their college composition classrooms, and the teaching of writing to non-native speakers has likewise improved significantly as research and pedagogy in English as a Second Language have burgeoned. However, those nonimmigrant students who bring to the college classroom various dialects of American English—regional and ethnic—often are learning from teachers unprepared to help them to recognize the patterns of their dialects and the ways they influence their writing. Principles and methods such as those outlined by Arnetha Ball—recognizing "how the characteristic patterns of students' spoken language are reflected in their written texts" (239), reconceptualizing the writing conference as places "where students can feel free to respond to teacher inquiries without censure" (240), and developing "attitudes of ethnosensitivity" in our evaluation of student work (241)—ought to be central areas of coverage and learning in all our teacher-preparation activities. More teacher-focused publications such as Redd and Schuster Webb's book *African American English: What a Writing Teacher Should Know* are needed at all levels of the curriculum. However, as Ball and Lardner point out, simply informing teachers about dialect differences is probably insufficient to result in the reform of pedagogical practice; "the cognitive internalization of information is not enough to increase teacher efficacy because there is a difference between knowing that and knowing how, between knowing and feeling and between knowing and transforming knowledge in practice" (102). These scholars advocate for teachers a process of transformation that involves "self-analysis, studying one's own journey toward efficacy, reanalyzing personal beliefs and assumptions and recentering one's sense of oneself in professional and extraprofessional dimensions" (103; see also Anson, "Reflective Reading"). Finally, broader national discussions of appropriate pedagogical and ideological positions are badly needed, regardless of the sentiments of politicians and a public largely uninformed about the nature and complexity of language (see Richardson; Young). Through continued education and sensitivity to this complexity, we may be able to move beyond simplistic and confounding approaches to literacy education.

ACKNOWLEDGMENT

We would like to acknowledge Dr. Walt Wolfram's support through grant NSF BCS 00-10224 and the William C. Friday Endowment.

WORKS CITED

Anson, Chris M. "Response Styles and Ways of Knowing." *Writing and Response: Theory, Practice and Research.* Ed. Chris M. Anson. Urbana, IL: NCTE, 1989. 322–66.

____. "Reflective Reading: Developing Thoughtful Ways to Respond to Students' Writing." *Evaluating Writing: The Role of Teachers' Knowledge about Text, Learning, and Culture.* Eds. Charles R. Cooper and Lee Odell. Urbana, IL: NCTE, 1999. 302–24.

____. "Talking About Text: The Use of Recorded Commentary in Response to Student Writing." *A Sourcebook on Responding to Student Writing.* Ed. Rick Straub. Norwood, NJ: Hampton, 2000. 165–74.

____. "Response and the Social Construction of Error." *Assessing Writing* 7 (2001): 5–21.

Auten, Janet Gebhart. "How Students Read Us: Audience Awareness and Teacher Commentary on Writing." *The Writing Instructor* 11 (1992): 83–94.

Balester, Valerie M. *Cultural Divide: A Study of African American College-Level Writers.* Portsmouth, NH: Boynton/Cook, 1993.

Ball, Arnetha F. "Evaluating the Writing of Culturally and Linguistically Diverse Students: The Case of the African American Vernacular English Speaker." *Evaluating Writing: The Role of Teachers' Knowledge about Text, Learning, and Culture.* Eds. Charles R. Cooper and Lee Odell. Urbana, IL: NCTE, 1999. 225–48.

Ball, Arnetha F., and Ted Lardner. *African American Literacies Unleashed: Vernacular English and the Composition Classroom.* Carbondale: Southern Illinois UP, 2005.

Bowie, Robert L., and Carole L. Bond. "Influencing Future Teachers' Attitudes Toward Black English: Are We Making a Difference?" *Journal of Teacher Education* 45.2 (1994): 112–18.

Campbell, Kermit E. "'Real Niggaz's Don't Die': African American Students Speaking Themselves into Their Writing." *Writing in Multicultural Settings.* Eds. Carol Severino, Juan C. Guerra, and Johnella E. Butler. New York: Modern Language Association, 1997. 67-78.

Connors, Robert J., and Andrea Lunsford. "Teachers' Rhetorical Comments on Student Papers." *College Composition and Communication* 39 (1996): 395-409.

Daiker, Donald. "Learning to Praise." *Writing and Response: Theory, Practice, and Research.* Ed. Chris M. Anson. Urbana, IL: NCTE, 1988. 103-13.

Delpit, Lisa D. "The Silenced Dialogue: Power and Pedagogy in Educating Other People's Children." *Harvard Educational Review* 58.3 (1988): 280–97.

Denzin, Norman K., and Yvonna S. Lincoln, eds. *Strategies of Qualitative Inquiry.* Thousand Oaks, CA: Sage, 2003.

Ede, Lisa, and Andrea A. Lunsford. *Singular Texts/Plural Authors.* Carbondale: Southern Illinois UP, 1990.

Elbow, Peter. "Inviting the Mother Tongue: Beyond 'Mistakes,' 'Bad English,' and 'Wrong Language.' *JAC: A Journal of Composition Theory* 19.3 (1999): 359–88.

Farr, Marcia, and Harvey Daniels. *Language Diversity and Writing Instruction*. New York: Teachers College/Columbia U, ERIC Clearinghouse on Urban Education, 1986.

Fasold, Ralph W. *Tense Marking in Black English: A Linguistic and Social Analysis*. Washington, DC: Center for Applied Linguistics, 1972.

Fife, Jane Mathison, and Peggy O'Neill. "Moving Beyond the Written Comment: Narrowing the Gap between Response Practice and Research." *College Composition and Communication* 53.2 (2001): 300–21.

Freire, Paulo. *Pedagogy of the Oppressed*. New York: Continuum International, 1970.

Fuller, David. "Teacher Commentary that Communicates: Practicing What We Preach." *Journal of Teaching Writing* 6 (1987): 307–17.

Gilyard, Keith. *Let's Flip the Script: An African American Discourse on Language, Literature, and Learning*. Detroit: Wayne State UP, 1996.

Halliday, M.A.K. *Language, Context, and Text: Aspects of Language in a Social Semiotic Perspective*. New York: Oxford UP, 1989/1997.

Heck, Susan. "Writing Standard English IS Acquiring a Second Language." *Language Alive in the Classroom*. Ed. Rebecca Wheeler. Westport, CT: Praeger P, 1999. 115-20.

Hill, Guy Y., and Milner, Joseph A. "What Instructional Strategies Do Teachers Use and How Do Teachers React When Students Use African American English in the Classroom?" *Proceedings of the Annual Research Forum at the Wake Forest University Department of Education Annual Research Forum, December 1995*. Ed. Leah P. McCoy. Wake Forest: Wake Forest Department of Education, 1995. 56–60.

Hillocks, George, Jr. *Research on Written Composition*. Urbana, IL: NCTE, 1986.

Howard, Rebecca Moore. "The Great Wall of African American Vernacular English in the American College Classroom." *JAC: A Journal of Composition Theory* 16.2 (1996): 265-84.

Hunt, Russell. "'Could You Put in Lots of Holes?' Modes of Response to Writing." *Language Arts* 64.2 (1987): 229–32.

Jimenez, Martha. "Educational Rights of Language-Minority Children." *Language Loyalties: A Source Book on the Official Language Controversy*. Ed. James Crawford. Chicago: U of Chicago P, 1992. 243-51.

Knoblauch, C.H., and Lil Brannon. "Teacher Commentary on Student Writing: The State of the Art." *Freshman English News* 10 (1981): 1–4.

Labov, William. *Language in the Inner City: Studies in the Black English Vernacular*. Philadelphia: U of Pennsylvania P, 1972.

___. "Can Reading Failure Be Reversed?" *Literacy Among African-American Youth: Issues in Learning, Teaching, and Schooling*. Ed. Vivian Gadsen. Cresskill, NJ: Hampton P, 1995.

___. "Academic Ignorance and Black Intelligence." *The Atlantic Monthly* June 1972: 59-67.

Labov, William, Paul Cohen, Clarence Robins, and John Lewis. *A Study of the Non-Standard English of Negro and Puerto Rican Speakers in New York City*. United States Office of Education Final Report, Research Project 3288, 1968.

Lees, Elaine O. "Evaluating Student Writing." *College Composition and Communication* 30 (1979): 370–74.

Murray, Donald. "The Listening Eye: Reflections on the Writing Conference." *College English* 41 (1976): 13–18.

O'Neill, Wayne. "The Politics of Bidialectalism." *The Politics of Literature: Dissenting Essays on the Teaching of English.* Eds. Louis Kampf and Paul Lauter. New York: Pantheon, 1972. 245-255.

Redd, Teresa M., and Karen Schuster Webb. *African American English: What a Writing Teacher Should Know.* Urbana, IL: National Council of Teachers of English, 2005.

Richardson, Elaine B. "Coming from the Heart: African American Students, Literacy Stories, and Rhetorical Education." *African American Rhetoric(s): Interdisciplinary Perspectives.* Eds. Elaine B. Richardson and Ronald L. Jackson II. Carbondale: Southern University Press, 2004. 155–69.

Rickford, John R. *African American Vernacular English: Features, Evolution, Educational Implications.* Hoboken, NJ: Blackwell P, 1999.

Rickford, John R., and Angela E. Rickford. "Dialect Readers Revisited." *Linguistics and Education* 7.2 (1995): 107-128.

Searle, Dennis, and David Dillon. "The Message of Marking: Teacher Written Response to Student at Intermediate Grade Levels." *Research in the Teaching of English* 14 (1980): 233-42.

Seymour, Dorothy Z. "Black Children, Black Speech." *Commonweal*, 19 Nov. 1971. 8, 175-81.

Shaughnessy, Mina P. *Errors and Expectations: A Guide for the Teacher of Basic Writing.* New York: Oxford UP, 1977.

Simpkins, G., G. Holt, and C. Simpkins. *Bridge: A Cross-Cultural Reading Program.* Boston: Houghton Mifflin, 1977.

Smitherman, Geneva. "Black English and the Education of Black Children and Youth." *Proceedings of a National Invitational Symposium on the King Decision.* Detroit: Center for Black Studies, Wayne State University, 1981.

Sommers, Nancy. "Responding to Student Writing." *College Composition and Communication* 33 (1982): 148–56.

Straub, Richard. "The Concept of Control in Teacher Response: Defining the Varieties of 'Directive' and 'Facilitative' Commentary." *College Composition and Communication* 47.2 (1996): 223–51.

Straub, Richard, and Ronald F. Lunsford. *Twelve Readers Reading: Responding to College Student Writing.* Cresskill, NJ: Hampton P, 1995.

Syrquin, Anna F. "Registers in the Academic Writing of African American College Students." *Written Communication* 23.1 (2006): 63–90.

Viechnicki, Gail Brendel. "Reading, Writing, and Linguistics: Principles from the Little Red Schoolhouse." *Language Alive in the Classroom.* Ed. Rebecca S. Wheeler. Westport, CT: Praeger P, 1999. 121-26.

Weiner, Harvey S. "Collaborative Learning in the Classroom: A Guide to Evaluation." *College English* 48 (1986): 52–61.

Wolfram, Walt. *A Sociolinguistic Description of Detroit Negro Speech.* Washington, DC: Center for Applied Linguistics, 1969.

Wolfram, Walt, Carolyn Temple Adger, and Donna Christian. *Dialects in Schools and Communities.* Mahwah, NJ: Lawrence Erlbaum Associates P, 1998.

Wolfram, Walt, and Natalie Schilling-Estes. *American English*. Hoboken, NJ: Blackwell P, 1999.

Wolfram, Walt, and Erik Thomas. *The Development of African American English*. Hoboken, NJ: Blackwell P, 2002.

Wolfram, Walt, and Marcia Whiteman. "The Role of Dialect Interference in Composition." *The Florida FL Reporter* 9 (1971): 34–38.

Yin, Robert K. *Case Study Research: Design and Methods*. Thousand Oaks, CA: Sage Publishing, 2003.

Young, Vershawn Ashanti. "Your Average Nigga." *College Composition and Communication*. 55.4 (2004): 693–719.

Ziv, Nina. "The Effect of Teacher Comments on the Writing of Four College Freshmen." *New Directions in Composition Research*. Eds. Richard Beach and Lillian Bridwell. New York: Guilford, 1984. 362–80.

8

WHY DENY A CHOICE TO SPEAKERS OF AFRICAN AMERICAN LANGUAGE THAT MOST OF US OFFER OTHER STUDENTS?*

Peter Elbow
Professor Emeritus,
University of Massachusetts at Amherst

"Black" language is sometimes more deeply stigmatized than "Black" skin. People who have learned to resist thinking that others are stupid if they have a darker skin, sometimes nevertheless think others are stupid if they speak the language coded Black. This stigmatization has been so pervasive as to be internalized by quite a few African Americans. Jesse Jackson famously called Ebonics "trash talk" and Bill Cosby at a big awards ceremony said (referring to young speakers of this language as "*it*"):

> It's standing on da corner. It can't speak English. It doesn't want to speak English. I can't even talk the way these people talk. "Why you ain't, where you is go...." I don't know who these people are. (Dyson xii)

But most readers of this chapter will have learned from the extensive testimony of reputable linguists that African American Language (AAL) is a full, sophisticated, and rule-governed language—like any other (see Palacas, Green, and Redd and Webb).[1]

---

*The present chapter builds on earlier essays of mine: "Inviting the Mother Tongue" and "Vernacular Englishes."

In this chapter I'm suggesting that teachers should offer speakers of African American Language the choice that so many mainstream writing teachers offer to mainstream White students: to start off serious writing projects using the kind of spoken vernacular language that naturally emerges in freewriting and fast exploratory writing, and wait until the end to get their final drafts into "correct writing" or Edited Written English (EWE). Ever since the maturing of the so-called process movement, teachers have routinely urged students not to pause and struggle over "proper language" and "correct grammar" while they are in the process of working out their thinking in writing.

That's my argument: invite both mainstream students and AAL speakers to write in their spoken vernacular language and edit later into "correct writing." In the end, I think it actually *is* that simple. Yet nothing is simple when it comes to language and race. So I can't stop here.

MORE ABOUT THIS MAINSTREAM APPROACH

It's not just African American Language that is wrong for final drafts of important essays in most school settings and many public settings. Let's not overlook that fact that the mainstream "White" spoken vernacular language that most mainstream students use in freewriting, drafting, and even mid-process revising is also wrong for writing. Even privileged speakers of so-called "standard" spoken English do not speak Edited Written English (EWE). I am an overeducated White teacher whose childhood "bad grammar" was often corrected, but some of my problems in writing came from the fact that my mother tongue is wrong for writing. I've only recently figured out the important general principle here: *"correct" writing is no one's mother tongue.*[2]

This mainstream approach to writing that I'm advocating is not only about managing language; it's also about managing one's thinking. "Don't stop in the middle of exploratory writing or even a mid-process draft and pull down a handbook and look for the rule that helps you decide between *There is a limited number of liquor licenses* or *There are a limited number of liquor licenses*. Wait until final editing.

What's central to this approach is an emphasis on learning to be more strategic in managing one's focus of attention. (For a useful analysis of the role of attention in writing, see Blau.) Many teachers have reaped big improvements by helping students notice the differences between three processes: *generating* or invention (finding lots of ideas and words); *revising* (choosing the best ideas and putting them in the best order and wording them clearly); and *editing* or *copy editing* (changing words to improve clarity and style and fixing surface grammar, spelling, and other conventions). This is part of a general approach that has been adopted by a large proportion of writing teachers (often called a "process" approach because of its emphasis on conscious awareness of one's writing process).

It's helpful to notice that this approach represents a kind of compromise between two extremes. At the "strict" or "conservative" extreme, *form* is a priority:

> *We must make students do all their writing in the correct language and form. They'll learn it best if they have to use it all the time and get in the habit.*

At the other extreme is a "liberal," "loose," liberatory, or forward-looking approach:

> *Let them write everything in whatever language comes most easily for them. In this era of multiple World Englishes and the "Students' Rights to Their Own Language," it's old fashioned and retrograde to force students to do any writing in EWE if they don't want to.*

Researchers still argue about whether this was the message of "Students' Rights to their Own Language" (see Committee).

It's this compromise between two extremes that I sense most mainstream teachers have come to adopt in dealing with more or less mainstream students. And it's the compromise I am suggesting for speakers of AAL. I have not taught primarily African American students, but I have plenty of authority and experience with this mainstream approach. I use it for my own writing and I use it in my teaching. Obviously my automatic command of written grammar is pretty good (though friends who read my drafts sometimes wonder), but I've found over many years of teaching that this approach also works well with many poorly prepared students who don't have much command over the grammar and conventions of the written dialect.[3]

CHOICE

I want to underline the word *choice* in my title. When I invite students to take this approach, I don't hide my belief that it's a good way to write. Sometimes I'll even say, "Even if you hate it, please give it a good try. It has great benefits." But I also acknowledge and accept that students who speak a stigmatized language might have various good reasons to decline the invitation:

- Many speakers of AAL might decide not to write it at all because they are comfortable and fluent at code-switching into mainstream sanctioned spoken English. They already have the ability to write in that language. They can use final editing for the smaller job of correcting from there into EWE.[4]

- Some may not want to use what feels like an intimate, precious home language for academic tasks, especially for ones they experience as impersonal, abstract, square—too alien from home rhetorical traditions.

- Some may feel they have too few allies in the class and so will prefer to use their vernacular language only for private writing.

- Some may not want to use it because they want to develop fluency in producing EWE. Toward this goal, they are willing to suffer reduced comfort, fluency, and power at the stage of putting words on the page.

- Of course a few may actually disapprove of AAL and feel that it's wrong, bad, defective, or broken. Some may have family members pushing them to "learn good English." The very mother they learned it from may call it "bad broken English." (I don't call this a good reason, but I feel I have to tread carefully when the student herself feels it strongly.)

A MAJOR OBJECTION

You oversimplify when you say that mainstream vernacular English and AAL are both "wrong for writing." The mainstream spoken vernacular is not so racially stigmatized and it's far closer to EWE. So it makes sense for mainstream speakers to write their drafts in their "wrong" language because it's not so hard for them to edit it into EWE at the end. The same goes for speakers of AAL who are good code switchers—since they too can write drafts in the mainstream vernacular. But for speakers of AAL who are not fluent code switchers—in effect they are monolingual speakers of AAL—this editing task is unfeasibly hard. Allowing these students to write in AAL will hamper their academic and economic progress. These students would be better off doing all their writing in EWE—or at least in mainstream spoken English.

Marcia Farr expresses a view like this. She is a notable figure in the fight against stigmatization of nonmainstream dialects, and in responding to my 1999 "Mother Tongue" essay, she wrote as follows:

> I worry a bit about trying to get them to write in their "mother dialect."
> . . . [U]sing it in the classroom (unless in creative writing) confuses form with function. I think it's more important to get them to fully realize the adequacy of all dialects. "Leave their oral language alone," as it were, but teach writing in SE [Standard English]. (e-mail response)[5]

I resist this objection. The approach that Farr suggests—keeping speech and writing apart—has been the traditional or "normal" approach that many teachers and writers have taken for granted for a long time. It can obviously work since it's probably produced much of the good writing in mainstream English by AAL speakers. But I'd argue that this two-track approach has actually kept us from getting lots of good writing by putting an unnecessary hurdle in the way of AAL speakers.

In effect, this approach asks students to try gradually to build a separate dialect or linguistic gear or space or track for writing. Admittedly, many speakers of mainstream English do the same thing when they learn to write *only* in fully correct written English or EWE—avoiding all informal vernacular language even when they write drafts. The goal of this two-gear approach is to help students become fluent or automatic in producing correct written English. It's a long path, but this approach can help monolingual AAL speakers develop right away the habit of simply *avoiding* their spoken language when they pick up a pen or put fingers to a keyboard. The goal is to reduce "language interference" so that they are not distracted by their spoken language when they write. For fluent code switchers, this approach seems natural. They already have a separate language gear—at least for mainstream *spoken* language—and they can use that language for drafting. Since they are good at code switching (unlike so many mainstream writers), they might even be able to learn to write *only* correct written English.

But what about speakers of AAL who are *not* fluent code switchers? Like so many mainstream students, they are more or less monolingual and have only one comfortable language gear. If they are going to get their writing into EWE, they will have to work at it. Their only choices are either to work at it *throughout* the course of writing something, or else to work at it during the *last editing stage* of writing. Neither choice is ideal. The deck is stacked against these students. They cannot prosper in school, college, or the workplace unless they learn to get important pieces of writing into a language that is not comfortable or easy for them.

I'll offer now five reasons why it makes sense to me to offer monolingual speakers of AAL the mainstream approach: drafting and even revising in their most comfortable spoken vernacular language and waiting until the end of the writing process to wrestle with the grammar, lexicon, and conventions of EWE.

1. *Easier writing.* When students can do exploratory writing and drafting in whatever language is most comfortable and inviting, they stand a better chance of finding writing to be more comfortable and inviting. In contrast, the traditional approach of trying to develop a separate linguistic gear for writing forces them to think about the grammar and conventions of EWE *as* they write. This gives them no relief from engaging in conscious linguistic decision making about which forms are right and wrong for writing. Why ask them to endure the Sisyphean task of trying to become automatic in a new dialect when very few will ever succeed? Why ask them to try to become, in effect, "native speakers" of correct writing, when we don't ask that of mainstream students? The only way they will ever learn to produce correct writing without having to constantly monitor their linguistic choices is by writing a *great deal* using this approach—much more than they'll ever have to write for school assignments. This can only happen if they come to love writing and write by choice—which is unlikely to happen if they have to write in an alien dialect. (Admittedly, the new media of e-mail and blogging may lead more of these students to love writing than in former times, but these new modalities carry much less pressure to write in EWE.)

   In short, the goal of the traditional approach of starting with EWE is to reduce language interference while drafting. But starting with AAL and waiting until the end to create EWE *eliminates* language interference while drafting.

2. *Better writing.* When speakers of AAL draft in the language they have most mastery over and postpone any worries about correct written English, they can almost always find more words and ideas. And when they write this way, their writing often has more energy, life, and voice. In contrast, when they try to use a language that's not comfortable for them, they often fall into awkward or even stilted language. In fact, the effort to follow unfamiliar rules can lead students into odd and linguistically peculiar constructions that teachers often see as merely "weird grammar" and read as "cognitive deficit." (Or even "stupid." These anomalous wordings are technically called "production errors.") If the student had simply written the AAL grammar that came easily to mouth, it would at least have been clear and strong—and often it would have been *correct* in EWE. When stu-

dents (and teachers) get too preoccupied by the *differences* between the syntax of AAL and what they call "standard" English, they forget to notice that AAL is *right* for EWE far more often than it's wrong.

In addition, people's spoken vernacular language is usually more connected to their unconscious than any dialect or language they learn later. This gives access to an additional range of experiences, memories, images, words, and ideas.

3. *More knowledge of AAL and how language works.* The goal of the traditional approach of writing *only* in EWE is to make EWE habitual and automatic and develop a separate language gear for writing—so writers don't have to think consciously or worry about "correctness." The more they succeed, the more they can put to sleep their conscious knowledge of the differences between AAL and EWE or mainstream spoken language. In contrast, when AAL speakers write in their vernacular language and wait until the end to worry about the rules of EWE, this final editing process forces them to notice and consciously compare the two grammars and lexicons. Constant practice in comparative linguistics of this kind will give them more conscious knowledge of AAL and help demystify the grammar and conventions of EWE. (See Gee and Palacas on the importance of this kind of meta-linguistic knowledge.)

4. *Helping AAL flourish as a language.* Writing is one of the safest sites for any stigmatized language. And we can make the writing classroom one of the most hopeful arenas for language: ideal for writing in stigmatized languages with pride—ideal for hiding them when needed. When AAL speakers talk to mainstream listeners, they invariably risk stigmatization unless they manage to remove even subtle accentual and intonational traces of their spoken vernacular. But when AAL speakers *write* to mainstream readers, they can do most of their work comfortably in their comfortable spoken vernacular, yet still end up with a text in correct EWE that won't make readers hear Blackness. Indeed, we can show *all* our students that writing provides a safer site for language use than speaking. Writing lets us write privately and write drafts that we don't show anyone until we are ready. When we speak we usually have a listener—who seldom forgets what we wish we hadn't said.

When we help speakers of stigmatized languages produce texts in their spoken vernacular that are carefully revised and edited, we help demonstrate that these languages are not just used for casual speech. One of my goals is for non-sanctioned versions of any major language—especially stigmatized versions—to survive and flourish. Few languages survive and flourish unless they are used for writing.

5. *More flexibility about what final drafts will look like.* When people hear the suggestion that speakers of AAL should be invited to write in that language, they often say, *But how will they learn to write in the "language of power?"* Obviously I've been trying to address this pervasive knee-jerk worry, but in doing so I may have allowed myself to sound as though I am accepting two common assumptions that are false: (a) that all writing has to be in EWE; and (b) that AAL and EWE represent a simple binary pair.

   a. Not all serious writing has to be in EWE. For a long time, there's been a good deal of writing in AAL published to high esteem (see appendix). But somehow teachers have tended to assume that all this published writing is irrelevant to the writing life of AAL-speaking students in our classrooms. In my teaching of students who speak stigmatized varieties of English (my limited experience has mostly been with speakers of AAL and Hawai'ian Creole English or so called "Pidgin"), I ask students to revise and copy edit their important essays, but I also invite them to revise and copyedit at least *one* important piece into a "non-standard" non-EWE final version. I want students to understand that revising and editing have no inherent link with EWE. I want them to learn to revise and edit for good thinking, clarity, liveliness and wit—and realize that EWE has no special claim on those virtues. Indeed they sometimes notice that EWE gets in the way. When they accept this invitation, they end up with a carefully revised and copyedited paper in their home language.

      In fact there are more and more opportunities for sharing and publishing writing in other versions of English such as AAL or Spanglish. School newspapers, school literary magazines, and even some local Sunday papers are often good sites for publishing strong, well revised and edited pieces as feature stories in nonmainstream versions of English. Personal letters and diaries have always been good sites for writing where there is no pressure for EWE, but now e-mail, blogs, and other internet arenas provide additional sites that are more deeply social. In my teaching of first year writing, I publish three or four class magazines each semester (see "The Role of Publication"). These are ideal sites—and often lead to useful discussions about different versions of English.

b. More and more scholars in our profession have been calling attention to how EWE is not a single monolithic dialect or register. For a recent telling argument, see Canagarajah's exploration in *College Composition and Communication* of what he calls "code meshing": pieces of writing that are hybrid or mixed as to dialect, language, and discourse. We see further evidence of this cultural development in John McWhorter's extended complaint that all kinds of casual and even "low" language is now accepted as correct standard English. The "grapholect" is not unilateral or single. Good writers have always enjoyed playing with mixtures of register and injecting energy and capturing readers' attention with unexpected changes of register.

"Correct" is not one thing. Teachers are notoriously variable in what they insist on as "correct." Some want students to avoid all informality, while others find it inappropriately stuffy for students to avoid all first person or narrative or statements of feeling (not to mention all contractions). If we wanted to lay out the rules for a single EWE "gear," we would be hard pressed to formulate them.

So one of the major benefits for students who start out writing projects in AAL is that this approach puts them in a better position to decide where they want to place their text on the spectrum from the "most correct" EWE to "basilectal" AAL—to decide how much mixing or hybridization they want to play with. Often, it's only in the last stages of a writing project that one can best make these decisions. If, on the other hand, students develop a dedicated "correct writing gear," they lock themselves into a single "proper" version of EWE where it's harder to use the kind of code-meshing that is more and more prominent in our culture.

One of Canagarajah's points—along with many other recent arguments for mixed genre writing (see Romano)—is that the traffic between discourses is two way: between formal and personal, between academic and "lay," and between written and oral. "Standard" discourses have always been changed and enlivened by writers using "nonstandard" discourses.

A note about fluent code switchers. These five arguments for starting off in AAL might not seem to apply to AAL speakers who are fluent code switchers. Such students can already write easily in a mainstream variety of English and thus have an easier time at the editing stage. But now I want to suggest that the last three arguments for starting off in AAL apply even to them. After all, code switchers too:

- might want to learn more about AAL and EWE by doing the comparative linguistics involved in that final process of editing between the two languages;
- might want to help AAL flourish by doing more writing in it and doing even some final drafts and publishing in it;
- might want to have more flexibility to play with hybrid registers and mixed genres.

ANOTHER OBJECTION

If speakers of AAL draft in that language, they will be left with a final task far more daunting than mere editing. In order to end up with a school or academic essay (what David Olson calls "essayist prose"), they'll have to dig deeper and change the very modes of thinking, arguing, reasoning, and organizing that's built into the fabric of their drafts. Frantz Fanon insists that "every dialect, every language, is a way of thinking." Arnetha Ball showed that the African American students in her sample tended more than comparable mainstream students to use the discourse of narrative and circumlocution for presenting their thinking and experience ("Cultural Preferences" and "Expository"). You can't learn a new discourse or rhetoric by working in the old one—you have to work in the new discourse or rhetoric itself.

Yes, there may often be *links* between a language like AAL and certain modes of thinking or self-expression that are discouraged for academic essays. But a dialect or language or register is *not* the same as a mode of thinking or rhetoric. It is this difference between language and thinking that mainstream teachers have been exploiting when using the process approach that I am advocating here for speakers of AAL. We see plenty of inappropriate thinking and rhetoric from mainstream first-year students in college. The whole point of the mainstream process approach is to put more focus on thinking, arguing, reasoning, and organizing by working on these new habits of academic thinking and rhetoric *without at the same time* having to worry about correctness of language. One of the most concretely practical consequences of this approach has been to help us get students to avoid a trap they so often fall into: when they are asked to *revise* they often just tinker or polish or correct their language. The main burden of revising is to take those early attempts to analyze or persuade and rework them until they reflect the kind of thinking, arguing, reasoning, and organizing that are needed for academic essays.

So what does this mean for students who started off writing in AAL? Perhaps their drafts will be further from academic discourse than those of mainstream students—or perhaps more of them will have this problem. (Perhaps not.) But their job in revising an essay will be exactly the same as the one for mainstream students: get the modes of thinking and rhetoric right for academic discourse; take that statement of feelings and rewrite it as an argument with clear supporting reasons and examples; reframe that story so it functions more clearly as supporting evidence for a more conceptually stated main point.

This is hard work for mainstream students; possibly harder for some speakers of AAL. Students can seldom be very successful at it unless they get feedback from teachers and/or peers on these substantive matters of rhetoric, reasoning, and organization—rather than on surface features of language. But it's the same job, and in both cases it results in the same interesting middle stage in the process of writing an essay: the student has put all her effort into creating better academic thinking and organization rather than jumping prematurely into trying to correct all the "wrong" grammar and spelling.

So at this stage, monolingual speakers of AAL will be rewriting their drafts to make them work like academic discourse, but not trying to change what Gee calls the "trivial" linguistic features that distinguish AAL from mainstream standardized English (530). Arnetha Ball writes specifically about this process:

> Students can continue to use their informal language patterns while acquiring competence in new academic registers. These kinds of curricula mandate further research on creating bridges between patterns used in students' home discourse communities and those required for school success. ("Cultural Preferences" 525)

So when these AAL-speaking students are doing the heavy lifting of revising, they are being invited to use their home vernacular spoken language while changing their rhetoric or discourse (i.e., their thinking, arguing, and organizing). Later, when *editing*, they'll turn their attention to changing the grammar, syntax, and lexicon to get them to conform to the conventions of EWE.

The important point here is that the use of a dialect or language does not lock someone into one way of thinking or organizing. There may be deep links between language, thinking, culture, and identity. But links are not chains. Even a knowledgeable authority about contrastive rhetoric like Ilona Leki insists that a culture does not consist of just one way of thinking. My central premise is that people can use any variety of English for any cognitive or rhetorical task.

Would anyone really want to argue otherwise?—to argue that people cannot analyze or think abstractly in AAL? Smitherman was at pains to contradict this notion when she sometimes wrote in AAL in both *Talkin That Talk* and *Talkin and Testifyin*. It's illustrative to look at the argument of a scholar who *does* insist that a dialect restricts thinking. Thomas Farrell maintains that Black children get lower IQ scores because their oral dialect lacks "the full standard deployment of the verb 'to be' and depends too much on additive and appositional constructions rather than embedded modification and subordination" (481).

Does mainstream English—or EWE—"own" certain kinds of thinking and certain discourses? Must people give up their cultural identity to take on certain rhetorical or intellectual or cognitive tasks? I believe we can validly invite speakers of AAL or other dialects and cultures to take on academic tasks and write an academic essay in their home dialects—as Latinos, African Americans, or Caribbeans. But even as they do genuinely academic thinking and rhetoric, this doesn't mean that they have to strip their thinking and rhetoric entirely of what Smitherman calls their own cultural "expressive discourse style." In her research she showed that this discourse style raised NAEP scores for the African American students who used it—as long as they didn't use stigmatized syntax or grammar from AAL ("Blacker the Berry").[6]

HOW CAN WE MAKE A WRITING CLASSROOM HELPFUL FOR SPEAKERS OF AAL?

There is no way we can make our classrooms ideal for speakers of AAL—especially those who cannot comfortably code switch. Their native language is heavily stigmatized in our culture and it's further away from EWE than mainstream spoken English. We cannot avoid asking them to use and master a language that often functions as hostile to their own language—indeed that they might understandably feel as bent on wiping out their culture. Still we can set ourselves the goal of making as good an experience as possible for these students:

- We can communicate to them that we respect and value their native language—without condescending.
- We can do our best to help other students respect and value that language—though we cannot always succeed.
- We can help them learn to write successfully for other teachers—and give them as good a start as possible for writing in other disciplines and on the job and for other audiences in the wider world.

- We can help them learn to like writing, to write by choice, and to use writing to help make sense of their lives—for example when confused or perplexed or hurt. (Writing in AAL will often be crucial here.)

When I try to think of ways to pursue those goals, here is what I come up with:

- We can help students understand how language works. They need to understand—and understand that we understand—that vernacular dialects of English are not "broken English" or mere "slang" but in fact fully developed, sophisticated, rule-governed languages—in no way linguistically inferior to standardized English. "I learned I had a language" wrote one of Irvine's and Elsasser's students (see "English" and "Ecology")—and it's what Palacas in this volume shows that many of his students learned as well.

- We can probably show all students that even though speakers of AAL may have to stretch further than mainstream English speakers to learn EWE, nevertheless many of them are more linguistically sophisticated than speakers of mainstream English. This is obvious with code switchers, but even those who cannot code switch will almost certainly be more aware of the political and ideological dimensions of language and culture. (Heath and Branscombe pioneered an approach that invites nonmainstream students to do anthropological research on language practices around them.)

- We can provide students with examples of powerful and successful writing published in vernacular dialects. (See the appendix for some examples). Students need to know that writing in vernacular dialects is not a weird experiment by some "radical teacher," but rather something proven by some of our best published writers, publishers, and large mixed-race audiences. They also need to know that much of our past prestige literature was written in vernacular dialects that were considered low, vulgar, and unsuitable for writing (consider, for example, much of the writing by Dante, the author of Gawain and the Green Knight, and Robert Burns). Indeed, for a long time in the British Isles, English itself was considered low and vulgar and unsuitable for writing—for which only Latin would do.

- We may need to fight against some of our deepest habits in reading and responding to student writing. Here's a comment by a dedicated and experienced teacher about a piece of writing by an AAL speaker: "Only now can I really address the underlying thinking and understanding problems—because previously the writing was so atrocious that I couldn't see them." (I took this from a composition list-serve, but we hear teachers saying it all the time—not all of them White.) Problems in thinking need to be the first thing we see and address.

Consider the primary criteria by which most teachers judge most essays: sticking to the topic or question or assignment; getting the information or concepts right; having good ideas; reasoning carefully; giving enough supporting evidence and examples; organizing effectively; and getting the meaning clear at the sentence level. Note: students can meet *all* those criteria and still write entirely in AAL and use lots of other language that violates the conventions of standardized written English. We need to help students meet all these criteria before asking them to try to get their grammar, syntax, spelling, and register right for correct written English. (Admittedly, a few matters of punctuation can affect sentence clarity, but we don't have to focus on punctuation problems until we get to the editing stage.)

So the job for many of us is one that we are uniquely trained to take on: to become better readers. When an essay needs to end up in the dialect of correct written English, we need to be more expert at *reading through* all the grammar, spelling, and other features we may experience as "wrong," so we can give them feedback to help them *revise* to meet all those substantive criteria. We can help students achieve every one of those strengths while entirely ignoring matters of dialect or grammar and syntax.

I find that most students need a palpable experiential understanding of the crucial difference between revising and editing—so they don't make surface improvements when asked to revise. So I set different due dates for revising and editing. The revision follows feedback from me and peers, but I make it explicitly clear that issues of mechanics and "correctness" don't matter at all for this revision. I get a little extra pleasure by shocking them with how I tell them their job: "Revise your paper until it's as *good* as it can be. But don't sweat correctness—language, grammar, spelling and other surface features. That's for later." When students do substantive revising and take their minds off the surface, the surface features often improve.

Admittedly, issues of register and voice can seem more "substantive" than issues of mere editing, but I find it helpful to delay much feedback on register until late. I want students to strengthen all those other criteria of thinking and clarity even if they are still using a register that is too colloquial, casual, or slangy. Register is really an issue of *propriety*—which is really the basis of EWE. When students try too soon for propriety, they sometimes fog up their thinking and fall into tangles of non-clarity.

Once a draft has become strong and clear on all the substantive criteria, the job of making the changes needed in grammar, syntax, and spelling—and register—is usually less scary and more manageable. Some of the ideological and political steam has gone out of the difference between the two dialects. I set a later due date for an edited draft—I often call it the "publication draft" (for the class magazine) or a "final final draft." It must be successfully copyedited into correctness for the conventions of standardized written English. (If I've already read the nearly-final draft, I save time by just spotchecking the final-final for copyediting. See "Mother Tongue" for a much fuller account of how I handle revising and editing.)

When we make it clear to students that they can ignore all matters of grammar, syntax, and spelling until after their major revision, we communicate more concern about thinking, organization, and clarity. We give them more feedback and hold them more responsible on these matters of substance. When feedback on dialect crowds out feedback on ideas, reasoning, and organization, it's another form of prejudice towards speakers of AAL. (See Matarese and Anson in this volume for citations of research showing evidence of that kind of skewing.)

To follow this route may not be easy. Errors in written grammar and syntax tend to grab the attention of readers and blind them to substance. But Nancy Sommers pointed out long ago that even mainstream dialect students need us to read through grammar and syntax to the substance. Countless students of all sorts get too little feedback on their thinking, organization, and clarity because teachers have taken the easy route of calling attention to violations of correct written English.[7]

In the end, I hope it becomes simple again: why not invite both mainstream students and AAL speakers to write in their spoken vernacular language and edit later to produce "correct writing."

APPENDIX: EXAMPLES OF PUBLISHED WRITING IN NONMAINSTREAM VARIETIES OF WRITTEN ENGLISH

AAL or Black English:

Childress, Alice. *Like One of the Family.* Boston: Beacon, 1986. *Wedding Band: A Love/Hate Story in Black and White.* 1966.

Hurston, Zora Neal. *Their Eyes Were Watching God.* Philadelphia: J.B. Lippincott Company, 1937.

Sanchez, Sonia. *Shake Loose My Skin: New and Selected Poems.* Boston: Beacon, 1999.

Sapphire. *Push: A Novel.* New York: Knopf, 1996.

Smitherman, Geneva. See her columns in *English Journal* (collected as chapter 20 in her *Talkin That Talk*. See also parts of her *Talkin and Testifyin*).
Walker, Alice. *The Color Purple*. New York: Harcourt Brace, 1982.

Caribbean Creole English:

Bennett, Louise. *Selected Poems*. 1982
Clarke, Austin. *The Polished Hoe*. New York: Amistead, 2003. New York: Warner, 2000.
Hodge, Merle. *Crick-Crack Monkey*. London: Heinemann, 1981.
Hopkinson, Nalo. *The Midnight Robber*. New York: Warner, 2000.
Lovelace, Earl. *The Wine of Astonishment*. New York: Vintage, 1984.
The Penguin Book of Caribbean Verse in English (see section on oral and oral-influenced poetry). Harmondsworth, England: Penguin, 1986.
Sistren, with Honor Ford Smith, ed. *Lionheart Gal: Life Stories of Jamaican Women*. London: Women's P, 1986.

Hawai'ian Creole English ("Pidgin"):

Lum, Darrell H. Y. *Pass On, No Pass Back*. Honolulu: Bamboo Ridge P, 1990.
Yamanaka, Lois-Ann. *Blue's Hanging*. New York: Farrar, 1997. *Saturday Night at the Pahala Theater*. Honolulu: Bamboo Ridge P, 1993.

Hispanic/Latino/a English:

Anzaldua, Gloria. *Borderlands/La Frontera: The New Mestiza*. San Francisco: Spinters-Aunt Lute, 1987.
Cisneros, Sandra. *Woman Hollering Creek and Other Stories*. New York: Random House, 1991.
Rivera, Tomás. *. . . y no se lo trag'o la tierra/And the Earth Did Not Devour Him*. Houston: Arte P'ublico, 1992.
Trevino, Jes'us Salvador. *The Fabulous Sinkhole and Other Stories*. Houston: Arte P'ublico, 1995.

Scots:

Kelman, James. *How Late It Was, How Late*. New York: Vintage, 1998.

NOTES

1. About terminology. I use the term African American Language (AAL), following Smitherman and Villanueva and contributors to their collection. I note also that

the University of Massachusetts Linguistics Department has used this terminology in recently establishing an active and ambitious *Center for the Study of African American Language*. But many other names have been given to this language: African American Vernacular English, African American English, Black English, and others. See Green's introduction for a good treatment of the naming issues. The most controversial term is Ebonics. When Robert Williams first used it, he used it to apply to a spectrum of languages including those of the Caribbean. He says that Ebonics refers to the

> linguistic and paralinguistic features which on a concentric continuum represent the communicative competence of the West African, Caribbean, and United States slave descendants of African origin. It includes the various idioms, patois, argots, ideolects, and social dialects of black people, especially those who have been forced to adapt to colonial circumstances. (qtd. in Smitherman, "Black English/ Ebonics" 29)

In a real sense, AAL is not one language. That is, even in the U.S., there is a spectrum of versions of AAL. Keith Gilyard points out that there's often a significant difference between the Black language young people find at home and the one they find and use on the street—and that peer pressure is often stronger than home pressure. Linguists sometimes lay out the spectrum with the terms "basilect," "mesolect," and "acrolect." This terminology, however, embeds a problematic metaphor of "low" to "high."

It's important to note also, that there are plenty of African Americans who grow up in homes where AAL is never spoken. Such speakers are, we might say, monolingual speakers of some version of standardized or sanctioned spoken English (though some might be bilingual in a non-English language like German or Vietnamese). This chapter ignores these monolingual speakers.

2. Some linguists use the term "grapholect" to distinguish the written dialect from spoken versions of a language. The linguists Walt Wolfram and Natalie Schilling-Estes make a comparable distinction, but frame it as "informal" versus "formal":

> Formal Standard English or Prescriptive Standard English tends to be based on the written language of established writers and is typically codified in English grammar texts. It is perpetuated to a large extent in formal institutions such as schools, by those responsible for English language education. If we took a sample of everyday conversational speech, we would find that there are virtually no speakers who consistently speak formal standard English as prescribed in the grammar books. (10)

I try to avoid the term "standard English" because that term masks the arbitrariness of that version, and "standard" is so often taken to mean "best quality." "Standardized" and "sanctioned" are more accurate adjectives for the mainstream variety of English.

But there's an important wrinkle here: there is no single sanctioned version of spoken English. There are only stigmatized versions versus "the rest." Here are Walt Wolfram and Natalie Schilling-Estes on this point:

> [S]tandard American English seems to be determined more by what it is not than by what it is. . . . If native speakers from Michigan, New England, and Arkansas avoid the use of socially stigmatized grammatical structures such as "double negatives" (e.g., They didn't do nothing), different verb agreement patterns (e.g., They's okay), and different irregular verb forms (e.g., She done it), there is a good chance they will be considered standard English speakers. . . . The basic contrast in North America exists between negatively valued dialects and those without negative value, not between those with prestige value and those without. . . . North Americans, in commenting on different dialects of American English, are much more likely to make comments about nonstandardness ("That person doesn't talk correct English") than they are to comment on standardness (e.g., "That person really speaks correct English"). (12)

Note, however, an important exception: North Americans often do comment positively on standardness when they expect a stigmatized version. It's not so unusual to hear, "She was a well-spoken Black woman" (race) or "He was a well-spoken gas station attendant" (class).

3. For much of my schooling I succeeded with the opposite approach—trying to write in the proper form and language right from the beginning of any project. But in graduate school (perhaps because the stakes got higher), I couldn't write my papers this way any more and I had to quit before being kicked out. I felt like a complete failure because I was a diligent student and it was the only approach to writing that I knew. When I finally went back to graduate school after five years of teaching, I learned—slowly, gradually—to write the language that came most easily to my mouth—a language that is unacceptable for serious essayist writing. I've found it helpful to be blunt in summing up what I learned: When I tried to write right, I failed; when I let myself write wrong, I succeeded—and could end up with right writing.

4. The term "code meshing" is sometimes used instead of "code switching." Traditionally, "code switching" has referred to the process of switching wholly into a different language or dialect and staying there for a while—for example, when a Spanish speaker uses English for a whole conversation with someone who wants or needs it. The term code meshing tends to highlight a different practice of moving back and forth between languages or dialects in mid-discourse so as to create a mixture—sometimes even hybrid forms that are not quite one or the other. But this distinction is not consistently observed. For in fact "code switching" has often been used to refer to mixing at a fine-grained level—as in certain kinds of Spanglish (see Kells). See Canagarajah for a rich and valuable exploration of code meshing. At this point in my chapter, I'm talking about code switching in the narrower sense, focusing on AAL speakers or writers who are comfortably

fluent at operating entirely in sanctioned English. Later in the chapter, code meshing in the more fine-grained sense will be an important topic.

5. Many people will assume that Lisa Delpit joins in with this objection and will cite
her *Other People's Children*. But her position is not simple. Her main criticisms
there were against teaching strategies unilaterally imposed on students and strategies that deprive them of access and control of the "language of power." That's
not the strategy I'm describing—a strategy where students don't just learn to
meet the standards of EWE for final drafts of certain important essays; they end
up with a more active and conscious knowledge of EWE than those who use the
traditional approach and develop a separate EWE writing gear. In fact, Lisa Delpit
writes specifically in favor of the kind of approach I'm advocating:

> Unlike unplanned oral language or public reading, writing lends itself to
> editing. While conversational talk is spontaneous and must be respon-
> sive to an immediate context, writing is a mediated process which may
> be written and rewritten any number of times before being introduced
> to public scrutiny. Consequently, writing is more amenable to rule
> application—one may first write freely to get one's thoughts down, and
> then edit to hone the message and apply specific spelling, syntactical, or
> punctuation rules. ("What Should Teachers Do" 25)

Geneva Smitherman makes a similar recommendation:

> I am often asked "how far" does the teacher go with this kind of writ-
> ing pedagogy. My answer: as far as you can. Once you have pushed your
> students to rewrite, revise; rewrite, revise; rewrite, revise; and once they
> have produced the most powerful essay possible, then and only then
> should you have them turn their attention to BEV grammar and matters
> of punctuation, spelling, and mechanics. ("Black English/Ebonics" 29)

My entire chapter could be thought of as nothing but an attempt to explore
and develop what they say here.

6. An interesting theoretical question or quibble arises when we consider these middle drafts revised by speakers of AAL but not yet copyedited into EWE. Are
these drafts "in AAL"? Geneva Smitherman deals with this question by distinguishing between African American *syntax* and African American *discourse* or
expressive discourse style: "BEV [Black English Vernacular] syntax and BEV discourse are not co-occurring variables" (*Talkin That Talk* 183, italics in original).

In talking about the relationship between language and thinking, I was
tempted to bring in Gee's treatment of what he calls *Discourse* (capitalized). He
sounds at times as though he's against the idea of writing in AAL—saying in
effect that you can *not* teach reading and writing outside a Discourse, and if an
AAL speaker writes in this language and then changes it at the end to conform to
EWE, this will do nothing to help a deeper Discourse problem of thinking, identity, or even perception:

So-called Black Vernacular English is, on structural grounds, only triv-
ially different from Standard English by the norms of linguists accustomed to dialect differences around the world (Labov, 1972a). Rather
these children use language, behavior, values, and beliefs [Discourse] to
give a different shape to their experience. (541)

But where I'm trying to write about two kinds of teaching, it turns out that
he is lifting this whole issue outside of the realm of teaching altogether. That is, he
insists that Discourse as a carrier of ideology cannot be taught: is "impervious to
instruction" (530). "Beyond changing the social structure, is there much hope [for
students to learn a new discourse]? No, there is not. So we better get on about the
process of changing the social structure" (531).

This prompts Lisa Delpit to accuse him of saying that it's hopeless for students who grew up with the Discourse associated with AAL to learn a new
Discourse or ideology. Delpit insists that instruction *can* help students "acquir[e]
a discourse other than the one into which he or she was born" ("Politics" 550):
"Individuals *can* learn the 'superficial features' of dominant discourses as well as
their more subtle aspects" (554).

7. Grateful thanks to Robert Eddy, Helen Fox, Keith Gilyard, Don Jones, Shondel
Nero, Arthur Palacas, Irene Papoulis, and Jane Smith for helpful responses on
earlier drafts.

WORKS CITED

Ball, Arnetha F. "Cultural Preference and the Expository Writing of African-
American Adolescents." *Written Communication* 9.4 (1992): 501-32.

_____. "Expository Writing Patterns of African American Students." *English Journal*
85 (1996): 27-36.

Blau, Sheridan. "Invisible Writing: Investigating Cognitive Processes in
Composition." *College Composition and Communication* 34.3 (1983): 297-312.

Canagarajah, A. Suresh. "The Place of World Englishes in Composition:
Pluralization Continued." *College Composition and Communication* 57.4
(2006): 586-619.

Committee on College Composition and Communication Language Statement:
Background Statement. "Students' Right to Their Own Language." *College
Composition and Communication* 25.3 (1974): 1-18.

Cushman, Ellen, Eugene R. Kintgen, Barry M. Kroll, and Mike Rose, eds. *Literacy:
A Critical Sourcebook*. Boston: Bedford/St. Martin's, 2001.

Delpit, Lisa. *Other People's Children: Cultural Conflict in the Classroom*. Rev. ed.
New York: Norton, 2006.

_____. "The Politics of Teaching Literate Discourse." Cushman et al. 545-54. New
York: New Press, 2006.

_____. "What Should Teachers Do? Ebonics and Culturally Responsive Instruction."
Perry and Delpit. 17-26.

Dyson, Michael Eric. *Is Bill Cosby Right? Or Has the Black Middle Class Lost Its Mind?* New York: Basic, 2005.

Elbow, Peter. "Inviting the Mother Tongue: Beyond 'Mistakes,' 'Bad English,' and 'Wrong Language'." *Journal of Advanced Composition* 19.2 (Spring 1999): 359-88. Rpt. in Elbow, *Everyone Can Write: Essays Toward a Hopeful Theory of Writing and Teaching Writing.* New York: Oxford UP, 2000. 323-50.

____. "The Role of Publication in the Democratization of Writing." *Publishing with Students: A Comprehensive Guide.* Ed. Chris Weber. Portsmouth, NH: Heinemann, 2002. 1-8.

____. "Vernacular Englishes in the Writing Classroom: Probing the Culture of Literacy." *ALT DIS: Alternative Discourses and the Academy.* Eds. Christopher Schroeder, Patricia Bizzell, and Helen Fox. Portsmouth, NH: Heinemann, 2002. 126-38.

Elsasser, Nan and Patricia Irvine. "English and Creole: The Dialectics of Choice in a College Writing Program." *Harvard Educational Review* 55 (1985): 399-415. Rpt. in Ira Shor, ed., *Freire for the Classroom.* Portsmouth, NH: Boynton-Cook, 1987. 129-49.

Fanon, Frantz. *Black Skin, White Masks.* New York: Grove, 1967.

Farrell, Thomas. "IQ and Standard English." *College Composition and Communication* 34.4 (1983): 470-84.

Gee, James Paul. "Literacy, Discourse, and Linguistics: Introduction" and "What is Literacy?" Cushman et al. 535-44.

Gilyard, Keith. "Cross-Talk: Toward Transcultural Writing Classrooms." Severino, Guerra, and Butler. 325-32.

Green, Lisa. *African American English: A Linguistic Introduction.* Cambridge: Cambridge UP, 2002.

Heath, Shirley Brice, and Amanda Branscombe. "Intelligent Writing in an Audience Community." *The Acquisition of Written Language: Response and Revision.* Ed. Sarah W. Freedman. Norwood, NJ: Ablex. 3-32.

Irvine, Patricia and Elsasser, Nan. "The Ecology of Literacy: Negotiating Writing Standards in a Caribbean Setting." *The Social Construction of Written Communication.* Eds. Bennett A. Rafoth and Donald L. Rubin. Norwood, NJ: Ablex, 1988. 304-20.

Kells, Michelle Hall "Understanding the Rhetorical Value of *Tejano* Codeswitching." *Latino/a Discourses: On Language, Identity, and Literacy Education.* Eds. Michelle Hall Kells, Valerie Balester, and Victor Villanueva. Portsmouth, NH: Boynton/Cook, 2004. 24-39.

Leki, Ilona. "Cross-Talk: ESL Issues and Contrastive Rhetoric." *Writing in Multicultural Settings.* Severino, Guerra, and Butler. 234-44.

LeCourt, Donna. "Performing Working-Class Identity in Composition." *College English* 69.1 (September 2006): 30-51.

McWhorter, John. *Doing Our Own Thing: The Degradation of Language and Music and Why We Should, Like, Care.* New York: Gotham, 2003.

Olson, David. "From Utterance to Text: The Bias of Language in Speech and Writing." *Harvard Educational Review* 47 (1977): 257-81.

Palacas, Arthur. "Liberating American Ebonics from Euro-English." *College English* 63.3 (2001): 326-52.

Perry, Theresa and Lisa Delpit. *The Real Ebonics Debate: Power, Language, and the Education of African-American Children.* Boston: Beacon, 1998.

Redd, Teresa M. and Karen Schuster Webb. *A Teacher's Introduction to African American English: What a Writing Teacher Should Know.* Urbana, IL: NCTE, 2005.

Romano, Tom. *Blending Genre, Altering Style: Writing Multi-genre Papers.* Portsmouth, NH: Boynton/Cook, 2000.

Severino, Carol, Juan C. Guerra, and Johnnella E. Butler, eds. *Writing in Multicultural Settings.* New York: MLA, 1997.

Smitherman, Geneva. "'The Blacker the Berry, the Sweeter the Juice': African American Student Writers." *The Need for Story: Cultural Diversity in the Classroom and Community.* Eds. Anne Haas Dyson and Celia Genishi. Urbana IL: NCTE, 1994, 80-101.

____. "Black English/Ebonics: What It Be Like?" Perry and Delpit. 29-37.

____. *Talkin and Testifyin: The Language of Black America.* Detroit: Wayne State UP, 1986.

____. *Talkin That Talk: Language, Culture, and Education in African America.* New York: Routledge, 2000.

Smitherman, Geneva and Victor Villanueva, eds. *Language Diversity in the Classroom: From Intention to Practice.* Carbondale: Southern Illinois UP, 2003.

Sommers, Nancy. "Responding to Student Writing." *College Composition and Communication* 32 (1982): 148-56.

Williams, Robert L.,ed. Preface, Introduction. *Ebonics: The True Language of Black Folks.* St. Louis: Institute of Black Studies. 1975. iii-xii.

Wolfram, Walt and Natalie Schilling-Estes. *American English: Dialects and Variation.* Malden, MA: Blackwell, 1998.

9

PLAY THAT FUNKY MUSIC . . . BLACK MAN

Rhetoric, Popular Music and Race in the Classroom

Earnest Cox
University of Arkansas at Little Rock

INTRODUCTION

"Popular music."

Those words often bring to mind images and sounds of teen pop stars, bouncing dance divas, rock-and-roll rebels, and hip-hop superstars. Popular music is so common that it is an unassuming and nonthreatening topic of interest for writing students. When students do not feel threatened by a topic, they seem more honest and open to learning. This chapter is about using popular music in the composition/rhetoric classroom to discuss the seemingly ever present issue of race but doing so within a comfortable context for students. Using music allows students to analyze race within familiar contexts without pressuring them to be too personal. I begin with a brief story about a classroom experience that sets up my discussion.

※ ※ ※

In Spring 2003, my first-year composition students and I were discussing critical thinking and seeking common ground with an audience. We read an essay by musician David Byrne called "I Hate World Music" that, despite its title, argued that listening to music from around the world allows us to better understand others. I thought the essay was perfect for that part of the course for two reasons. First, it advocated critical thinking and having an open mind, which are two of the goals I set up in the course. Second, it dealt with one of my favorite topics—music.

I have always used music in my classes, ranging from first-year composition to graduate rhetorical theory courses. Music has been a useful tool for me in explaining concepts in rhetoric and writing that students sometime have difficulty grasping.

In order to better explore Byrne's argument, I brought in the lyrics from a song by the group Oceania called "Union." Oceania is a musical project combining Western music with the music and language of New Zealand's Maori people. The song lyrics dealt with universal concepts such as pride, freedom, justice, and peace. We read and discussed the English translation of the song, and most of my students felt it presented a message with which they could identify. Then I played the song for them.

As soon as the song started and the Maori instrumentation and language filled the room, I knew something was wrong. I looked around the room at the faces staring at me in amazement. Some students shook their heads in disbelief while others fidgeted in their seats impatient with the strange sounds. A few students could not stop laughing at the song. After the song ended, they just sat in silence until a very familiar comment rang out, "That sucked!" An unintended discussion then erupted about the aesthetic merits of the song. Some students described it as "unique" and "original," whereas others termed it "stupid" and "senseless." Surprised, I then asked them to explain their reactions to the song. I also tried to explain that my purpose was not for them to evaluate the song but to consider Byrne's argument and the song with an open mind toward understanding others—those who might live and communicate differently from themselves but who ultimately have the same common human concerns. As the chaotic discussion continued, many of my students admitted they were far less open minded about music and difference than they had originally believed, and, in fact, they wanted to remain that way. I let the discussion and class end with my sense that at least I had gotten them to think a little about their own prejudices and assumptions about others. I did not push my students further at that time. I believe teaching should be a collaborative effort, and I didn't want to force my tastes on them. I saw our discussion as the beginning of a process. I hoped our conversations would eventually open some of their minds. Nevertheless, their initial lack of openness was disappointing, but not unique. That incident was not the first time I had played a piece of music for a class, only to have the class question my musical taste and sanity, but as my students left the room, a young African American female student stopped at my desk and looked at the CD cover.

"Is this really *your* CD?" she asked as she glanced over the cover image of a woman's shadowed face with only her eyes highlighted by a shaft of light pouring in from a lush green rainforest around her.

"Yes," I responded.

"And you like this music," she continued.

"Yes."

She shook her head.

"That's interesting. I didn't know Black men listened to that type of music. At least no Black man I've ever known," she stated as she looked at me strangely and then left the room.

Her questions and statement still haunt me.

My students often question the music I bring into class, as I often bring in not only popular music but some obscure music as well, but it was the first time I had been questioned openly from a perspective based on race. What was strange for her was not the song, but the fact that I, a Black man, had played it. I wondered how many others in the class were having those same thoughts. That encounter led me to explore and more closely consider how music could be used to discuss race in the classroom. It also made me consider how my use of music might construct a racial persona of myself as the teacher in the classroom. This chapter deals with some of my thoughts that emerged from my experiences with that particular class and how we, as a class, explored the links between music and race.

* * *

First, this chapter discusses why I see a very strong relationship among rhetoric, writing, and popular music. My use of music in the classroom serves to bridge academic culture and the students' home culture. The bridge is built on rhetorical similarities between popular music and academic writing. This bridge also contributes to the students' perceptions of their home culture having value in the academy. Understanding why I use music in the class provides a foundation for looking at how it can be used to discuss race.

The second part of this chapter addresses some ways popular music can be used as part of a critical discussion of race. I am specifically concerned with how some music constructs what it means to be Black in America. Since that Spring 2003 class, I have continued to observe that Black and White students often accept the values and images of Black culture presented in popular musical genres like hip-hop and R&B; they do not consider how narrow a version of Black culture is often being sold to the audience. Music therefore serves as a wonderful starting point for critical thinking about race as a social construct.

Finally, this chapter concludes with a self-reflection of what I think it means to be a Black male in the writing academy and how the choices I make, the manner in which I present myself as a teacher, and the tools I use—specifically music—contribute to a notion of Blackness. For many of the students with whom I work, a Black male writing professor is an unusual creature, and the diversity of music I use makes me even more unusual. I

think my presence and approach to teaching in the academy serve to emphasize the richness that exists in the Black community and the diversity of definitions of what it means to be "Black."

WHY POPULAR MUSIC IN THE COMPOSITION CLASSROOM?

Before discussing the specifics of *how* I have used popular music to address
race in my composition and rhetoric classes, I should first give some background on *why* I use music in all my rhetoric and writing classes. I have three
primary reasons for my belief that music has been successful in helping my
students to understand rhetorical theory and to improve their writing.

The first reason I use music is because it seems most people enjoy it. I
have yet to find a student who does not enjoy some type of music in his or
her life. The very nature of music—rhythm, melody, lyrics, and sound in
general—connects to the rhythmic and sense-based nature of being human.
We are seemingly conditioned from the earliest ages to appreciate the presence of music.

Second, music permeates most aspects of our modern society. Even when
we do not want to hear it, it is difficult to avoid in many public arenas. It is so
common we often do not notice it as it works on us in malls, on television
shows, in movies and through our MP3 players. Because it is so common,
popular music provides an excellent bridge between students' home lives
(those places they consider to be their own, where they have fun, and in which
they seem most comfortable) and the academic world presented in class.

The third reason I use music is because music is rhetoric, or at least
music has rhetorical characteristics. A functional and historical relationship
exists between the two disciplines. First of all, music is a persuasive tool in
our modern world. We find music playing an integral role in commercials, in
the soundtracks of motion pictures, and in the selling of those motion pictures. Other persuasive examples of music can be found on the internet,
where information is often presented on both a visual and musical level, and
any attempt to play a video game reveals, in blasting clarity, the role music
plays in that context. Music is a familiar rhetoric for our students. Therefore
looking at or listening to music from a rhetorical perspective can be very
informative for them because of the relationship between rhetoric and music.

One excellent source of material concerning this relationship is Mark
Evan Bonds' *Wordless Rhetoric: Musical Form and the Metaphor of the
Oration*. In this book, Bonds examines the nature of musical form in instru-
mental music in the eighteenth and nineteenth centuries by concentrating on
the shifts in metaphors used to describe music in music criticism and theory. What Bonds illustrates is that often perceptions of music, as a commu-

nicative tool, are directly connected to societal attitudes toward rhetoric. Bonds explores eighteenth-century musical aesthetics, for example, and notes that many terms associated with music during that century and even at present are rhetorical terms. The concept of *composition* now used in both rhetoric and music was first a rhetorical idea adopted by music composers. In a chapter entitled "Rhetoric and the Theory of the Compositional Process," Bonds writes that in "eighteenth-century accounts of musical form, the manner in which a composer 'puts together' his work is perceived as analogous to the manner in which an orator constructs an oration" (80). I think that view can also be seen in the popular music of today.

Modern popular music can be seen as a very effective social and cultural rhetoric. Music is constantly being used to send social, political, and commercial messages, and modern musical artists are persuasive rhetoricians. They are rhetoricians whose ethos is tremendously appreciated by their listeners and fans. Think about how many young people were and continue to be influenced by the rhetoric of musical artists such as Tupac Shakur, Kurt Cobain, and Bob Marley. Even overtly commercial artists such as Britney Spears, Janet Jackson, and Madonna have used their music to have an effect on their audiences' fashion, language, and ideas about culture.

Music is also used in political rhetoric. During the 2004 Democratic National Convention there were performances and songs by musical artists—ranging from The Black Eyed Peas to Sly and the Family Stone—that were all aimed at persuading the audience on a very basic level. The same was seen at the 2004 Republican National Convention with musical artists such as Michael W. Smith, Donnie McClurkin, and the Gaitlin Brothers performing. All of these examples point to the rhetorical importance of music. Bonds writes that music can act as rhetoric if one considers rhetoric from Aristotle's perspective as

> "the faculty of discovering the possible means of persuasion in reference to any subject whatever." Rhetoric by this definition is not a specific body of rules or devices, but rather the rationale, as one modern writer has described it, "of the informative and suasory in discourse." In this sense, form is the manner in which a work's content is made intelligible to its audience. (5)

Music persuades and informs; music is a reflection of our society yet can also affect how we perceive society. This perspective and definition of rhetoric—as persuasive discourse—provides the basis for the way I use popular music in the classroom. In my classes, we often examine music within the social context of how it is used and perceived by popular audiences. In our modern world, the social context in which music exists also naturally leads to the topic of race.

TEACHING RHETORIC AND WRITING WITH MUSIC

Many of my students come to class with minimal experience with writing in general, and academic writing specifically. The first thing I try to do is to make them comfortable with the idea that writing and rhetoric are topics they are already familiar with by using analogies to music.

For example, when I discuss the logic and rationale for documentation in writing, I bring in songs and news articles dealing with the use of samples in music. Artists in hip-hop, dance, and rock have dealt with the problem of incorporating other's artistic ideas into their own work—some successfully by giving credit to the originators and smoothly incorporating the samples, and others in unsuccessful ways. Those examples allow me to easily address the topic of plagiarism and its consequences in both the popular culture and the academy.

In some of my rhetorical theory courses, we have analyzed rhetorical style and delivery by comparing different versions of popular songs. One of the most effective songs for classroom use has been Bob Dylan's "Lay Lady Lay," which was covered by 1980s pop group Duran Duran and the industrial metal band Ministry. Another great song I have used for this purpose is The Smith's "How Soon is Now," which has been remade at least four times in the last ten years in various styles by various artists. Having my students compare these different versions brings them to a much better understanding of the effects that changes in style and delivery can have on an audience.

A final example of how I have used music to teach rhetoric is my use of the songs "Dancing Queen" by Abba and "Super Freak" by Rick James to talk about ceremonial rhetoric, the rhetoric of praise and blame. In class I argue that both songs celebrate specific cultural values: One extols dancing ability and the other highlights what can only be termed "super freakiness." These songs are not pieces of classical rhetoric, but they are classic songs that show ceremonial rhetoric in a new light. Bringing music, all sorts of music, into the classroom allows students to see the rhetorical value in a discourse they might not have considered a "school" topic. Musical examples allow many students to better connect with the subject matter and content of my classes.

MUSIC, CULTURE, AND RACE IN THE CLASSROOM

How does the topic of race fit into my use of music in the classroom? It usually didn't seem to do so until I reflected on the incident with my student in Spring 2003. Being raised in the Black community, I believed the concepts of "race" and "culture" were often used interchangeably, and music often played—and plays—an important role in the establishment and support of Black cultural identity. My experiences and those of my African American students can attest to that point. But the role of music in culture can also be viewed in broader terms. If one considers almost any culture, or even sub-culture, one will most likely find a type of music that is a part of that culture's existence and social structure. Music is very important in both the socializing within most cultures and also in establishing the identity of many like-minded groups. Let us first consider the role music plays in social contexts.

According to Walter Ong in *Rhetoric, Romance, and Technology,* "Sound always tends to socialize," and he continues to note that oral expression often brings about "the drive toward group sense and toward participatory activities, toward 'happenings'" (284). The same could be said of aural expressions such as music. Many social activities carry with them specific and appropriate types of music; one can think of a number of "happenings" or ceremonies that have and even require soundtracks. For example, parties, weddings, graduations, funerals, football games, and church services have definite musical soundtracks. Sound and music, as Ong implies, compel a certain type of participation or involvement, whether it be physical actions like dancing and singing along, or just the involvement of being immersed in a certain emotional or cultural mood. By using music in the classroom, I hope to exploit its participatory potential. Music's ability to induce cooperation and group involvement is what is important for me as a teacher. Music gets students involved through the process of listening, and involved students tend to engage more in a conversation of learning I hope to have in my classes.

The communal effect of a group of individuals listening to music also fits well into Ong's notions of what defines the culture of secondary orality in which the modern writing student lives. Ong writes that "this new orality has striking resemblances to the old in its participatory mystique, its fostering of a communal sense" (*Orality and Literacy* 136). Music is just one way that members of this community foster that "communal sense" as Ong calls it, and in regard to the students in the writing classroom, they are also very aware of music's effect in this manner. Another very helpful rhetorical theory that can explain this effect of music is found in Kenneth Burke's concepts of "identification" and "consubstantiality."

In his book *A Rhetoric of Motives*, Burke presents his theory on the role of "identification" in rhetoric (21). Applying this concept to music can give some insight into why music works in a socially constructive manner. The music, as used in social contexts, provides a means by which members of a group can identify with one another. As Sonja Foss, Karen Foss, and Robert Trapp note in their discussion of Burke's concepts of identification and the term "consubstantial," "As two entities are united in substance through common ideas, attitudes, material possessions, or other properties, they are consubstantial" (174). The attitudes that music enables in listeners in social contexts such as a concert reveal this aspect of the possible relationship between rhetorical theory, like Burke's, and its use in discussing the influence of music. Burke's theory can explain one aspect of the cultural pull and influence of music.

Certain types of music are often listened to by certain types of people, and in this manner music comes to be associated with the construction of a cultural, and sometimes racial, identity. In modern cultures, or subcultures, music and image are closely related. According to Joseph Harris and Jay Rosen in the text *Media Journal,*

> Few things in our culture have more to do with our sense of who we are (or who we want to be) than the music we listen to. . . . Punk, disco, metal, rap, funk, country. The words conjure up not only sounds but images; they invoke not only certain kinds of music but certain kinds of people. (61)

From my experiences with many of my African American students, I have found music often helps them to define and maintain their notions of race—what it means to be "Black" and conversely what is "not Black." That fact in part explains the reason for the question my student asked me during the incident recounted at the beginning of this chapter. The connection between music and image also extends to the idea of music and race—which is so often defined primarily by the "image" of skin color. As a Black man, I did not "look" like the type who would be listening to aboriginal music from New Zealand. Like it or not, many students get their ideas of what is expected of their culture, their race, and themselves from popular media like music. With this thought it mind, I talked with the students in that class about their perceptions of the relationship existing between race and music.

CLASSROOM CONVERSATIONS AND ASSIGNMENTS ABOUT RACE AND MUSIC

One of the first issues I brought up in the class was the perceived connection between race and specific genres of music. I asked my class if they thought certain types of music were associated with specific racial classifications. Although some exceptions and other genres were discussed, most of my students felt R&B and hip-hop were "Black" forms of music, whereas hard rock and country were "White" forms of music. From my perspective, I know music is a part of the culture that produces it, but I do not think music has a "color." I think this is especially the case when one sees how many genres of music in popular culture borrow from other genres. For example, it is very common to hear Indian musical samples in hip-hop today from artists such as Missy Elliot and Dr. Dre. Do those samples make hip-hop an Indian musical genre? Many examples support arguments against the racial classification of music, and I told my class about the exceptions to these classifications. I found it interesting, and somewhat disappointing, that my Black students were a great deal more hesitant to accept the argument that certain types of music were not race based, or more specifically, racially directed. For them, some music is like the FUBU fashion line, "for us, by us." I also found it interesting that my Black students were more accepting of Whites listening to R&B and hip-hop than they were of Blacks listening to hard rock and country. I think if you look at the current music charts and the history of popular music, you might see a precedent for Blacks "accepting" Whites playing "Black" music. My students were all very familiar with artists such as The Beastie Boys and Eminem in hip-hop or Justin Timberlake singing R&B, and many of my White students stated they also listen to hip-hop music. Both Blacks and Whites buy hip-hop and R&B in great numbers. This explains the make up of the Billboard Singles charts. "Black" genres are readily accepted by the general American culture, and this is a very positive situation. A common and accepted fact in popular music is that Black music is "cool"; being Black is "cool." For some of my White students, it also seems that "Blackness" and Black music is a rebellion against their own White home cultures. I recall Ice-T once commenting that rap was not considered "dangerous" until young White kids started bringing it home to the suburbs. This phenomenon seems to partially explain the popularity of "gangsta rap" in the 1990s, and most of my students agreed with this fact. For my students it seemed very acceptable for Whites to listen to and perform Black music, but when I asked about the other side of the coin, Black artists performing hard rock and country, the reactions were very different.

None of my Black students listened to music in those genres, and many commented that they just could not relate to what the songs were about. In fact, my African American students showed some hostility toward the idea of listening to "non-Black" music. Whereas crossing the musical race line could be seen as an act of social rebellion or just the act of broadening one's horizons, for many Black listeners, crossing that line is often perceived as culturally "selling out." They have an attitude that Blacks who do not listen to "Black" music are trying to distance themselves from their culture. On a personal note, a young, intelligent African American woman once told me that because of my musical tastes she did not consider me "Black enough" to date. As crazy as that sounds, it is an attitude about race present in some of my students.

Of course, this attitude bothered me because it seemed to represent a narrow perspective of the world and specifically a restrictive definition of Blackness. I believe one purpose of education is to open students' minds to new possibilities. I recently "witnessed" a conversation on a Black Internet forum where a young Black man discovered Led Zeppelin after years of being told and believing it was "White boy" music. To his surprise, he discovered the obvious blues foundations of the band's hard rock. He took a chance and opened his mind past racial stereotypes. As a Black man, I think of all the ideas I have been exposed to by having an open mind. I decided I wanted to expand the experiences of my students, especially my Black students, with an assignment aimed at having them think about and maybe question the perceived relationship between popular music and race. The following is a series of exercises and a writing assignment that I gave to the class:

Exercises:

1. *Genres and Race Analysis*

   a. *I brought in samples of music from the four genres we discussed in class—hip-hop, R&B, hard rock, and country—and I played a song from each genre for them.*

   b. *I had each member of the class individually analyze the musical style, instrumentation, and lyrics of the songs for characteristics that would define the song as a representation of that genre.*

   c. *As a class, we compared and contrasted the different genres by discussing their analysis of the music.*

   d. *I asked the class to produce an informal writing explaining the connection, or lack thereof, between those stylistic conventions and their notions of race, supporting their views with the evidence found in the songs.*

   e. *I asked the students to go on the Internet and listen to some more music within those genres, and come back to class ready to argue whether any of the genres can be seen in strictly racial terms.*

When we returned to class, many of my students reported that they found exceptions that made it difficult to say a type of music, especially the lyrical content, was "Black" or "White" based on what they could hear. One of the most telling comments was from a Black male who primarily looked at country and hip-hop music. He commented that "many of the country songs talked about the same things that rappers talked about—women, partying, getting drunk, and love."

The next time I do this exercise in class I will identify more artists such as Cowboy Troy for the students. Troy is a 6'4" Black musician who has coined the term *hick hop* to describe his blend of rap and country. An example like Troy shows Black music goes beyond what is commonly accepted. Another source of information I could point to is the Web site Afropunk.com, which supports a documentary about Blacks in the punk rock movement. The Web site even sells T-shirts with such sayings as "Some Sista's Want to Rock" and "Punk Rock is Black Music."

What I hoped to do by pointing out such examples in my class and giving this exercise was to have all my students question their assumptions about race and music—ideas they had always believed were true. After that discussion, I played some more music for the class, and had them comment on how race fits into their perceptions of the music. I used the following artists and songs, but other examples would work as well:

1. "Stand," Sly and the Family Stone: a multiracial band from the 1960s and 1970s.
2. "I Against I," Bad Brains: a Black hardcore-punk band from the 1980s.
3. "Emergency of Planet Earth," Jamiroquia: a White soul band from Britain.

I chose these examples because the sounds of the artists do not fit into dominant racial stereotypes. After listening to these three songs, we discussed how sound and musical image can be deceiving when it comes to identifying race in music. My point is music often deals with universal topics, and the different genres just communicate those topics in slightly different ways. In addition to these discussions and exercises, I gave them the following formal research project that was to serve as a capstone for our discussion of this topic:

Essay 3: Musical Research and Understanding

Consider a genre of music you do not normally listen to and do research on the origins of the music, the prominent artists involved, and the popularity of the music. Listen to as much of this music as you can find, including CDs and videos, over a period of at least a week. Then write an essay (1,000-word minimum) in which you detail your new experience with the music. Be sure to discuss the effects the music had on you and what you learned about the music from your research. Also be sure to refer to specific artists and songs to develop your essay.

I assigned each student a genre of music to research based on an earlier brief survey that asked, "What types of music do you not listen to or understand?" I didn't tell the students the purpose of the survey because I wanted honest responses. I wanted them to open their minds and to research new topics, not just for them to research a type of music they listen to all the time.

Although the assignment was not specifically a project about race, because of the exercises and discussions leading up to this assignment, race was an implicit topic of discussion. I think most of the students learned a great deal about their subjects, at least those who put in the needed effort did, but a few just could not get past their resistance to exploring music outside of their established interests. The resistance I saw was also manifested in some less than successful essays, which allowed me to once again emphasize the importance of critical thinking and good research in the writing process. I told my students they did not have to like the music after their research was complete, and many still do not like their assigned musical genres, but I wanted them to have some *understanding* of the genres. I think understanding—whether it is achieved or at least attempted—can do a great deal toward promoting the questioning of many social constructions including, of course, race.

STEREOTYPES OF RACE IN POPULAR MUSIC

Another topic to emerge from the discussions of music in my writing classes has to do with the idea of music presenting images and concepts of what it means to be Black and White in America. I refer back to my student's comment about a Black man listening to "that type of music" and all the comments about race and specific genres of music my students made. Even though many stereotypes have their basis in reality, I, being a Black male, am very conscious of the types of ideas and images presented in the media, including music, about what it means to be a Black man today. I am especially concerned because for many people, Black and White, who have limited exposure to diverse groups of people, what is presented in the media is their reality. The accurate and diverse presentation of racial groups is an important social issue, and it is also a topic that can make students more aware of making assumptions about audiences, both in their writing and in their lives, which are not beneficial for effectively communicating with one another. I believe having students talk about the stereotypes they perceive in the music they listen to allows them to think critically about audience and also allows them to see how musical rhetoric contributes to a construction of race in America that might not be entirely positive for the social development of individuals and the society at large.

In order to address this issue, I concentrated on two genres of music my students said present definite stereotypes of race—both Black and White. Those genres are hip-hop and hard rock. During our discussion on race and music, my students highlighted the following characteristics of the performers of and audiences for hip-hop and hard rock:

"Hip-hop performers were players, pimps, and thugs who curse, smoke weed, were uneducated, and who treated women as 'bitches' and 'hoes.'"

"Hard rock performers were satanic, crazy, drug-using rebels who celebrated suicide and destruction."

What was interesting about our discussion was that most of the stereotypes were based on male artists; very few female performers were brought into the initial class discussion. Considering the many studies and social comments on the lack of positive, Black male role models, I found our concentration on the male artist very appropriate. If there is a lack of "real-world" male role models in the Black community, then one needs to be overly critical of those "role models" in the media whom young men follow. With this in mind, I asked them to consider what hip-hop and hard rock music teach/show about what it means to be a Black man or a White man in America. What did they think of these images? If you were new to this country and all you had to listen to and look at were hip-hop and hard rock songs and videos, what would you think it meant to be Black or White in the United States? These are just some of the possible questions that might be explored in class in order to analyze the rhetoric of race as constructed in popular music.

On a similar note, every semester in my senior-level rhetorical theory classes, we have approached this topic from a slightly different perspective by reading Joan Morgan's article "The War on Girls: Sex, Lies and Videos" and then looking at hip-hop videos from artists such as Snoop Dog, Nelly, and Ludacris to discuss how the media's definition of a Black man today is often constructed by his relationship with women. As a class, we observed a pattern; most of the women in these videos were used as signs of the materialistic wealth of the male performers. As one of my students noted, "The videos tell Black men they should define themselves by the things they can acquire, including as many women and as much 'bling-bling' as possible. Success is defined by superficial standards." This was a common theme in many of the videos and also in the music. Some other observations by my students included the way woman were always seen as subordinate to male artists, being there for the pleasure and use of the men. They also pointed out how female hip-hop artists such as Lil Kim, Trina, and Jacki-O have to sell themselves as "hypersexual" beings, wearing skimpy clothing and singing sexually explicit songs, whereas many male performers do not. We all noticed how, in a sea of half-naked women, the male performers show almost no skin whatsoever. I know not all hip-hop artists present these and similar themes, but it seems the most popular artists, songs, and videos do. What is troublesome to me is that popular music of this type often presents a very stereotypical view of what it means to be a Black man in America.

I am even more concerned about the effects of these images on my young Black students. Many of my students seem to think doing anything that goes outside of the popular media images of being Black is, in essence, an attempt to distance oneself from the Black culture—an attempt to be "White." Often, the notion of trying to be "White" is perceived in the way some Blacks speak, write, think, and dress, and it is also presented in the type of music one listens to. It is ironic and somewhat disturbing that many of these notions of Blackness are presented and supported by Whites who are the heads of entertainment corporations. Whether this popular notion of Blackness is the result of overt racist attitudes or ignorance is not clear, but what is clear is that the status quo means more money for all those involved. The selling of "race" is a big business, and I hope my students will consider this fact critically so they are not sold a product that will ultimately harm them. Rejecting the negative stereotypes is not the rejection of one's race. Besides, who can honestly say what it means to "act White" or "act Black" without succumbing to very dishonest and potentially racist views of the many diverse experiences we have in America? I think we should take the opportunity to get students, all students, to look critically at how race is presented in music and translate that awareness into a better understanding of how race is rhetorically constructed and how the limitations of those constructions can be overcome. Just because the media tends to present Blacks, or other racial minorities, in one particular fashion does not mean that single presentation is the limit of what it means to be a part of that culture.

In addition to dealing with the subject in my classes when it occurs, I think my very presence in the classroom, as the instructor, allows many students to begin to question many of their racial assumptions.

CONCLUSION: A PERSONAL REFLECTION ON RACE

There are so many things I think should be said about this topic, but I really do not want to get on a soapbox about all my thoughts on race in the classroom. Most of the time, I try not to make race the center of my class discussions. In fact, I never really speak about it unless it comes up in class discussions, readings, or in the music I use. It seems that often minorities are expected to be natural specialists in minority issues in the academy. Students and sometimes other professionals assume an African American is versed in and totally interested in African American literature and rhetorical studies. At least that is the impression I often get, but that is not really the case for me. For example, when I was in graduate school I was the only African American student in the English graduate program. I remember once taking a modern poetry class, and when we got to the poetry of the Harlem Renaissance, everyone looked to me as a representative of the "Black perspective." I did not feel I could be a representative, yet I was by virtue of my presence in the class. It is a position I have to always remember. The same can be said about my position as a teacher. In the classroom, I always am, and I always will be, a representation of being "Black."

Even though I do not bring up race in the classroom, I will not hide from the topic either. I cannot. No member of a racial minority can avoid it, because it is written on our faces and in others' perceptions of our skin color. I had an "interesting" experience in a Wal-Mart a few months ago that reminded me of this fact. I was shopping for a picture frame, and as I browsed down the aisle, I passed a group of three White women. As I always do, I gave them a friendly nod and an "excuse me." They had left their shopping cart at the end of the aisle, and as I moved past them and toward their cart, I heard one of them say, "Oh that was stupid of me." She then raced past me to get her cart. I instantly knew I was the reason for her actions, and as they quickly left the aisle, and turned the corner, I heard a comment about all the "niggers in the store." Their ignorance did not shock me, but it did remind me that my race can be the first, and only, thing some people see.

I also know many of my students have not seen many Black males as English and writing teachers. I therefore, again, become a representative of "Blackness" whether I want to be or not. But what does that mean? What is Blackness?

My Blackness comes from my background; I grew up in a predominately Black neighborhood in Little Rock, Arkansas in a family consisting of myself, my mother and my younger sister. My father died when I was an infant. Music played an important part in our home. My mother listened to blues, gospel, and soul records, my sister listened to R&B, funk, and soul, and I listened to movie soundtrack records—and that was accepted by my family and friends.

My Blackness comes from my interests; I enjoy reading and writing poetry, fiction, literary nonfiction, and rhetorical theory. I also enjoy science-fiction, fantasy, horror, and action films. I subscribe to academic journals in the field of rhetoric and writing, along with Black men's lifestyle magazines, *Smooth*, *Black Men*, and *King* with their photos of beautiful women of color and articles on Black popular culture. As a female friend once told me while browsing through those magazines, "Even Black intellectuals like ass." Her point being that you can be an intelligent Black man and still appreciate the aesthetics of urban culture.

My Blackness comes from my education; I attended fairly racially balanced public schools, and I was the first person in my family to go to college. I received my undergraduate and master's degrees in English and writing from a public, state university, and then received my doctorate from a private, predominately White university.

And of course, my Blackness comes from my musical tastes; I regularly listen to pop, classical, extreme metal, gothic, industrial, opera, world music, synthpop, new age, soul, and trip-hop just to name a few of my favorite genres.

So, what does it mean to be Black? To be a Black man in the classroom? For me, Blackness is the pride of being myself. It is pride and comfort in being oneself.

It is the richness of individuals that make up the Black culture and not the stereotypes often presented in the media. Blackness ranges from gangster and players to professors and lawyers. What I hope I represent is the freedom to be what one wants to be, the freedom to write and rewrite the racial scripts often presented to everyone as the way things *should* be. This is the best way to deal with race in the classroom, and it is what I think is most important about this topic, no matter how one decides to define race. The next time a student questions my taste in music and its relationship to my race, I will explain to them who I am and why I listen to the music I do. I hope the experience will allow them to add to their understanding of what it could and should mean to be Black, and I will continue to play that "funky" music and dance to my own beat.

WORKS CITED

Bad Brains. "I Against I." *I Against I*. SST Records, 1986.

Bonds, Mark Evan. *Wordless Rhetoric: Musical Form and the Metaphor of the Oration*. Cambridge: Harvard UP, 1991.

Burke, Kenneth. *A Rhetoric of Motives*. New York: Prentice-Hall, 1950.

Byrne, David. "I Hate World Music." *Mirror on America: Short Essays and Images from Popular Culture*. eds. Joan T. Mims and Elizabeth M. Nollen. Boston: Bedford, 2003.

Foss, Sonja K., Karen A. Foss, and Robert Trapp. *Contemporary Perspectives on Rhetoric*. 2nd Ed. Prospect Heights: Waveland, 1991.

Harris, Joseph and Jay Rosen, Eds. *Media Journal: Reading and Writing About Popular Culture*. Boston: Allyn and Bacon, 1995.

Jamiroquia. "Emergency on Planet Earth." *Emergency on Planet Earth*. Columbia Records, 1993.

Morgan, Joan. "The War on Girls: Sex, Lies and Video." *Essence*. June 2002.

Oceania. "Kotahitanga (Union)." *Oceania*. Point Music, 1999.

Ong, Walter. *Orality and Literacy: The Technologizing of the Word*. New York: Routledge, 1982.

_____. *Rhetoric, Romance and Technology: Studies in the Interaction of Expression and Culture*. Ithaca, NY: Cornell UP, 1971.

Sly and the Family Stone. "Stand." *Essential Sly and the Family Stone*. Sony Music, 2003.

10

DABBLING IN THE ABNORMAL

Blackening the Text in the Composition Classroom

Dorothy Perry Thompson
Winthrop University

with an introduction by

Teresa M. Redd
Howard University

In 1991, the faculty at historically Black Howard University adopted an Afrocentric text for its first-semester composition course (ENGL 002). Entitled Revelations *(Redd), the text was "Afrocentric" because it consisted of essays written by and about Blacks—essays penned by Ishmael Reed, Ralph Ellison, Steve Biko, James Baldwin, Gloria Naylor, Zora Neale Hurston, Martin Luther King, Jr., and other writers of African descent. These essays explored topics ranging from the Civil Rights Movement to the Black Power Movement, from racist stereotypes to racial pride, from the African continent to the African Diaspora. Thus, consistent with Molefi Asante's definition of Afrocentrism, the anthology portrayed Black people "as the subjects rather than the objects of education" (Asante 171-172).*

Howard's faculty adopted Revelations *because at that time traditional composition anthologies did not feature enough essays by and about Blacks. For instance, Blacks had written less than 5% of the essays in the anthology Howard had been using,* The Norton Reader *(shorter edition, 1988). Since* Revelations *encompassed so many essays by and about Blacks, the faculty hoped that the book would motivate students to read, think, and write with clarity and authority.*

To determine whether Revelations *was fulfilling these goals, Howard's writing program surveyed the 1,305 students who were completing ENGL 002 during the 1991–1992 academic year. Of those students, 911 filled out the questionnaire, responding as follows:*

- *94% enjoyed reading about the Afrocentric issues, whereas 64% enjoyed writing about them.*

- *89% thought more carefully about the Black Experience as a result of reading the essays; 79% did as a result of writing.*

- *80% felt more positive about writing in general because they had read so many essays by Black writers.*

- *75% thought they had something worthwhile to say when writing about the Afrocentric issues, whereas only 6% said they did not. (Redd, "Afrocentric" 5-9)*

Although these results confirmed the value of Revelations *in Howard's composition program, they shed little light on the value of an Afrocentric text in most U.S. composition courses. Not only were Howard's composition students almost exclusively Black, but they had chosen to attend a historically Black university. Therefore, it was hardly surprising that they appreciated the Afrocentric focus of the ENGL 002 curriculum. But how would Black students at majority White institutions respond to an Afrocentric text in a course where some or most of their classmates were White? And how would their White classmates react? Indeed, who would dare require an Afrocentric text for such classes?*

Dorothy Perry Thompson, an African American teacher, dared to do just that. Beginning in 1995, Thompson adopted Revelations *as a required text for her composition classes at Winthrop University, a majority White institution of, at that time, nearly 5,500 students. Thompson first introduced* Revelations *to two predominantly African American Writing 101 classes in Winthrop's Summer Term Enrichment Program (STEP). However, the following semester she began to require the text for non-STEP Writing 101 classes that were predominantly European American.*

Thompson summed up her experiences in a paper entitled "Dabbling in the Abnormal: Blackening the T's (Text, Topics, and Teacher) in the Composition Classroom." After presenting the paper at the 1997 meeting of the Conference on College Composition & Communication, she continued to require Revelations *in predominantly White composition classes through the Fall semester of 2001. Sadly, Thompson died soon afterward, but she left her story behind. The rest of this chapter will present excerpts from her paper (slightly rearranged) to document how Black and White students at a majority White institution responded to an Afrocentric composition text.*

THOMPSON'S STORY: BLACK STUDENTS' RESPONSE TO AN AFROCENTRIC TEXT

Expecting to have a majority African American student population in two sections of STEP Writing 101, I chose Teresa Redd's *Revelations: An Anthology of Essays by and about Blacks*. The students in STEP are first-generation college students, underachievers in math and/or English who are, according to recommendations from their high school teachers, highly motivated. The old savior mentality in me bristled. Here I was, the only African American in my department, and our composition program director diplomatically had implored me to take the STEP students. I said "Yes" and rolled up my sleeves. That was August 1995.

On November 20, three months later, I found myself writing in my journal "Take this job and shove it. I ain't working here no more."

So, what happens when one Blackens the T's—text, teacher, and topics in the composition classroom, expecting all of the positives of culture identification from a majority African American student population? In Rock Hill, South Carolina, at a majority White institution of approximately 5,500 students and 300 faculty members, a complex system of racial dynamics resulted, at first, in Frustration with a capital F. That frustration was not mine alone. For the students it culminated in writer's block, refusal to write on suggested topics, assumed assaults to their integrity and beliefs, and suspicions that their teacher would not or could not enable them to operate in linguistically appropriate ways in the dominant culture. In short, what was Black could not, in their minds, be "normal."

In what I refer to as Class 1, there were 17 African Americans and 2 European Americans; in Class 2, 9 African Americans and 5 European Americans. For me, the tension and general discomfort eventually included (around November 1995) that overriding realization that there might not be a great epiphany for these students at the end of the semester—no "Eureka, we've been gypped. We missed something in high school. We missed (to appropriate a Nikki Giovanni title) Black feeling, Black talk, Black thought." In fact, one African American female in Class 1 (I'll call her Robin) said that she felt most uncomfortable with "all of this Black stuff" because of Sean, a White male student. "We must be making him feel bad," she worried. I responded, "But Robin, didn't you feel uncomfortable in your high school classes? You told me you've never studied anything Black; you've never even had a Black teacher." "Exactly," she replied. "I didn't feel uncomfortable because I was used to it." TRANSLATION: The Whiteness of this African American student's education, to her, seemed *normal.*

I, then, had alienated my students, on purpose, from a mainstream curriculum designed to facilitate their easing into the *normal* population of market-driven consumers. I was dabbling in the abnormal.

After a couple of weeks of dry in-class discussions, late assignments handed in, one of two European American students constantly missing class, and at least one I'm-too-sleepy-to-keep-my-head-up-off-the-desk whiner, I said, "Time out. Let's talk." Unfortunately, in class, I ended up doing most of the talking, asking questions about what was going wrong. Some students did pipe up and offer that they really were enjoying the class, despite all of the reading and writing required. But I was concerned about the quiet ones. Robin was one of those. I decided to schedule conferences in my office, which is where Robin explained her discomfort with the class text and topics, and her preoccupation with what Sean must have been feeling and thinking.

I had assumed that working with comfortable topics, those grounded in the African American students' own culture, would facilitate ease with the subject matter. African American students would be glad to write about Malcolm X's "conk" and/or their own experiences with hair perming. They would jump at the chance to explain the importance (as does Bernice Reagon Johnson) of African American music in their lives. After all, she was one of the famous founders of Sweet Honey in the Rock, and if nothing else, African American students would love simply seeing her essay in their book.

However, I found that most African American students tended to stay away from what I thought were excellent topics related to the essays— Black English, African cultural concepts, Black self-identification, and African spirituality, for example. They were not comfortable discussing these topics and had little background in these subject areas. Actually, quite a few of the African American students did write their process papers on the horrendous hair-perming process that so many of us suffer through, but, in class discussion, when White students expressed unfamiliarity with the entire procedure as it applies to Black hair, Black students seemed reluctant to discuss it. I found out that some of them were reading for the first time Malcolm's view of conking as self-degradation for Black people, a middle-class appropriation of White beauty standards. They were embarrassed, as many of them sat there with elaborately permed hairdos. Malcolm was a hero figure for many of them, but a hero missing from their high school curriculum and their home bookshelves. The media, the history books and, perhaps, their own families and communities, especially in the South, had embraced, not Malcolm, but his contemporary, Martin Luther King, Jr. They could recite parts of "I Have a Dream" and even identify King's home church in Atlanta, but they had not read Malcolm's "House Negro vs. Field Negro" philosophy and could not identify the Organization of African American Unity. (There were a few exceptions in the three semesters I used Malcolm's essay. Some African American students had studied Malcolm X, but reported having done so on their own, not in a high school class).

Fortunately, two students in Class 1, Julise and Manny, filled their journals with entries describing how much they were learning and how they were inspired to read more about African and African American history. Manny, for example, did extra research on African spirituality after reading Steve Biko's essay, "Some African Cultural Concepts." However, in the beginning, these two students' responses were the minority's view. Most of the members of this class showed obvious discomfort.

I began to think that a part of the problem was my own personal dynamic as teacher. Did the students see me as an Afrocentric crusader bound and determined to make them espouse my own perspectives? I decided to let them hear other voices. I called in two of their peers (upper classmen) to discuss race and writing on the Winthrop campus. The first student speaker was appalled that these African American students were leery of their Black text and Black teacher. She appealed to them to try to understand the importance of being comfortable in their own culture. The second student speaker came armed with a visual aid. She held up her reader from her Writing 102 course, explained that the text was a special one that her instructor had put together, and began reading the names of the essayists from the table of contents. After reading about a dozen names, she stopped and explained that only one of the essays in the entire reader was by a Black author. The class then began to discuss the implications of the text that the teacher had generated.

One of the students in Class 1 expressed his opinion that it was, indeed, my identity that turned some students off. On my campus, I am also the coordinator of the African American Studies Minor and lots of times my reputation reaches students before they reach me. This student reminded me that his classmates, during the course of their summer orientation studies, had worked very hard for a European American teacher. His ultimate point was that perhaps his fellow students did not view me as someone who could help them move into the mainstream. I was stuck in the abnormal—Afrocentrism. (A personal note of irony for me here was that the summer school writing instructor for whom my students had reportedly "worked hard" was one of my former graduate students, who often thanked me for helping her broaden her horizons when she took an African American literature course with me.)

I decided that frank and open discussion with my students about the issue of race and about my own background might be in order. Some students were surprised to hear that I had taught in segregated public school systems in South Carolina. They seemed even more surprised when I explained that I did not see my use of an all-Black text as an act of separation, but rather, one of celebration. I reminded them that we celebrate other specific cultures—on St. Patrick's Day, for example.

This open discussion was a turning point for some of the students. I think I became a more believable voice for them, and they became more willing to tackle culturally rooted writing topics that, heretofore, they had been reluctant to choose. In retrospect, I have concluded that some of these students simply needed to be told that there was nothing wrong with writing about the culture and history of African and African-descended people. One of the most gratifying turn-arounds here was that the I-just-want-to-keep-my-head-on-the-desk whiner showed up a bright-eyed note-taker the next semester in my African American Studies 300 course.

THOMPSON'S STORY: WHITE STUDENTS' RESPONSE TO AN AFROCENTRIC TEXT

Spring 1996, I decided to do it again—same text, same teacher, same topics, mostly, with some necessary student-driven changes. But this time, I had a majority European American non-STEP section of Writing 101 (Class 3). This was going to be interesting. In retrospect, I can say that it was, but not in the ways that I expected.

My approach to the use of *Revelations* changed slightly after the first two semesters. With Class 3 made up of a majority of European American students, I decided to treat the text as "normal," that is, to make no highlighting comments at the beginning of the course about its Afrocentric focus. Students responded by not even mentioning the book's all-Black authors and topics. Did the class go smoothly because students were allowed to choose their own topics, topics not related by culture to the essays but by subject matter? Was it because I did not treat what we were doing as an "abnormality?"

Whatever the answers, the fact is that most students in Class 3 did not write any of their five out-of-class essays about African-descended people and their culture. When I made bidialectalism the topic for the midterm in-class paper, several of them had problems, even though I had prepared them with discussion and extra handouts by Geneva Smitherman and Dorothy Seymour. They took a long time getting started, and many of them wrote shorter papers than usual with more general examples.

Nevertheless, in Spring 1997, I found myself ordering *Revelations* again for two sections of freshman composition (Classes 4 and 5)—again classes that had enrolled primarily European American students. To substantiate my suspicions that most of my composition students had not been exposed to the "narrative" of Africa and African-descended people, I gave the Spring 1997 classes a rather simple survey. Of thirty-six students in two classes, only two students reported having had any high school study of Africa or African Americana. Quite a few had never had an African American teacher. Some mentioned that their teachers briefly discussed African American achievements during Black History Month, but for the survey item that required them to list Black achievements, most could cite only Martin Luther King, Jr., George Washington Carver, and Maya Angelou. Not one student could list any accomplishment by ancient African civilizations or by modern-day Africans.

On his survey, one European American male in Class 5 stated that he did not like the *Revelations* text at all as it does, in essence, the same thing that traditional (all-White) texts do: discriminate. His classmate, David B., a nontraditional student (in this case, a local European American businessman in his forties) totally disagreed. He stated, quite dramatically in class, that he felt fortunate to be in the class because he was learning not only about writing but a culture about which he knew precious little. On one occasion, David B. held up his hands and arranged his fingers as if pinching a grain of salt to give us a picture of how much he knew about African Americans before enrolling in the Writing 101 class.

By now I had two and half semesters and five classes of "Blackening the T's" under my belt. During this period, I had heard White students express their misconceptions about Malcolm, confessing one-sided views of him as the militant, violent man who hated all White people. Few knew about the post-Mecca Malcolm. One European American female articulated grave concern after having read Malcolm's essay as the first assignment. She asked, "Am I going to get a bad grade if I don't understand the essays? I mean, I read the assignment, but I still don't know what a conk is." (For the record, she made a B in the course. She had a basketball scholarship and was determined not to lose it. Although she experienced some discomfort because of the all-Black text, that discomfort had less to do with race and more to do with getting good grades to get out of college, to get a good job, to buy a nice house, etc.).

Another European American female, Heather R., in Class 2, also had problems with the text. In fact, she confessed, near mid-semester, that she had read only one of the assigned essays: Ivan Van Sertima's "They Came Before Columbus: The African Presence in Ancient America." To get more of the students involved in the discussions, I had made group assignments, and Heather's group had asked her to be responsible for responding to some of the discussion questions at the end of Van Sertima's essay. The author, a respected anthropologist, linguist, and literary critic from Guyana, carefully and specifically identifies similarities between the ancient Egyptian/Nubian culture and that of the Olmecs to prove the early presence of Africans in the Americas. The essay, as articulated by two African American students in Class 1, is an "eye-opener," especially for students who, having never had much African history, learn for the first time that Africans visited the Gulf of Mexico at least 900 years before the birth of Christ. However, Heather R.'s response was somewhat indifferent. She did not consider the information important, and her responses to the discussion questions in the text were brief. Moreover, one European American male voiced his surprise when told that the essay was not "fiction."

In conference, Heather explained that the essays in *Revelations* simply did not interest her and that the topics for writing that we generated in class in response to them usually had nothing to do with her personal interests. Like many of her classmates, Heather suffered from writer's block as she pondered each essay assignment sheet. Ultimately, she posed what I consider a question that intersected in very significant ways with her writing in the course. She asked, "Why are African Americans always harping on *their* history and *their* culture? "Other ethnic groups don't do that," she continued, offering Jewish people as an example. Finally, she asserted, "We're all Americans."

THOMPSON'S ANALYSIS: SILENT WHITENESS

Overall, my "dabbling in the abnormal" showed me that we, as teachers, have lots of work to do in handling with our students the results of many years of "silent whiteness" in their reading and writing. Various analysts have begun to understand that whiteness often is not an articulated or rhetorically recognized "difference." For instance, Ann Louise Keating, in "Interrogating 'Whiteness': (De)Constructing 'Race'" states that "whiteness has functioned as a pseudo-universal category that hides its specific values, epistemology, and other attributes under the guise of a nonracialized, supposedly colorless 'human nature' " (904). Indeed, Nobel laureate Toni Morrison suggests, in *Playing in the Dark*, that whiteness is a construct realized only when White authors "play" it against blackness. For example, Willa Cather's Black character in *Sapphira and the Slave Girl* is the other pole in a binary system that gives the White mistress her identity. This unarticulated whiteness allows the author to dwell on the Black "other" in ways that make the latter beastly. The Black servant is so unfeeling that she is willing to participate in a plot to have her own daughter raped. The implied definition of whiteness then becomes "something more moral, human, good"—most importantly, normal. Whatever is not white becomes, syllogistically, not normal.

The problem of silent whiteness crystallized for me when I decided to use an all-Black text in my freshman composition classes. Morrison's and Keating's theories of an unarticulated whiteness played out in the dynamics of my classroom. For example, Heather's question "Why are African Americans always harping on *their* history and *their* culture?" is characteristic of readers who tend not to see the focus on a White middle-class culture in traditional curricula and are thus unsettled by Afrocentricism. When I copied, from other sources, model essays that were obviously not by or about Blacks, students missed the silent whiteness: one was about a man who runs a pizza shop, and the other was a comparison of two of the author's friends from "average" European American families. These were considered simply *normal*.

Even African American students trained in the public school system's culture-laden curricula tend not to see silent whiteness. From their elementary school primers to their twelfth-grade British literature texts, they are trained to think of White culture as normal and Black culture as not normal. Keith Gilyard makes this point in *Let's Flip the Script: An African American Discourse on Language, Literature and Learning*, when he analyzes Morrison's mock-primer rhetoric in her novel *The Bluest Eye*. He writes:

> The story opens with a paragraph that could have been excerpted from a typical primer: "Here is the house. It is green and white. It has a red door. It is very pretty. Here is the family. Mother, Father, Dick, and Jane live in the green-and-White house. They are very happy." (7)

> The major trouble with primers is that characteristically they have depicted the happy, white, suburban, nuclear family which discounts the reality of most of the nation, including, of course, African American children like Pecola Breedlove who wishes for, above all things, a set of blue eyes.

> In the second paragraph of the novel, Morrison repeats the wording of the first, only she removes standard punctuation marks. The spaces between the lines of type are smaller. In the third paragraph, she removes the spaces between the words and even ignores conventional syllabification.

> The reader soon realizes . . . that a narrative of domination contributes directly to Pecola's plight and eventual insanity. (105)

Gilyard concludes that in the absence of an adequate language system and an enabling tale, Pecola and her family suffer from a narrative of domination. From my more than twenty years of teaching, I can assert that many African American students suffer from the same absence. Not having been taught their own linguistic history, not having seen their own culture reflected in school texts, and most importantly, having been trained to accept assimilation to the dominant narrative in order to participate in a market-driven society, they too begin to see the non-White as abnormal. Perhaps "flipping the script"—introducing them to articulated blackness—is a necessary step toward making them more perceptive readers and writers, communicators who no longer have to choose between binary poles in order to make their world coherent.

WORKS CITED

Asante, Molefi. *The Afrocentric Idea*. Philadelphia: Temple UP, 1987.

Cather, Willa. *Sapphira and the Slave Girl*. New York: Random House, 1975.

Eastman, Arthur M., ed. *Norton Reader: An Anthology of Expository Prose/Shorter Edition*. New York: Norton, 1988.

Gilyard, Keith. *Let's Flip the Script: An African American Discourse on Language, Literature, and Learning*. Detroit: Wayne State UP, 1996.

Keating, Ann Louise. "Interrogating 'Whiteness': (De) Constructing 'Race.'" *College English* 57 (1995): 901–18.

Morrison, Toni. *Playing in the Dark—Whiteness and the Literary Imagination*. Cambridge, MA London, England: Harvard UP, 1992.

Redd, Teresa. "An Afrocentric Curriculum in a Composition Classroom." Paper presented at the annual convention of the Conference on College Composition & Communication, San Diego, CA, 1993. ERIC. ED362898.

____. *Revelations: An Anthology of Expository Essays by and about Blacks*. 1st ed. Needham Heights, MA: Ginn Press, 1991; 4th ed. Boston: Pearson, 2002.

11

"WE ARE ALL BOUND UP TOGETHER"

Racial Literacy and Pedagogical Dialogue

Litasha Dennis
Winthrop University

Kelly L. Richardson
Winthrop University

Noting the oppression of both African Americans and women in her 1866 address to the Eleventh Women's Rights Convention, Frances E.W. Harper reminded her audience that "We are all bound up together in one great bundle of humanity, and society cannot trample on the weakest and feeblest of its members without receiving the curse on its own soul" (156). Although Harper's proposition that we all suffer when domination and racism are the cultural norms may ostensibly have a more positive widespread reception in contemporary society than in her time, racial discrimination, unfortunately, remains a reality. In addition to overtly discriminatory acts, racism exists subtly because of its institutionalization, often making it more difficult to examine. As Frances Maher and Mary Kay Thompson Tetreault, authors of "Learning in the Dark: How Assumptions of Whiteness Shape Classroom Knowledge," explain, "Whiteness, like maleness, becomes the norm for 'human'; it is the often silent and invisible basis against which other racial and cultural identities are named as 'other,' and are measured and marginalized" (71). Margaret Andersen and Patricia Hill Collins, editors of *Race, Class, and Gender: An Anthology*, likewise explain:

> Racism is a system of power and privilege; it can be manifested in people's attitudes but is rooted in society's structure and is reflected in the different advantages and disadvantages that groups experience, based on

their location in this societal system. The concept of institutional racism reminds us that racism is structured into society, not just into people's minds. (71)

Contributing to this process of institutionalization is the lack of authentic dialogue about the subject. Individuals from all backgrounds in discussions about race may refrain from expressing an opinion because they do not know how it will be publicly received. Will they sound racist? Will they be offensive or offended? Is it acceptable to acknowledge race instead of being "colorblind"? If race is discussed explicitly, doesn't that equate to refusing to put the past behind us and move on? Will it create disharmony?

Teachers who have attempted to have conversations about race with students may recognize some of these questions, and it was as teachers of composition and American literature who had observed some of these reactions that we began this chapter. Originally, we had planned to examine how we both employ class discussion as a pedagogical strategy for introducing race in the American literature classroom and use this strategy as a means of "prewriting." We were also fairly comfortable in our understandings about our racial sensibilities, and we had known each other for several years. When we began to collaborate, however, we quickly realized that we had never before had intense, ongoing discussions about our racial understandings, and we had not anticipated the extent to which our personal interrogations would overwhelm our original purpose. Attempting to unravel some of our own assumptions, we had to engage in a conversation that did not simply state abstract ideas but also challenged us to consider how those ideas influenced our pedagogy and daily life. Overall, Litasha reaffirmed the centrality of her African American race to the construction of her identity. While Kelly felt she had been open and understanding about racial issues, she began to understand that her reality was filtered through a veil constructed by her White skin, which gave her access to a power structure she had not been aware of. Litasha also analyzed how her experiences had somewhat narrowed her perceptions of whiteness.

When we reviewed research to supplement our exchange, we found that there were clear threads of conversation: definitions of race as a "sociohistorical" concept as noted by sociologists Michael Omi and Howard Winant (3-10), the importance of facilitating conversations about race in classrooms for democratic purposes, and the dissemination of techniques designed to help this process. When we put these ideas into the context of a conversation between us as colleagues, we realized that this cross-racial conversation was more important than our original intent as we engaged in not just reflective pedagogy but *critically* reflective pedagogy as it pertains to both personal and professional discussions of race. In other words, we realized that we needed to explore more fully what Jane Bolgatz, author of *Talking Race in the Classroom*, calls "racial literacy." As she explains, "Racial literacy is a set of social competencies. Being racially literate means being able to interact with others to challenge undemocratic practices" (1). Bolgatz stresses that key to this process is conversation: "Becoming racially literate, however, also involves learning how to engage in talk—even when that talk is difficult or awkward" (2). In this chapter, we describe our backgrounds, process, and recommendations for others interested in a similar project. Some of what we say may sound naïve at times or may not resonate with readers; however, we hope to inspire others to have conversations with colleagues as well as students and to participate in these discussions actively and honestly. Still ongoing and far from closure, our conversation has taught us that there is a difference between talking about race as an abstraction and talking about race in a way that is authentic and personal; admittedly, such talk can be difficult, messy, and challenging; but also potentially transformative in helping us understand our relationships in the "great bundle of humanity."

UNDERSTANDING OUR RACIAL BACKGROUNDS

What prompted this investigation in part was the realization that we share a surprisingly similar educational history. We both obtained degrees from the same schools, we both specialize in American literature, and we teach at the same institution. We are both in our early thirties, having grown up in South Carolina. Kelly is from a lower middle-class background, whereas Litasha grew up in a working-class home. Although education was certainly valued and emphasized, college was not necessarily the next logical step after completing high school. Certainly, college, as an *idea*, was something we were both aware of, but there was a gap in our understanding of that idea and how it would manifest itself in our personal lives. For both of us, the degree to which college could be an achievable goal was directly dependent upon financial issues. Higher education, then, was a desired, yet illusive, dream that was almost unattainable. It is ironic to us that we have devoted our life's work to this institution, the academic community, yet were almost unable to participate in it, and were even confused by it in many ways as a social and political reality. Having this relationship to college as a concept definitely brings to bear on our interpretations of our roles in academia, specifically as professors in the classroom. How we relate to our students derives from this experience.

In terms of teaching, we also have similar styles, especially in our consistent use of classroom discussion. We value it as a means of instruction as well as a way to build community in the classroom. Also, because we both use writing frequently as a pedagogical strategy and have backgrounds in composition, we see these conversations as a form of prewriting. Furthermore, we agree that this technique needs support and structure.

These personal and educational parallels have given us some comparable training and perspectives; however, as we talked, we discovered that our awareness of race in the classroom is very different. While we covered many of the same texts and made similar observations, we differed in our approaches to introducing race into the conversation. Certainly, some of these differences are the result of our personalities, but we cannot ignore the impact of our racial awareness.

Our relationships to this region have a significant influence on how we personally define and view our racial and cultural sensibilities. Kelly was brought up identifying strongly with the South, whereas Litasha, even though also brought up in the South, does not have a particularly regional identity. Interestingly enough, despite growing up in a racially-charged region, Kelly describes her perception of race, as an idea, as something that took her a long time to develop and understand; in short, she was naïve about the impact that race has on a daily basis. For example, she recalls having an African American student tell her that her parents taught her never to trust White people. That moment was one of many more that would come, forcing Kelly to think about race, not in personal terms, but in more external ways. Before, her understanding of race and her status as a "White" woman was something that she never really consciously had to *think* about; therefore, she wasn't as aware of how race can be an active part of someone's daily life. Even after these conversations with Litasha, she feels that she still tends to focus on issues of gender and class unconsciously first, more so than race.

In contrast, Litasha is very concerned with issues of race and the resulting dynamics. This "preoccupation" has always been a part of her perceptions of herself and the world around her. For her, growing up in the South, in Charleston, was a very different experience from Kelly's. As she was surrounded by the history and marketing of the "Old South" through school field trips to various plantations, for example, Litasha grew up seeing the exploitation of race for commercial means. Those experiences, coupled with a family that is very aware of racial boundaries, created a strong racial identity as opposed to a regional one. Although she was not taught to hate White people, she *was* made aware that the world is a very different place based on one's racial background. Thus, for Litasha, race is the primary lens through which she views the world.

In the classroom, personality styles coupled with these differences in racial awareness have translated into the ways that we conduct, foster, interpret, and sometimes misinterpret the communities we seek to create. As noted earlier, classroom discussion is a primary pedagogical technique for both of us. In any community, it is inevitable that there may be conflict, and conversations about race carry with them the potential for more conflict among the students than "safer" topics. A signal difference is the way that Kelly and Litasha respond to this conflict in classroom settings. Extroverted by nature, Kelly views talk—in and out of the classroom—as a vital way of making meaning; however, she acknowledges that she has trouble when conversations move toward tension and unpredictable emotion. As a result, she sometimes chooses indirect routes to introduce and facilitate discussions about controversial subjects such as race. Over her years of teaching, she has also come to understand her authority more critically. Because she seeks to be approachable, she did not always consciously consider the power dynamics potentially involved in asking students' opinions regarding controversial subjects. Moreover, she thought that her feelings of alienation resulting from class status were sufficient to establish common ground with students who had been racially alienated; however, now—especially after these conversations—she understands that her whiteness had granted her access to power in ways that she had not understood. Kelly began to see that although one can make conversation approachable, the issues themselves can often be anything but "nice," and, as a White woman, how could she engage her students in dialogues about race when she herself had not experienced the kind of racism that many of her students had? Now more aware of her role, Kelly finds herself still talking about race, yet she does not presume to understand as she once did. She has also learned that conflict in a classroom space does not necessarily negate community; rather, it can be a powerful sign of community. However, she does find that she has to work against her naturally indirect approach in order to have students deal with the issues.

In contrast, Litasha chooses to introduce race directly, maybe even assertively, as a classroom practice. In her thinking, the classroom is a microcosm; ideally, there will be diversity. Because we should respect each other as members of a community, she sees it as a part of her job to make students address issues of race so that they can explore them and get a better understanding of other members of the community who are different than they are. In her opinion, talking about race in a way that is open, honest, and direct is her contribution to eliminating racism. There are some students who come from backgrounds where they have never had to deal extensively with people of other races, which means that they may have very little experience not only with understanding these different perspectives, but also identifying them. Whereas Kelly struggles with interpreting conflict as a breach in community, Litasha sees conflict as a natural part of the experience that will, hopefully, lead to a fuller and deeper understanding not only of these issues in the literature but about these issues in our real lives.

Admittedly, introducing race assertively is a risky technique, and Litasha, too, is always a little nervous about what might develop. But very early in the semester she begins encouraging her students to disagree with her if they have a different interpretation; she is very clear that she is interested in their thoughts. Thus, when they get to more heated issues of race, there are typically some students who think she may be making race too big an issue and are comfortable enough to say so. Again, not only does this enhance the community, but also it introduces her to a different perspective because she is aware that she has a highly defined racialized sensibility. It helps the community, therefore, to see that we *all* have to think through and process our opinions and feelings about race, as well as measure those feelings and opinions against the feelings and opinions of others. In short, she enjoys having students confront their own ideas as well as the ideas of others about this touchy area; the literature is simply a tool for her to get them there.

GROUNDING THE DISCUSSION THROUGH LITERATURE

Composition classrooms certainly provide an environment that exposes students not only to the conventions of academic discourse but also to discussions about the multiple discourse communities that are vying for their attention and in which they participate. In fact, one key challenge of composition courses, we have found, is to balance these discussions of self and society with writing instruction while also creating a sense of community that facilitates authentic dialogue; however, we wondered how the conversations changed as students moved through their college curriculum, experiencing new opportunities to consider issues of race and education across boundary and discipline.

Here, we specifically examine American literature and the literature classroom, taking into consideration a slightly diversified student population at a predominantly white university. Because American literature is based on a very complicated and complex history, having students address this history engages them in discussions of multiple perspectives and voices just as they would in their composition classes. As teachers of these courses, we are trained in composition and bring that training into our course design. To help us understand the differences our backgrounds may have had on our pedagogical approaches, we decided to compare how we would teach three key texts of American literature: *The Declaration of Independence*, Nathaniel Hawthorne's "The Birthmark," and Harriet Jacobs' slave narrative *Incidents in the Life of a Slave Girl*. Not only are these popular selections, but they also provided us a means of comparing our views of race using different genres and voices of American literature. We chose *The Declaration of Independence* because its status as a founding document provides us an important foundation to examine racial consciousness in America during a time when the idea of America was very new. Hawthorne's "The Birthmark" offers a selection from a canonical author whose writings embody race, albeit in a way that is less than obvious. Finally, Harriet Jacobs's slave narrative draws attention directly to racial questions by inviting readers to witness her struggle for freedom. Certainly, we could have chosen others; however, these three documents provided us with a diversified selection that led us to think about our own views of race critically. To that end, we found it equally important for us to talk about how we *read* these texts because those responses inform our assumptions of how we *teach* these texts. Our backgrounds are reflected in our responses. Although we both create courses that present and then challenge the idealism of American literature, our styles differ to a large degree.

We both read *The Declaration of Independence* as a historical document, a cornerstone of American letters, and an articulation of core American values. Because it provides us with a clear and accessible example of democratic process in action and because it is a political document, it allows us an opportunity to talk with students about what we define as "literature": that texts, especially from the eighteenth century, often challenge our contemporary definitions. Once students become comfortable with the idea of reading a political document in a literature classroom, we can begin to interrogate that text not only in terms of what it says politically and socially but also what it does not say about those things. Specifically, as readers, both of us are aware of the underlying hypocrisy of declaring freedom in a time when slave owners were in existence, and the writer and editors of the document were also slave holders. As readers, we both examine the creation of the argument and its style; however, we tend to differ in regard to the focus on Jefferson. Litasha follows the class discussion of the text with specific reference to Jefferson's biography, telling her students plainly: "We are not going to leave this text until we discuss the fact that Jefferson was a slaveholder." Because literature is a tool for her to evaluate social issues, she invites her students to challenge the text, setting the tone for the class and for their relationship as student and teacher. She sometimes sees surprise register on the students' faces as she points to the problematic biography of Jefferson; she believes that students expect a sanitized version of these issues. Because, too, these documents are so respected, she wonders if students view it as a betrayal of our American idealism. She sees this as a good text to illustrate to her students that to engage in reading American literature critically means to tackle complex and uncomfortable issues. Community thus is created; her direct style shows her students that not only is she going to engage with these questions, but she expects them to do the same.

For Kelly, the questions themselves tend to take priority as she focuses on the underlying tensions in the text; however, her reading tends to place Jefferson in a more contextualized space by focusing on how the document was edited by a large group of men with conflicting agendas that overrode some of Jefferson's individual intentions. In this way, she feels she can draw attention to the larger social and political influences that led to the creation of this document and in the particular way it was crafted. Because of this approach, Jefferson's personal biography would get less focus than it does in Litasha's class. As a result of Kelly's concerns about how her race could impact the discussion, she tends to prefer to raise rather than answer ques-

tions to encourage students to take ownership. For example, Kelly is probably not going to say "Jefferson was a slaveholder, and *I think* that is what
should dominate discussion." Rather, she would more likely ask: "How does
Jefferson's status as a slaveholder affect the reading of these words? How
does the political climate affect the reading of the final version?" In this way,
she feels that she deals with the issues but also establishes that the questions
are going to dominate rather than her individual answers. This dialogue with
Litasha and her own increased understanding of explicit racial discussions
will lead Kelly to address Jefferson's role as a slaveholder more directly.

We next examined our readings of Nathaniel Hawthorne's "The
Birthmark." As a canonical author, Hawthorne's writing provides us an
opportunity to focus on more "familiar" ground with students, as we do not
have to explain why we are including him in the course. Because his writings
so often deal with internal conflict and social responses to that individual
conflict, they can often work against discussions of social and cultural issues
in a global sense. We can talk, for example, about how the Puritan community reacts to Hester Prynne's "sin" more easily than we discuss how
Hawthorne views issues of race. However, "The Birthmark" provides an
interesting text that raises questions about race and gender as Aylmer, the
husband-scientist, seeks to eradicate the blemish from his wife's fair skin in
order to reinstate her perfection of complete "whiteness." The Crimson
Hand, the Bloody Hand—both of these labels suggest that for Aylmer, color
is a sign of contamination to be controlled rather than a sign of her individ-
uality. This focus on perfection equating to a white surface is something that
Kelly explicitly draws attention to in her reading, tying it to standards of
beauty for white women. In this way, Kelly draws race and gender together
and would feel very comfortable asserting her authority to speak to these
issues.

What became interesting to us as we were discussing this point is that
although Kelly was very aware of this story's focus on race, Litasha did not
see race as an issue at all. Even though Georgiana is a White woman struggling with a problematic color on her face, because the color in question is
red rather than black, she does not link Aylmer's need to remove that color
to a racial cleansing. She saw perfection and standard of beauty as themes in
the story, but she only saw these issues through a gendered lens—she never
once saw them as tied to race. Why not? One explanation could be that
whiteness, as a racial category, is not *always* as readily apparent to her as
blackness as a racial category. This explanation, however, is unsettling and
incomplete. From Litasha's perspective, she is always aware of the categorical nature of race for everyone, yet she did not see that color flaws
Hawthorne's character. She is much more inclined when talking about
canonical American literature to see race as an issue between two opposing
groups. Because there are no people of color in the story, she is not as accustomed to thinking about this text in racial terms. Furthermore, Litasha rec-

ognizes that she readily associates White, as a racial category, with the dominant power structure; therefore, even though Georgiana has a blemish, in the eyes of most she is still more perfect than she is flawed, and this "flaw" is the perception of a male. Thus, when reading this story, her issue appears more gendered than raced for Litasha since Georgiana is still a member of the privileged race. In short, Litasha just does not see that Georgiana's subjugation results from her whiteness.[1]

Incidents in the Life of A Slave Girl by Harriet Jacobs serves as a text to discuss both race and gender in explicit and clear ways. In our readings and class discussions, we both focus on the story as a subversion of the sentimental form, where slavery interferes with the role of motherhood and a woman's sexual freedom. This subversion also suggests Jacobs's construction of a relationship between slave women and White women.

Litasha has had consistently positive experiences teaching this narrative. Surprisingly, however, she finds that she is the most nervous when preparing to discuss this text with students. Unlike *The Declaration of Independence* and "The Birthmark," there is nowhere for students to "hide," so to speak, from race. This is a text about a slave who is trying to persuade White women to be sympathetic to her plight and the plight of those like her. The path to examining the import and urgency of Jacobs' situation leads directly through a discussion of slavery proper. Thus, to talk about Jacobs' experiences is to talk about the relationship between Blacks and Whites during a time when such interactions were of a blatantly turbulent nature. Although she knows she will not shy away from the discussion, Litasha does wonder if her White female students will be made particularly uncomfortable, as it can be helpful to teach Jacobs by referring to Barbara Welter's "Cult of True Womanhood" and the fetishization of White women. Furthermore, the fact that there are still vestiges of this way of thinking in contemporary society drives this issue even more for Litasha as a teacher. Before every discussion of this text, she wonders if the White women in the course will feel conflicted—on the one hand, they will more than likely identify the disparities between the White women and the slave women in the text, but will they feel conflicted as White women speaking negatively about White women?

Or will they have trouble speaking at all, as Kelly found with one class? This work taught her about the perceived danger that class discussion can pose to students when examining racially-charged issues. One class of all-White students, for example, surprised her by not wanting to talk about the piece. When she asked about their hesitation, many of them revealed in their response journals that they felt like talking would be tantamount to "opening up old wounds," seeing silence as an appropriate response to helping us "move on." Silence for these students seemed the appropriate response because it appeared to be a way to quiet an ostensibly settled conflict for them; however, the conflict was still there under the surface. The silences in the class taught Kelly about the dangers of making assumptions about discussion. Not only did she assume that students would readily want to talk, but she also realized that for this class race was not a "safe" topic. How could she facilitate a discussion without having White students feel guilty or without her feeling that she was too directive in leading them? The experience taught her to reflect about and reconsider her role more deeply, and again, led to her more indirect style of asking questions, and encouraging the students to answer, but letting the questions linger, if necessary, if the group found a forced dialogue too threatening. Still, she continues to seek ways to show students that conflict and disagreement do not equate to a breach in the classroom community or in their ethos as students.

INVITING PEDAGOGICAL DIALOGUE

As educators, we often locate the concept of dialogue within the classroom, associating it with a teacher facilitating discussion of student thoughts, and certainly our work validates this association. Limiting this view to one location, however, runs the risk of assuming that teachers have already had these conversations with colleagues. In fact, our process unknowingly reflected this assumption as our initial topic dealt with class discussion as a form of thinking. In composing this piece, however, we were repeatedly struck by how our personal epiphanies and questions kept leading us to explore our primary experiences not only in the classroom but also within our own lives. Overall, Kelly learned how she did not, for all her liberal views, understand the privilege she had experienced.[2] Litasha has explored her views of whiteness more fully. Despite the importance of these individual lessons, what has been even more striking is having the conversation about race in a way that has allowed for critical debate and conversation. Our experiences of authentic listening and dialogue—asking probing questions, being honest in our responses, agreeing to respect each other's standpoints, confronting uncomfortable beliefs, taking the time to nurture the conversation, and determining ways to move beyond our comfort zones—have led us to a shift not only in the way we think about race but also in how we view the value of the dialogue. It exists not only in the classroom between teacher and student; it must exist within the professional and interpersonal worlds of teachers.

Again, we are still in the process of exploring some of these questions, and we probably always will be, to some extent. Based on our experiences so far, we offer a description of how our dialogue evolved, hoping that others may see in it the value and possible applicability to their own pedagogical experiences.

PREPARATION TO ENGAGE

Understand Your "Positionality"

Maher and Tetreault define "positionality" as

> the concept advanced by postmodern and other feminist thinkers that
> validates knowledge only when it includes attention to the knower's
> position in any specific context. While position is always defined by
> gender, race, class, and other significant dimensions of societal domina-
> tion and oppression, it is also always evolving, context dependent, and
> relational, in the sense that constructs of "female" create and depend on
> constructs of "male"; "Black" and the term "of color" are articulated
> against ideas of "White." Thus, people's locations within these networks
> are susceptible to critique and change when they are explored rather
> than ignored, individualized, or universalized. (70)

Maher and Tetreault essentially articulate the need for teachers to develop a fundamental understanding of the ways in which our collection of
experiences, ideas, and opportunities shape and influence our perspectives.
Often, we are not always as aware of these influences because they are so
inextricably tied to the way we understand our personal identities. This
work is necessary, however, because failure to understand the relationship
between our positions and our perspectives can have a subtly negative
impact on not only the way we facilitate discussions but on our abilities to
even begin the dialogue for and with our students.[3]

Understand That Talking Is a Vital Action

When conversations focus on social issues, the tendency is to believe that
talk is not equivalent to action; however, such a view ignores the transformative power of dialogue. Bolgatz reminds us, for example, of the dynamic
and creative power of language:

> Talking together is a core activity with which to develop racial literacy.
> Talk is a powerful tool. It develops our ideas and influences who we are.
> Talk is also a form of action. Playwright Bertold Brecht said that art was
> a hammer with which to shape reality. I believe that talk, like art, does
> not simply mirror reality; it influences reality. Race and racism do not
> need to be the centerpiece of a curriculum, but these topics need to be
> brought up when they are relevant and addressed when they come up,

even if our attempts are flawed. . . . Moreover, *not* talking is its own form of action. A teacher's silence leaves his or her students' assumptions unexamined. Silence denies us the opportunity to try out and share new ideas, positions, or ways of working together. (10-11)

The danger of silence was something that we came to realize while working on this project, as we noticed that our preconceptions about race were unconsciously silencing potentially valuable exchanges. After we observed that we were limiting ourselves in this way, we embraced the centrality and significance of talking as the vehicle to developing our own racial literacy.

Value the Silences as Well as the Narratives

This point may seem to contradict the previous recommendation, but it does not. Silence for us was more often than not positive because it allowed us the time and space for listening. Racial literacy is a complicated concept, and we realized that we had to analyze the process, the pause, the half-articulated thought as much as the coherent, transition-filled narratives. As Bolgatz reminds us, "we foster our racial literacy precisely in those moments when we bump into disagreement and even antagonism" (2). In our conversations, the basis for our disagreements were often easily identifiable; however, the more we talked, the more we discovered that we sometimes had to help each other process our ideas in order to articulate our questions, beliefs, and experiences clearly. This kind of work involved silences as well as thorough discussions that were sometimes difficult and confusing but always enlightening.

ENGAGING: BEGINNING THE DIALOGUE

Start with Something Concrete

Using specific works of literature was probably one of the most illuminating activities as it was in our different reactions that we became aware of some of the larger questions that would occupy us. Our readings also gave us a concrete place to go when we needed to ground our remarks. Literature was our vehicle in this case, but any texts—student essays, nonfiction pieces, student comments, and visual forms such as film—could be just as effective for inspiring critical dialogue.

Be Open to the Process

Numerous times while collaborating, Kelly could not believe that she had not grappled with some of these questions before. Litasha was concerned that she sounded too harsh at times. Again, when we turned the lens on ourselves instead of our students, we realized that talking about race as an abstraction was much more comfortable than concretely examining it in everyday life. Consequently, this chapter was difficult for us to conclude because the conversation still feels so much in process, and rightfully so. Is there ever really a point when a person can consider herself completely racially literate?

FURTHERING THE DIALOGUE

Work to Create an Atmosphere of Trust

It sounds obvious, but these dialogues will not be possible without a foundation of trust. We knew that when we questioned each other, it was out of a sense of respect. Establishing that sense of community was critical in enabling us to be honest and vulnerable in our thinking.

Engaging to Learn

Conversations about race and racism, in the varied forms in which they appear, are simply necessary. Teachers must be prepared to listen and engage in dialogue with each other as well as with their students. After all, if we feel naïve and in flux about our thoughts, imagine how our students may feel? Also, if we don't talk, how will anyone ever learn to listen?

In the final analysis, our conversations illustrate one example of engaging with Bolgatz's idea of racial literacy. Our process remains dynamic, and again, appropriately so, given how dynamic society remains. What has stayed constant is teacher's role in effecting change. The truth is that our classrooms are not as homogenous as they once were; consequently, it is imperative to help our students and ourselves understand the value of diversity. Engaging in authentic, qualitative conversations in order to cultivate racial literacy has implications not only for the classroom but also in embracing this "great bundle" that is "humanity."

NOTES

1. Litasha's reading echoes Keating's assertions in her article "Interrogating 'Whiteness,' (De)Constructing "Race." Here Keating explains that her students often have trouble seeing the impact of Thoreau's whiteness on his creation of *Walden.* Although Litasha's reaction does not exactly mirror that of Keating's students, the sentiments are similar in that there is difficulty seeing the influence of race in the absence of a competing race.
2. Peggy McIntosh explores this idea in her essay "White Privilege and Male Privilege: A Personal Account of Coming to See Correspondences Through Work in Women's Studies." She compiles a list of everyday activities that she can rely on that her African American counterparts cannot. For example, McIntosh cites that she knows her children will be given materials in schools that attest to their race's existence.
3. Stephen Brookfield underscores this notion in discussing how people can become critically reflective. Specifically, Brookfield notes that teachers must become aware of their "[a]utobiographies as [l]earners and [t]eachers" in order to assume "the role of the 'other'" (29). This practice, he argues, helps teachers to identify, more strongly, with their students.

WORKS CITED

Andersen, Margaret L., and Patricia Hill Collins, eds. *Race, Class, and Gender: An Anthology.* Belmont, CA: Wadsworth, 1998.

Bolgatz, Jane. *Talking Race in the Classroom.* New York: Teachers College, 2005.

Brookfield, Stephen D. *Becoming a Critically Reflective Teacher.* San Francisco: Jossey-Bass, 1995.

Harper, Frances E. W. "We Are All Bound Up Together." *Nineteenth-Century American Women Writers: An Anthology.* Ed. Karen Kilcup. Cambridge, MA: Blackwell, 1997. 156–158.

Keating, Ann Louise. "Interrogating 'Whiteness,' (De)Constructing 'Race.'" *College English* 57.8 (1995): 901–918.

Maher, Frances A., and Mary Kay Thompson Tetreault. "Learning in the Dark: How Assumptions of Whiteness Shape Classroom Knowledge." *Race and Higher Education: Rethinking Pedagogy in Diverse College Classrooms.* Eds. Annie Howell and Frank Tuitt. Cambridge, MA: Harvard Educational Review, 2003. 69–95.

McIntosh, Peggy. "White Privilege and Male Privilege: A Personal Account of Coming to See Correspondences Through Work in Women's Studies." *Race, Class, Gender: An Anthology.* Eds. Margaret Andersen and Patricia Hill Collins. Belmont, CA: Wadsworth, 1998. 94–105.

Omi, Michael, and Howard Winant. "On the Theoretical Concept of Race." *Race, Identity, and Representation in Education.* Eds. Cameron McCarthy and Warren Crichlow. NY: Routledge, 1993. 3–10.

AUTHOR INDEX

SUBJECT INDEX

Academic community, 17-18, 22, 25, 27, 187
    Expectations and traditions of, 3, 39, 50-52, 79, 89, 97-98, 106-107, 116, 146, 148, 154
Academic discourse, 4, 7, 18-21, 24, 28, 50-52, 95, 97, 104, 111, 139-140, 146-147, 190
    Academic literacy and, 4, 18-19, 24, 26, 28-29, 31, 140, 147, 164
    Academic rhetoric and, 97-98, 100, 103-108, 146-147, 163-164
African American culture, 8, 10, 26-28, 35, 37-38, 40-47, 65, 97-99, 107, 143, 147-148, 166-167, 170-175, 177-182
African American discourse community, 10, 15-17, 35, 38, 41-47, 100-104, 107, 165, 179
African American English (AAE)
    As a bridge to learning Standard American English, 10, 15-16, 54, 112-113, 138-142, 145, 147
    Attitudes toward, 6-7, 12, 15-17, 49-51, 56, 62-64, 67, 69, 95-96, 108, 112-115, 137, 139-140, 142-143, 146-151, 167
    Defined, 32, 65, 152-153

Grammar and grammatical features of, 56-61, 70, 95-96, 111, 118-122, 124-29, 142, 147-148
Interpersonal nature of, 5, 56-57, 62, 99-104, 140
Monolingual speakers of, 50-52, 140-142, 148-149
Oral nature of, 7, 60-63, 96, 100-101, 121, 141
Rhetoric, characteristic features of, 5, 11, 31, 59, 96-97, 100-108, 146-148
African American Language (AAL), defined, 13, 152. *See* African American English
Afrocentrism, 175-176, 179-180, 182
Assimilation. *See* Mainstream culture
Audience or reader, 5, 75, 80, 106, 143, 150

Basic writing, 29, 39
Bilingual or bidialectal, 7, 16, 21-22, 68, 73, 84-87, 89, 92, 114, 140-141, 143, 145, 180
Black English or Black English Vernacular, defined, 13, 65. *See* African American English
Blackness, 8, 44, 143, 161-162, 167, 170-171, 173-174, 182-183, 188, 192, 195

LaVergne, TN USA
19 December 2010
209361LV00002B/7/P